HUMAN LANDSCAPES FROM MY COUNTRY

ALSO AVAILABLE FROM PERSEA

Poems of Nazim Hikmet
Translated by Randy Blasing & Mutlu Konuk

HUMAN LANDSCAPES FROM MY COUNTRY

An Epic Novel in Verse

By
NAZIM HIKMET

Translated from the Turkish by
RANDY BLASING & MUTLU KONUK

Foreword by
EDWARD HIRSCH

A Karen and Michael Braziller Book
PERSEA BOOKS / NEW YORK

Grateful acknowledgment is made to the editors of *The American Poetry Review* for first publishing part of this book.

Persea Books
853 Broadway
New York, NY 10003

Library of Congress Cataloging-in-Publication Data
Nazim Hikmet, 1902–1963.
    Human landscapes from my country : an epic novel in verse / Nazim Hikmet ; translated from the Turkish by Randy Blasing & Mutlu Konuk.
        p. cm.
    ISBN 0-89255-273-5 (alk. paper)
        I. Blasing, Randy. II. Blasing, Mutlu Konuk, 1944– III. Title.
PL248.H45 H86 2002
894'.3513—dc21   2001058805
Manufactured in the United States of America
First Edition

CONTENTS

TRANSLATORS' PREFACE

TWENTY YEARS AGO, when Persea Books published our abridged version of this poem under the abbreviated title of *Human Landscapes*, roughly one-third of the original had to be left out for reasons of economy, and this uncut version restores all the omitted sections. In fact, we have newly translated the entire epic, substantially revising it from beginning to end. We have also restored the many passages that, until recently, had been censored and banned from all Turkish editions of the work, so that we finally have in hand the first English rendering of Hikmet's magnum opus as a whole.

Our thanks to Muzeyyen Dursunoglu and our son, John Konuk Blasing, for their help with this edition, and to our friends and publishers, Karen and Michael Braziller, who for twenty-five years have gone all-out to put Hikmet on the map for English-speakers. This translation is dedicated to the author's stepson, Memet Fuat, whose editorial genius and generosity of spirit have preserved—for more than half a century—the integrity of the original for readers both at home and abroad.

> *R. B.*
> *M. K.*
> *September 2001*
> *Çeşme, Turkey-Providence, Rhode Island*

FOREWORD

Mustafa stopped.
Mahmut was a little taken aback:
"That's a strange epic," he said,
    "this guy in prison has written a different kind of epic.
He's stirring up something.
But your voice is sad, son,
        and it reads like music:
        it touches a man."

Book Two, Section III

NAZIM HIKMET is one of the necessary poets of the twentieth century. His voice is sad and reads like music; it is joyful and sounds like happiness. It is compassionate, lonely, heartbreaking, unashamed. It is vulnerable and impure, at times offhanded, at times didactic. It is strikingly direct, ruthlessly honest. It is sorrowful and filled with struggle.It is plaintive and hits a note of pure feeling. To read Hikmet deeply is to be stirred up and confronted by unabashed emotion, connected to something mortally, even nakedly human. "Who touches this," as Whitman said, "touches a man."

Hikmet is one of the great poets of social consciousness. He is a figure comparable, say, to Federico García Lorca and Miguel Hernández, to César Vallejo and Pablo Neruda, which is to say that he was a Whitmanesque poet of the empathic imagination who felt his way into the lives of other people, who put his wild creative energies at the service of a humane vision. Like the major poets of the Spanish Civil War, Hikmet was politically minded and devoted to the international left, romantically inclined to utopianism, but also temperamentally allergic to socialist realism, to authoritarian constraints on the literary imagination. He essentially valued people over ideology and thus created what Vallejo called *poemas humanos*, human poems. His poetry radiates with human presence. He took suffering personally—it instigated his writings—and compassion flowed through his work like a deep river. It is possible to read Hikmet in English because of the path-breaking collaboration of Randy Blasing and Mutlu Konuk, who since the mid-1970s have made him available to us as a major poet. They have shown the range of his achievement, both in short and long poems, and consistently captured his idiomatic free verse cadences, his fresh tonalities, his openheartedness, and his ferocious humanity. It is a noteworthy event in world literature that they have now translated into English for the first time in its entirety the 17,000 lines or so of Hikmet's masterpiece, *Human Landscapes from My Country*, a collage-like work to put beside Ezra Pound's *Cantos* as a heroic achievement, one of the majestic epic sequences of the century just past.

Hikmet called poetry "the bloodiest of the arts," and *Human Landscapes* is, in a crucial sense, a war poem. It is written in flesh and blood, and baptized in dark water. It is empowered by the idea of the poet as a singer of tales telling the tale of his tribe, and it simultaneously employs and plays with the traditional notion of the epic as a long narrative poem, exalted in style, heroic in theme. Hikmet shared Pound's concept of the epic as "a poem including history." He evoked the historical events he considered fundamental both to the development of his country and to an understanding of the modern world, and thus his work has a long memory. It takes place in time. One thinks of it as a written poem (the lineation has a strong rhythmic economy) that bears traces of the oral, that often sounds spoken, as if Wordsworth had confronted real people in an actual prison setting. The people so brilliantly characterized are ordinary people, and the exalted epic style becomes in Hikmet's hands something playful and daily, something musical but also social and even novelistic, almost Joycean. Like Joyce, too, Hikmet was inspired by the local, instigated by his native realm to try to create a universal pageant. From a Turkish prison cell, he imagined nothing less than his own human comedy, and hence the title: *Human Landscapes from My Country*.

"How fast the earth passes!" Hikmet writes in one of the key refrains of his poem. How quickly it passes, and how deeply we need to cherish it. Hikmet's epic poem is filled with social information usually reserved for novels, but it is animated by lyric feeling, by human wishes. It remembers what has come before us, it holds fast to what is rapidly passing away, and it is driven forward by a fundamental faith in the future, by something immutable that he is not afraid to define as love:

> *Night falls in the mountains.*
> *Distances disappear,*
> *but love stays in the heart.*

Edward Hirsch

INTRODUCTION

NAZIM HIKMET, the first and foremost modern Turkish poet, is known in more than fifty languages around the world as one of the great international poets of the twentieth century. In his native Turkey he is both popularly recognized and critically acclaimed as one of the best poets ever to write in Turkish. What such a consensus means becomes clear in the light of his masterwork, *Human Landscapes from My Country*. Hikmet began this epic poem in Bursa Prison in 1941, sending sections of it to friends and relatives for safekeeping as he finished them, and it was largely completed by 1945; he continued revising it until 1950, however, when he was finally released in a general amnesty and subsequently driven into permanent exile. Parts of the epic were published first in translation, in Italy in 1960 and 1965 and in the former USSR in 1962; it did not appear in Turkey until after his death in 1963. In 1966-67, the five books of the poem appeared in separate volumes under the editorship of his stepson, Memet Fuat. Since then, the poem has gone through multiple printings in numerous editions and has been translated into French and German. This is the first English translation of the poem in its entirety.

Hikmet's long imprisonment was crucial to the creation of the epic and the development it represents in his work. When Hikmet was arrested in 1938 on charges of inciting the army to revolt, convicted on the evidence that military cadets were reading his poems, and sentenced to twenty-eight years in prison, he was thirty-six years old and already had established himself as the most important poet of his generation. In the preceding ten years he had published nine books, which had revolutionized Turkish poetry by introducing free verse and flouting the proprieties and conventions of Ottoman verse. During the same period he had been in and out of prison, serving almost five years on a variety of trumped-up political charges. It was the thirteen years he spent in prison between 1938 and 1950, however, that radically changed his poetry in manner and content: a more serious tone, a simpler and more direct style, and a growing interest in the lives of common people mark this change. As a pasha's grandson and an Istanbul intellectual, Hikmet had had no real contact with Anatolian peasants, who made up nearly ninety percent of Turkey's population. The lengthy prison stay gave him a true education in what it meant to be a "poet of the people," and the experience enabled him to write *Human Landscapes*, which is filled with characters based on real-life models from Bursa Prison. Hikmet wrote: "At least half the people depicted—sometimes in five lines, sometimes throughout the first three books—in *Landscapes* are people whose lives I personally witnessed; the other half are heroes of my imagination."

The evolution of *Human Landscapes from My Country* offers valuable insights into its aims. In September 1940 Hikmet started what he called "The Encyclopedia of Famous Men," a long poem that represented in its scale and style an early attempt to deal with his new experience. The fact that he could no longer publish his poetry—his books were banned in Turkey after he went to prison—led him to abandon the rhetorical mode of the topical poems on current political figures and events that he was writing immediately before his imprisonment. He came to realize that his time in prison would be best spent producing a poetic history of the present, which might be of use to the future. Hikmet conceived of his "Encyclopedia" as a series of portraits, ranging from two-or-three-line epitaph-like notations to more fleshed-out life stories and arranged alphabetically by the names of the "famous" men and women. As Hikmet described them, his heroes were not "generals, sultans, distinguished scientists or artists, beauty queens, murderers or billionaires; they were workers, peasants, and craftsmen, people whose fame had not spread beyond their factories, workshops, villages, or neighborhoods." Such a series of portraits done in the manner of biographical dictionaries and encyclopedias would constitute, he felt, an abbreviated social history. The individual portraits were not intended to stand alone but meant to function as parts of a whole, as separate "lines" of the whole "poem." In Hikmet's view, just as a poem combines lines of different values—plain as well as brilliant lines, both muted and resounding lines, lines of one syllable and thirty syllables—the variety of "lives" in his "Encyclopedia"— some modest and indistinguishable from their epitaphs, others more complex and sketched in greater detail; some presented through their thoughts only, others seen in their milieus—would, when combined, create a new entity, a document delineating a historical period and reality yet not exceeding the bounds of poetry.

Hikmet's simile reveals the compositional principle that would become the method of *Human Landscapes*: he emphasizes less the units of separately "finished" lines or portraits and more the variety that constitutes the larger unit of the poem and lends it greater range and flexibility. This conception defines a social and aesthetic position that would yield a new style, even though the "Encyclopedia" itself remained an experiment.

In June 1941 Hikmet embarked on another long poem upon hearing of Hitler's invasion of Russia, which convinced him of the need for an epic—a history of the twentieth century: "To start with Hitler's attack and work back to the Boer War, then to work forward again, and to keep at this history till the end of my life, was my goal. I had no doubt that fascism would be defeated and that I would get out of prison." This poem, eventually entitled *Human Landscapes from My Country,* superseded the "Encyclopedia"; yet many of the original portraits survive in the opening section of *Landscapes.* The title of the new work indicates a less encyclopedic and more compositional approach, stressing the relationships among people as well as their interplay with their social and natural settings. And Hikmet's statement of his intentions projects the scope of the poem: the personal life of the imprisoned poet and the history of modern Europe would mark its boundaries. For *Landscapes* ranges beyond Turkey, and the ongoing war in Europe provides Hikmet with a context for epic action—the possibility of heroism not confined to national examples. In fact, war became his central theme. *Human Landscapes* has no single hero; its hero is a composite "fighter," and the "war" includes the First World War, the defeat of the Ottoman Empire and the Allied occupation of Turkey; the subsequent Turkish War of Independence and the establishment of the Republic; the Second World War, which Turkey mobilized for but never entered; and the civil "war" Hikmet's political prisoners are engaged in.

Hikmet initially envisioned a 10,000-line poem. In 1941 he reports in a letter, "I'm writing fifty lines a day. It will be finished in six months and have 10,000 lines." But the poem kept growing, and he kept revising it in content and conception; in 1944, for example, he writes, "I pass my days in uninterrupted work from 8:30 a.m. to midnight, and I am happy. *Landscapes* is proceeding full speed ahead. It's getting longer and longer, but what can I do? Life is so various, people and their lives so curious, and I am so greedy, so eager to put it all in one book, that I can never call an end to it." As the poem expanded, so did Hikmet's conception of his form, until he became unwilling even to call it a poem. *"Landscapes,"* he explains, "is not a poetry book. It has elements of poetry and sometimes even technical stuff like rhymes, etc. But it also has elements of prose and drama and even movie scenarios. And what determines the character of the whole, the dominant factor, is not the element of poetry. But it's not any of the others, either. I'm trying to say that I've stopped being a poet; I've become something else." He was not afraid to say this, because he valued what he had gained more. In *Landscapes,* he felt, there was no dichotomy between poetry and prose, and he referred to the work both as an "epic" and as a "novel."

Hikmet regarded his language as a historical synthesis of oral poetry—

which, designed to be sung, relied heavily on such devices as rhyme, meter, and repetition—and its antithesis, the printed prose novel designed to be read silently in private. Such a synthesis, which he argued was necessitated by developments in the non-print media, represented a new language that could both be memorized and read aloud on the radio to large numbers of people and be taken in by the eye by solitary individuals. While he aimed to synthesize poetry and prose, the techniques of poetry offered advantages over prose. For one thing, poetry was more economical: it could say so much more so much faster than prose. Thus Hikmet employs poetic techniques, but not for self-protection or to distance himself from his material. For someone of his literary education in Russian Futurism and European modernism, *Landscapes* represents something of an act of courage. Here poetic language is not allowed to mark the poet's distance from the lives he is portraying, and Hikmet's discovery of such a language opened up for him an immense area—a store of material for fiction. The lives of ordinary people, which in European and other "advanced" literatures had been relegated to prose, was essentially unclaimed in Turkish literature at Hikmet's time. His use of such material places *Landscapes* at the source of modern Turkish fiction as well; the contemporary novelist Yashar Kemal, for example, has repeatedly cited the poem as a major influence on his work. In fact, one of Hikmet's models for the poem was no doubt the epic novel *War and Peace*, which he translated into Turkish while working on *Landscapes*.

A compendium of all Hikmet knew about human life, *Human Landscapes* is also a compendium of various modes of representing it. Indeed, this blurring of the distinctions between genres contributes to the epic stature of *Landscapes*. Ezra Pound defined an epic as "a poem including history." Hikmet's poem is, and was meant to be, a short history of Turkey since the Constitution of 1908. Yet epics are also histories that include poetry. Suzanne Langer's definition of "epic" conveys its peculiar status. The epic, she writes, "is the great matrix of all poetic genres. There are lyric verses, romantic quests, descriptions of ordinary life, self-contained incidents that read like a ballad." Moreover, as C. S. Lewis points out, primary epics like the Homeric poems and *Beowulf* always contain descriptions of "poetical performances, at feasts and the like, proceeding in the world which they show us." The "feast" with its epic recital occurs in Book Two of *Landscapes*, when the waiter serving the upperclass passengers in the dining car recites to his fellow workers Hikmet's "Epic of the Independence War." As Hikmet admitted, his "Epic of the Independence War" was not an autonomous work created in isolation;

the poem commemorated a social environment and a history that transpired within it. *Landscapes* provides the "social context" or setting for the "epic" of the Independence War, which is distinguished by its stylized diction and form. Thus *Landscapes* encompasses not only social and political history and varieties of literary genres but epic poetry itself.

There is no doubt that Hikmet consciously placed *Human Landscapes* in the epic tradition. The episodic plot, the central motif of a journey (complete with a descent into the "underworld" in Book Two, Section III), and the stylistic devices of repeated epithets and digressions looping away from the main action all constitute conscious "epic" allusions. Hikmet even gives us a transformation of the figure of the "blind bard," who traditionally signified the imagination and the necessity of preserving the past in memory. The political prisoner Halil, one face of Hikmet's composite epic hero, who is growing blind alludes to this figure of the oral tradition.

Halil has no gift of song—of memory or prophecy—but as a writer and scholar he has knowledge of historical necessity: he is the scholar as poet, the historian as seer of the past and the future. His alter ego is the poet Jelal, whom we never meet. Together they comprise the Marxist poet, the two faces of Nazim Hikmet. The epic hero, however, has still more faces and includes, for example, the farmer Kazim and the worker Fuat. The multifaceted epic hero corresponds to the multiplicity of styles, techniques, genres, and points of view, which renders *Landscapes* something of a cultural product. Indeed, there is a sense in which the poem is literally a cooperative venture, for the prisoners Hikmet knew provided not only the characters for his poem but the audience and criticism that helped shape it. As he wrote his epic, Hikmet would read it to his fellow inmates, and any phrasing, diction, or episode that did not ring true to them was immediately revised. Thus *Landscapes* is the joint fiction of novelist and poet, social historian, folklorist, and dramatist, author, characters, and audience, and it presents life itself as a joint human creation. This is the meaning of the inclusiveness of the epic genre, and this is ultimately the only political "message" of *Landscapes*: human beings have the power to make and change human life.

The plot of *Landscapes* is episodic yet carefully structured by dramatic mirrorings of characters, scenes, and actions. Drawing on his experience not only as a playwright but as a screenwriter, Hikmet composes his story as a montage and alludes—in his radical juxtapositions of different tenses, images, and perspectives—to such cinematic techniques as pans, zooms, and freeze frames, jump cuts and dissolves, flashbacks and even forward flashes. The action fans out from a single point,

Haydar Pasha Station in Istanbul. We start with one man on the steps of the station; we shift to the other people he sees; they board the Ankara train; and we witness the whole range of lower-class social life on the train, while taking in the passing spring countryside and learning about the people who inhabit it. Book Two mirrors this plan, one man in the station café serving to introduce us to a different cast of characters. We follow the express train, along the same route to Ankara on the same day, and get to meet the middle and upper classes. The device of parallel train journeys enables Hikmet to move freely among people from different social backgrounds and classes, ranging from the dispossessed and the unemployed to senators and industrialists, from soldiers and prisoners to students and merchants, from factory workers and peasants to doctors and professors' wives. Such a variety of lives and experiences the journey brings together provides for a corresponding mix of levels of diction, including different dialects and styles of speech as well as allusions to various sorts of folk material, proverbs, folk tales, and popular beliefs and practices. The form of a journey also allows Hikmet to depict the varied geography of Turkey and the sharp contrast between rural and urban life. Finally, the device gives him historical mobility, since the terrain crossed includes major battle sites of the Independence War, and the places passed en route trigger in the passengers memories of events in national history.

While Book Three is stationary and presents a prison and a hospital in a town on the steppe, Books Four and Five move in radical ways. For example, we change scenes by following first the course of nature in the seasonal migration of birds and, later, radio waves and the mail. These books establish the wider networks of communication characteristic of a shrunken globe, where the Atlantic war touches life in a Turkish town on the Mediterranean. Thus Hikmet can stage private lives, hopes, and griefs in the larger contexts of natural, national, and global history. And the background of the Second World War enables him to cut across his various parallel stories in order to relate them in and as a present, thereby animating them with historical reality and significance.

The scale of *Human Landscapes from My Country* shows that Hikmet indeed took on "life in the twentieth century." Yet his preface to the 1962 Russian translation comes to a rather modest conclusion: "I'm curious about just one thing. As you watch these pictures flash past, will you be bored or not?" For the ultimate purpose of *Landscapes* is to convince us that every human life is interesting; this is its supreme and wonderful fiction.

Mutlu Konuk

BOOK ONE

Hatijé Pirayé.
Where she was born,
how old she is,
I did not ask,
I did not think to think,
I do not know.
The kindest woman in the world
and the most beautiful.
My wife.
Here
        facts don't count . . .
This work, begun in 1939 at the Istanbul House of Detention
and completed . . . . ,
is dedicated to her.

Haydar Pasha Station,
spring 1941,
                    3 p.m.
On the steps, sun
                    fatigue
                              and confusion.

A man
          stops on the steps,
                    thinking about something.
Thin.
Scared.
His nose is long and pointed,
and his cheeks are pockmarked.
The man on the steps,
                    Master Galip,
                              is famous for thinking strange thoughts:
"If I could eat sugar wafers every day," he thought
                                        when he was 5.
"If I could go to school," he thought
                    at 10.
"If I could leave Father's knife shop
before the evening prayers," he thought
                    at 11.
"If I could buy a pair of yellow shoes
so the girls will look at me," he thought
                    at 15.
"Why did Father close his knife shop?
And the factory is nothing like his shop,"
                                        he thought
                              at 16.

"Will my pay go up?" he thought
                    at 20.
"Father died at fifty—
will I die early, too?" he thought
                              when he was 21.
"What if I get laid off?" he thought
                    at 22.
"What if I get laid off?" he thought
                    at 23.

"What if I get laid off?" he thought
                    at 24.
And out of work from time to time,
he thought "What if I get laid off?"
                    till he was 50.
At 51 he thought: "I'm old—
          I've lived one year longer than my father."
Now he's 52.
He's out of work.
Stopped on the steps now,
      he's lost
            in the strangest of thoughts:
"When will I die?
Will I have a bed to die in?"
                    he thinks.
His nose is long and pointed.
His cheeks are pockmarked.

Spring comes to Haydar Pasha Station
with the smell of fish in the sea
                    and bedbugs on the floor.

Baskets and saddlebags
      go up and down,
            stopping to rest
                  on the steps.

A child
      about five
      comes down the steps with a policeman.
There is no record of his birth,
but his name is Kemal.

A saddlebag climbs the steps,
                    a carpetbag.

Kemal coming down the steps
      without shoes or a shirt
            is all alone
                  in the universe.

Hunger is all he remembers,
                    plus the shadowy figure of a woman
                              in some dark place.

The saddlebag going up the steps
is embroidered red, black, and blue.
Carpetbags
        used to ride wagons, horses, mules;
now they ride trains.

A woman comes down the steps.
Cloaked,
        fat.
Adviyé Hanum.
Originally from the Caucasus.
She got measles in 1895
        and married in 1902.
She washed clothes.
She cooked.
She bore children.
And when she dies, she knows
        her coffin will be covered with a shawl
                from one of the sultan's mosques:
one of her son-in-laws is an imam.

On the steps, sunlight
            a stalk of green onion
            and a man:
            Corporal Ahmet.
He fought in the Balkan War.
He fought in the Great War.
He fought in the Greek War.
"Hang in there, brother, the end's in sight,"
                        he's famous for saying.
A girl goes up the steps.
She works at the stocking factory
in Galata—Tophané Street.
Atifet is thirteen.
Master Galip
looks at Atifet:

"If I'd married,
        I'd have a granddaughter her age,"
                        he thinks.
"She could work and look after me,"
                        he thinks.
Then he suddenly remembers Shevkiyé.
Emin's daughter.
With the bluest eyes.
Last year,
        before she'd even had her changes,
                they ruined her in Shahbaz's field.

Baskets and saddlebags
        go up and down,
                stopping to rest
                        on the steps.

Corporal Ahmet,
a soldier once again,
caught up with the carpetbag
and kissed his hand.
The carpetbag
        (and blue shirt, overcoat, black shalvars,
                        and sneakers,
                        felt hat, beard,
                        and Lahore
                                sash)
                patted the corporal on the shoulder and said:
"Don't sweat a couple loans.
I won't put the squeeze on you.
        We'll just add a little interest."

In Haydar Pasha Bay
sea gulls rise and fall
        over the carrion in the sea.
A gull's life
        is nothing to envy.

The station clock reads
        five past three.

Down by the silos
        they're loading wheat
                on an Italian freighter.

The carpetbag parted with the corporal
                and entered the station.

On the steps, sun
                fatigue
                        and confusion—
        plus a gold-headed dead butterfly.
Heedless of the huge human feet,
ants drag the dead butterfly
                across the longest, whitest stone.

Adviyé Hanum
walked up to the policeman.
They discussed something.
She patted little Kemal.
And all together they left
        for the police station.
And though
        he'll never again see
                the shadowy woman
                        he dimly remembers,
        the child Kemal
                is no longer all alone
                        in the universe.
He'll wash a few dishes,
                carry some water,
and live at Adviyé Hanum's knee.

A group of prisoners goes up the steps,
joking
        and laughing:
three men,
one woman,
and four guardsmen.
The men with handcuffs,
the woman without,

the guardsmen with bayonets.

On the steps, an apricot rose
                 a cigarette package
                       a newspaper.

The prisoners stopped.
Guardsman Hasan
       shook hands with Corporal Ahmet.
Guardsman Haydar
       picked up the empty package
          and stuck it in his pocket.
And the woman prisoner
       kissed Atifet, who came running up to her,
          on both cheeks.
Handcuffed Halil looked down
at the newspaper next to the apricot rose:
       "A single-column soldier.
       Unclear what uniform.
       Unshaven.
       Head in white bandages.
       Blood on the bandages.
       Then airplanes
          like winged sharks—
             'dive-bombing,' it says.
       And then a harbor
          with tiny white circles drawn on it.
       Can't read the name—
       the ink's dissolved by a kerosene stain."

Three ladies
       in pointed hats
       and platform shoes
ran up the stairs—
commuters.

Handcuffed Suleyman
         saw the ladies.
He pictured a young woman.
Aiming at the apricot rose,

          he spat.
Handcuffed Fuat
          called out:
"Master Galip,
          you're thinking strange things again."
"Just thinking, son.
You take care."
"Thanks.
But thinking doesn't change life."

Fuat
is a fitter in the dockyards.
He went to prison at nineteen
          for pulling down the shades
          and reading a book with two friends.
He's been inside two years.
Now they're sending him to the interior.

Galip looks
at Fuat's handcuffs
and has a scary thought
                    this time.
Things that have built up unknown
          until this moment
          rush
                    all together
                              in torrents
          like water bursting from a capped spring
                    —muddy,
                              clear—
          and flood his head:
"So many factories in Istanbul,
          so many in Turkey,
so many in the world you can't count them!
The lathe-turner Drunk Kadir was found dead
last night outside the university gates
          —one of the women students fainted.
So many belts and pulleys,
          so many flywheels,
                    so many motors

turning and turning and turning, forever turning,
so many people, so many people thinking,
'What if I get laid off? What if I get laid off?'
The typesetter Shahap went blind
                      and goes begging in the print shops.
Textile looms, drill benches, lathe benches,
pile drivers, rollers,
planes,
      planes,
           planes.
[Galip was a planer.]
Who knows how many in the world,
                how many are out of work?
But maybe they're soldiers.
When an unemployed man joins the army,
      doesn't he count as unemployed?"

"You're getting deep again, Master Galip."

Galip touched Fuat's handcuffs:
"May God"—
      his own voice scared him—
                "see all ends well,"

                            he said.

Fuat smiled
      under his fine black mustache:
"Our end is good for sure."

Galip's bleary eyes were moist,
      and his long nose quivered.
And without letting on to the others,
      he slipped twenty of his fifty-five kurush
           into Fuat's pocket.

The station clock reads eight past three.
This train leaves at 3:45.

In the third-class waiting room
              they sit

or pace
or sleep face-down.
They're not waiting for any train.

The fabric printer Omer
has crouched here since morning,
beard in his palms,
bare feet on the concrete.
And also since morning, Rejep has paced
                    back and forth in front of him,
                                        back and forth.
His long thin arms jerk up and down
                    as if juggling invisible knives.
Ali lies face-down on the table,
            his shirt torn in the back,
                    his blond head on his wrists.

In the third-class waiting room
                    they sit
                    or pace
                    or sleep face-down.
They aren't waiting for any train.

Aysel:
age unclear.
Maybe thirteen, maybe twenty.
Dark.
Skinny.
Nejla:
not quite fifteen.
Red nose,
        round face.
And her breasts are surprisingly big
under her green slicker.
Vedat:
eighteen.
Thick neck, white tie with six arrows on it,
                    and pimples.
Vedat says:
"The Bursa baths are like nowhere else.

Especially the 'Open Air.'
A hotel in a garden.
Clean customers.
Three bills a visit.
One's for the owner.
Last year I took an Armenian girl there.
Armenians are sharp,
              not like us Turks.
She made a bundle.
Put together a dowry.
You know heathen customs.
She's engaged now."
Aysel asks:
"How much do we give you?"
"I'll take five bills for you each from the owner
                    against your accounts,
                    as commission.
It's the season—
if you girls stick,
fifteen times a day,
              maybe more.
              Know what that adds up to?
Let Bursa see some class goods.
The papers said Kadikoy girls
are the most beautiful in Istanbul."

For the first time
              since morning,
the printer Omer straightened up.
He called to Rejep:
"Give me a cigarette."
Rejep raced past,
              spun around,
                    and tossed him a cigarette.

The printer Omer's father had been a mufti.
He had coconut-wood rosaries in the house,
                         gold-thread prayer rugs,
and gilt volumes hand-lettered by the calligrapher Osman,
but not a single deed to any property,

                                        a single savings bond,
or a single Hejaz Railway share.
Mufti Effendi was a pale, plump man;
                        Omer was a sickly child.
He couldn't learn Arabic;
he couldn't learn Persian.
But he took one look at the Gates of Heaven in the Book of Ahmet
            —they were just like the doors of Dolmabahtché Palace—
                and started to draw designs.
The mufti died before the Constitution.
During the Constitution the women ran off,
        taking the rosaries and prayer rugs.
Back then
        Omer must have been twenty.
He burned the calligrapher Osman's pages at Les Parisiennes.
He enlisted during the Balkan war,
was taken prisoner during the Great War,
came back, and began printing in Kalpakchilar.
The designs on Ahmet's Heavenly Gates
                        unfolded on cambric.
Wood blocks
        wood spoons
            wood shop
and, in the evening, a clay jug of wine
and (a holdover from prison camp)
        a little pederasty—
            the mufti's son Omer Effendi lived happily.
Until
        ready-made patterns arrived from Italy.
The paper patterns
        closed the doors of the printing shops
                        one by one
                            for good.

Racing past again, Rejep
                turned
                    and threw Omer the matches.

Ali lies face-down on the table,
            his shirt torn in the back.

Aysel went to piss.
Nejla told Vedat:
"Brother,
let's not take that skinny thing.
She has gonorrhea.
She got it in Izmit last year.
She's dripping everywhere.
And don't believe her, it's a lie—
              she's not from Kadikoy."

Spring comes to Haydar Pasha Station
with the smell of fish in the sea
            and bedbugs on the floor.

In the third-class waiting room
two red-bearded Bulgarian immigrants
with blue buttons on their shirts
and homespun yellow pants worn at the knees
            squat
            on the concrete
            against the wall,
            instead of sitting on the wood benches.
One says, sad but not angry:
"If bad then,
now worse than bad.
Enough of that.
Money's brass.
Men bastards.
But that's not all—
        there's good, too."

Outside,
the 3:45 train pulls away from the platform.
Despite its sleeping car,
        it's the sorriest of trains,
        something like a six-kurush cigarette . . .

Galip saw the prisoners off
and went into the third-class waiting room.
He sat next to the printer Omer.

Ali lay face-down on the table.
Rejep suddenly stopped in front of the dead radiator,
turned the knob from cold to hot, from hot to cold,
then gave the pipes a kick,
and yelled at the top of his voice:
"All the Jews in the world should be butchered wholesale.
What's keeping you, Uncle Hitler? Come quick!"

Rejep was a dealer.
He'd been waiting all morning for Moishe
                    to show with heroin.
Galip was no friend or foe of Hitler.
But he got mad at Rejep.
He looked at the Bulgarian immigrants.
One of the redbeards said
            with the same sadness without anger:
"...a man goes to the prophet Abraham and says,
'I saw crows
rise from manure
to perch on branches
and read calls to prayer.
I saw a man
sitting at a wellspring;
he won't let the water flow,
he drinks it all.
I saw deer:
they don't run away
but chase the hunter—
go on, shoot us...'
Prophet Abraham tells the man:
'Those crows you saw
are imams and hodjas.
They dwell in manure
and read the calls to prayer...
The man drinking up the stream are nations;
they drink their people's blood,
they drink and drink, and never drink their fill,
they won't let the stream flow
            where it will.
The deer you saw are our sins,

they run to the hunters.
The hunters are money.'"

Ali lies face-down on the table,
                his shirt torn in the back,
                        his blond head on his wrists.

Rejep yelled:
"Hey, you! Is this an all-night coffeehouse, a hotel?
                                        Wake up!"
Ali didn't move.
"I'm talking to you!"
Ali didn't move.
Rejep grabbed the young man
        and rolled him over on his back.
Ali's head
        flopped.
Ali was long dead.

                        II

Near the Kiziltoprak station,
        in the garden of a wood-frame villa,
                stands a great big pistachio tree.
It leans a little to one side.
Under this pistachio,
        a woman in a yellow dress
        hangs out clothes.
The 3:45 train goes screaming past.

Concrete villas.
Lined up all the way to Pendik.
The trees are mere saplings,
the grapevines just greening.
The 3:45 train goes screaming past.

Concrete villas.
The Secretary Pasha's summer house,

a forty-room marvel,
has been torn down.
Now it's concrete villas,
concrete villas
all the way to Pendik.

Afternoons like this,
the Goztepé station is deserted,
except for a black eunuch of the Harem
           sitting by himself
                always on the same bench.
He's very tall,
very thin.
One of the last.
The oldest.
Concrete villas.
The 3:45 train goes screaming past.

Schoolgirls in shiny black satin uniforms
walk among the pines, looking awfully serious.
Proud of their breasts.
Books in their hands.
The 3:45 train goes screaming past.
Concrete villas.
Concrete villas.

The sea looks milky.
It's lost its color to the sun.
Along the asphalt road
      people walk to the beach.
Their broad straw hats
      sway like huge yellow flowers.
Concrete villas.
The 3:45 train goes screaming past.

Islands appear in the distance,
detached from the sea floor.
Like ships,
they float on the surface.
All the way to Pendik.

Concrete villas.
The Kartal cement factory
            covered with sad,
            thick dust.
And on the shore, camouflaged gasoline tanks.
The 3:45 train goes screaming past.

Pendik.
The train stopped.
Fuat tapped Halil on the knee
            with his handcuffs
and pointed out the plainclothesman on the platform:
beady little eyes,
        pug nose,
jug ears.
Shoulders hunched.
Navy-blue suit,
        tan shoes,
                and crumpled black felt hat.
Hands probably sticky-soft.
Something's in his back pocket—
        his jacket bulges
                just above it.

The 3:45 train left Pendik.

The locomotive.
The engineer Aladdin
        undid one more button of his blue overalls.
He stuck his head out
        and looked back:
the baggage car,
            five passenger cars
                    (counting the sleeper and the diner)
                        and six boxcars
came rocking along
                one after another.
Whenever Aladdin looks back
                        —especially on inclines—
he feels as if the cars were roped together

and harnessed to his shoulders.
And on descents
> he feels their awful weight
> between his shoulder blades.

The cars came rocking along.

Eskishehir-Haydar Pasha; Haydar Pasha-Eskishehir:
since '28,
passengers have come and gone,
engines have changed,
but Aladdin is in his place,
Aladdin hasn't changed.

The cars came rocking along.

To get on the Simplon Express at Sirkeji Station
—not this mail train—
like a passenger with a linen-covered suitcase!
To sleep in the *wagon-lit.*
And, especially,
to sit by the little red lamps at night
> and sip raki in the *wagon-restaurant . . .*

The cars came rocking along.

"Hey, boss!"
Aladdin turned to the fireman Ismail:
"What is it, Ismail?"
"Boss, how will this war end?"
"It'll end well."
"How's that?"
"We'll drink raki in the dining car."
"Us?"
"Us."
"Who'll shovel the coal?
> Who'll drive the engine?"
"We'll do that, too."
"Seriously, boss,
who'll win?"

"Us."

Ismail didn't really understand,
              but he let it go.
He rubbed his thick black eyebrows
and said: "Boss,
        I have another question.
        These rails here,
              do they go around the whole world?"
"They do."
"So if there's no war,
and not just no war
but if no questions are asked at borders,
and we let the engine loose on the rails,
it'll go from one end of the world to the other?"
"When you say 'sea,' it stops."
"You get on ships."
"Airplanes are better."
Ismail smiled.
One of his front teeth was chipped.
"I can't get on an airplane, boss—
my mother made me promise."
"Not to get on an airplane?"
"No,
        not to hurt even an ant."
Aladdin slapped Ismail's long bare neck.
"Well, aren't we pious!
No problem, man,
we'll get on airplanes anyway—
not to kill people
but just for the fun
        of breezing through the sky.
Now you go
              stoke that fire."

The cars came rocking along.

Third-class car 510.
The prisoners and guardsmen occupy the first section.
The sergeant hasn't smiled once.

Though the Mausers have been laid on the racks,
                    the handcuffs remain locked.
The two sides are in different worlds.

The prisoner Halil has opened his book.
He has mastered
                    turning the pages
with cuffed hands.
This is his fifth trip
                    in thirteen years
                              with books and handcuffs.
Lines under his eyes
and white at his temples,
        Halil may look a little older.
But his books, handcuffs, and heart haven't aged.
And now,
his heart more hopeful than ever,
Halil thinks of his handcuffs
        as he reads his book:
"Handcuffs, we'll beat
your steel
into plowshares."
And he finds this idea so well phrased
that he's sorry
he doesn't know the art of writing poetry,
measured or otherwise.

The train entered and left the Gebzé station.
It crossed a high iron bridge.
On the right, the earth dropped off sharply
                    maybe a hundred,
                              maybe a hundred and fifty fathoms,
and there,
        way down
                below,
the "Old Fort" village and fortress,
the two horsemen on the long narrow road,
the olive trees, and even the empty sea
look like toys just taken out of their boxes,
                    so small

and colorful,
so distant
    deep
and clean in the spring light,
      because so quickly left behind.

The prisoner Fuat
saw and would not forget
    the deep road and its two horsemen
    sinking into the distance toward his big city.
And because Istanbul was lost to him for the first time,
he suddenly started talking about home.
"My grandfather," he said, "my grandfather
    was a strange man.
He was a lieutenant commander in the navy.
We've only got one photograph of him.
You can tell that under his long pointed fez
    his head's been shaved with a razor.
He was incredibly reactionary.
Imagine: when the Constitution came,
he renewed his marriage license
    out of allegiance to Sultan Abdul Hamid.
He retired three years later anyway
and opened a corner store in Kulaksiz.
He died in 1922
during the liberation of Istanbul,
in October.
They found his body in the kitchen,
all alone
beside the food cupboard.
Children were singing marches in the street."

The prisoner Suleyman kidded Fuat:
"Your social origins are pretty mixed—
      reactionary militarism
      and petty bourgeoisie."

Fuat ignored him and went on:
"I can still see my father.
A man with long yellow fingers.

He was a master wood-carver
          in the carpentry shop of the dry docks.
He was very fond of old calligraphy.
Mornings he would read the call to prayer,
          and you could hear him as far as the fairgrounds.
He sulked
          and wouldn't read it
                    after Arabic was outlawed.
He died of TB at thirty-five."
Suleyman asked:
"And your mother?"
"Died giving birth to me.
I grew up in the carpentry shop—
          in my father's toolbox.
It was a green box.
He'd take the tools out at the shop
          and put me to sleep inside it."

Third-class car number 510.
The corridor.
A university student paces up and down.

Third-class car number 510.
Second section.
Canned sardines, lemons,
          bread, cheese,
                    bottles:
men and women
          drinking.
The National Operetta Company
—eight performers
and the famous composer Mehmet Ali—
is on tour.

Third-class car number 510.
First section.
Handcuffed Fuat laughs, flashing his white teeth,
because handcuffed Suleyman can't stand
                    the university student
                              peering in the window,

probably at Melahat.
Uncuffed Melahat,
flaunting the freedom of her pale thin wrists
and happy she can use her hands,
                    eats an apple.

The student kept staring.
Suleyman spoke up.
Guardsman Haydar agreed
        with him and lowered the shade
        on the glass door.
And so began
        the friendship of the prisoners
                and the peasant guardsmen.

Handcuffed Halil
        (maybe he'd noticed everything,
        maybe nothing)
                looked up from the book on his knee
                        and asked Guardsman Haydar:
"How many households in your village?"
"Around fifty."
"How many have more than one pair of oxen?"
"Two."
"How many with just a single ox?"
"With a single ox, about fifteen."
"Without any?"
"Five or six, I guess."
"And the rest?"
"One pair of oxen."
"You?"
"I've got a pair."
Suleyman asked:
"Any families without land?"
"Sure, some."
Fuat broke in.
The talk went on.
And such a moment of friendship occurred
                (beyond suspicion and orders)
                        that the peasant guardsmen exchanged glances

and, joking in their thick voices
as if doing some happy job together,
unlocked the handcuffs.

The corridor.
The student paced up and down.
Someone from the fifth section bolted out of his compartment.
It was a short, potbellied pair of pants.
All in a sweaty rush,
he threw open every single window.
And leaning out the last one,
he took three deep breaths.
Suddenly he spun on his heel.
He had a low narrow forehead
and broad full cheeks.
His head sat on his shoulders
like a huge pear.
His crossed blue eyes lit on the student:
"My good man," he gasped,
"I almost suffocated!
They're a bunch of pigs in my compartment—
the filth
the sweat
the stink.
They won't open the window."

He approached the student:
"You're a student?
I could tell.
From the gray wolf on your cap.
Except a lot of funny fellows
wear those caps.
So I've heard.
That's what they say.
I haven't seen it myself.
I've got no cloth in that loom.
Except I'd be lying if I said I hadn't tried it.
When the English came to Istanbul,
those Scotch boys with no pants . . .
And the poor Persians, they just have a bad name.

Except a man should sample every pleasure.
Pleasure
        is what life's all about.
Except, brother, you got to have money.
Love, life, and all that—
        it all comes down to dough.
Now try telling this to the pigs in there.
Those jerks won't open the window.
Look,
here's some fatherly advice:
your health is sacred.
You have to take care of your body.
A raw egg every morning is a must.
I've got three little donkeys at home.
Except each morning they drink three raw eggs.
And we have this custom:
when I come home from work,
                I find out from their mother
                        if they've been bad
                        or good.
And depending on that,
        a bird brings a little something to the window:
                        it could be an apple,
                                an orange,
                                        or a candy bar.
Of course, it's not a bird—
                I bring it.
But my youngest
                caught on one night.
                The next day he told his mother:
                'The bird looks just like Daddy.
                        His spitting image.'
Except I'm convinced
you gotta test your kids' I.Q.
I test it all the time.
There's a famous story:
one of the sultans wanted to teach his son how to tell fortunes."

The student smiled:
"I know that story," he said.

And then, just to say something, he asked:
"Are you in the civil service?"
"Well,
you could say so.
I'm an accountant at the Istanbul Nursing Home.
The name is Nuri Ozturk.
We're on the government pay scale.
But I once sold tickets at Salajak.
I was in business, too—
         a salesman, a merchant.
I've done just about everything
         but run a coffeehouse.
That's the one thing I didn't get to do.
I even drove a cab.
Had my own car.
The golden age of taxis.
I'll never forget one summer day,
                  late afternoon,
I'd dropped a fare at Chiftehavuzlar
                  and headed back.
I saw a woman walking up ahead.
In a black coat.
Her legs caught my eye—
            well-turned.
When I got up next to her, I stopped the car.
I looked at her face:
         classy, somebody's wife for sure.
And she had these big black eyes.
The Devil got into me:
         I opened the door
              and said, 'Please.'
She got in.
I drove off.
Where to?
She doesn't say and I don't ask.
I can see her eyes in the rear-view mirror:
            they're so black,
                  so big,
         just so.
We turned up at Jaddebostan.

Erenkoy, Upper Erenkoy, fields.
I stopped the car.
Under a nice plane tree.
Not a soul around.
I took her out of the car.
She doesn't say a word.
I lay her on the ground.
Still not a word.
Except I'm kissing her.
She's just like a statue.
Anyway, to make a long story short,
we finished our business and got up.
Into the car again.
We started back.
Back to where?
Like before, she doesn't say and I don't ask.
Like before, I can see her eyes in the mirror:
       her eyes are still, like I said, so black,
          so big,
        just so.
We came to Kiziltoprak.
The lights were on downtown.
I stopped in front of a fruit stand.
I opened the door.
The woman got out,
       walked away, turned, and disappeared.
Now, what do you think of that, my man?
Except how can I say—
    or, as the Albanians say,
       how can I make it said?
I mean, it's been thirteen or fourteen years—
I can't get that pasha's wife out of my mind.
Because she was a pasha's wife for sure.
Well, I didn't have this belly then,
and my mustache was like silk,
    yellow as an egg yolk.
I cut a wide swath through the Parisian quarter of Kadikoy.
I've lived, my man,
       I've lived my life.
Now try telling all this

to the pigs in there.
Those jerks won't open the window."

Those who wouldn't open the window
                    were in the fifth section.
The owner of the carpetbag
sat at the head of the section,
          in the corner seat
                    on the left,
like an enormous,
          cunning
                    bird of prey.
Felt hat on his head, overcoat on his back,
his black shalvars spread out in easy folds,
and with his sneakers off,
his feet in white wool socks
                    were as animated as his hands
                    beside them on the wooden bench.
And he didn't listen to the conversation with his hairy ears
                              but with his feet.
The subject was demons.

Across from him, Blond Seyfettin
          (the mayor of a Circassian village in Adapazari)
          talked away,
                    his Adam's apple bobbing up and down:
"Don't ever undress without asking God's blessing.
All things need God's blessing.
Or the demons steal your clothes
          and raise Cain all night."
The carriage driver Selim—from Eskishehir, fiftyish, bald—
                    agreed with Seyfettin:
"It's the same with horses.
If you tie up a horse in the stable at night
                    without asking God's blessing,
the demons get on it
and ride till dawn.
Plus, they weave the horse's hair into tiny little braids.
It's happened to me lots of times:
I go into the stable in the morning,

the animal's tied up in there all right,
              but it's frothing at the mouth
                    soaking wet,
and its hair's braided like a bride's.
Most of the braids won't comb out—
                nothing to do but cut them.
Where do the demons go at night,
          riding these horses under the moon?
People have enough trouble as it is.
Because we forget to ask God's blessing,
He sets these demons on us.
Wonder what they're like?
          Are they like people?
They act like people:
          thieving,
                seeking their pleasure,
                      making trouble . . . "

The Tartar-faced man sitting by the door
          (from a Bursa village, a watchman at the Merino factory)
                answered Selim:
"I was visited by them.
They appeared to me.
Six weeks, day and night.
It happened because of a lute.
The sultan of strings is the nine-string *jura*.
Whenever I heard of a *jura* master somewhere
                      —even at seven days' distance,
                      in raging winter—
                      I'd sit him on my donkey
                      and take him to the village.
But I can't learn the *jura*, no way.
There's this famous *jura* player.
A Gypsy.
Known as Master Alish.
He told me:
          'A curse must descend on your wrist
          before you can master this instrument.'
'Okay,' I said,
'but how will a curse descend on my wrist?'

'On the Night of Revelation,' Alish said, 'on the 27th of Ramazan,
       you'll take the *jura* and go to the bathroom.
And you'll sit backwards in there
       and start playing.'
I followed Alish to the word.
Revelation Night was close anyway.
I went to the bathroom.
Sat backwards.
Touched the strings.
But no sound.
I adjusted the frets.
No use.
But no sound,
as if the thing called 'sound' had disappeared from the earth.
I threw away the cherry pick
                       and plucked the strings with my fingers.
The strings don't break
       and they don't make a sound.
They stretch like rubber and snap back.
Alish, help,
       what *is* this?
              I'm losing my mind—
then they appeared.
Some smaller than a lentil seed,
                  some tall as a minaret.
Their clothes look like ours,
but they have cone hats—
              red, green, long, and pointed.
All on horseback.
They draw their swords
       and attack me.
I must have thrown myself out of there.
Night and day for six weeks, they never left.
My grandfather broke and burned my instrument.
They say they chained me in the basement.
They called in hodjas to exorcise them.
No use.
Finally, they called Master Alish.
Gypsy Alish
put his own *jura* in my hands.

And I started to play.
The more I played, they say, the more I came round,
        the more I could play.
Then I passed out.
When I came to, no swords or horsemen—
                    they're gone.
But from that day on,
no one in all of Bursa
        can play the *jura* like me."

He fell quiet.
The driver Selim glared at him.
The owner of the carpetbag
stroked his wool socks
as if petting two white lambs.
Across from him came a weak voice
        like the squeal of a beaten animal:
"The water in my belly
        is probably their work, too."
The speaker
was a tiny man
        (or else he'd shrunk);
his face was thin and yellow,
            the skin drawn at the temples.
And his eyes glittered
        in his bony face.
Death often begins in the face
        with protruding temples.
And death
had begun in the face of the Sakarya peasant Shakir.
"This water in my belly
        is probably their work, too."
Shakir has cirrhosis.
"I know what I know.
The doctor took ten buckets of water out of my belly,
                and it swelled up again in three days.
No way I'll get well.
The demons got in my belly.
I know
        I'll die.

I said: 'Doctor, don't discharge me—
I got wounded for my country on so many fronts,
what would it hurt if I died in a bed with springs?'
The doctor wouldn't listen.
I guess they wanted to save the bed with springs
                    for someone they still had hope for.
I have the wounds, I have the pain,
                    but I have no hope.
The city gave me money for the train,
                    and I'm going back.
What luck,
                    what fucking bad luck—
of all the people in the world, it had to find me."

The train stopped at Hereké Station.
The engineer Aladdin stepped down from the locomotive
                    and checked something near the rear wheels.
The engine looked alive,
as if it had nerves and a heart—
                    young, impatient, and sleek as a racehorse.
Hereké Station is a quaint little place.
Hereké itself
        is an hour away
                    and out of sight.
At the station they sold cherries, dangling
from long sticks like red earrings.
            (From here on, cherry and olive trees line the tracks.)
Across from the station stood the textile factory,
                    facing the sea.
You think you can almost see inside it from the train.
The prisoner Suleyman leaned out the window and bought cherries.
By the time the student finished drinking from the spigot,
                    the train had started moving.
Suleyman saw him:
"He'll miss the train, the dirty womanizer," he thought happily.
But the student jumped on.

The train headed for Yarimja,
now and then losing the sea
                    —for just a moment—

and coming full upon it once again.
In the fifth section of car 510
              they discussed the war.
The owner of the carpetbag listened,
from time to time
              pulling at the tip of his nose
                    —a nose curved like a knife handle—
              above his black beard.
The carriage driver Selim from Eskishehir said:
"The Germans are doomed to defeat—
whatever happens, they'll be brought down for good.
Thugs, those who wreak havoc,
          always die like dogs or end up pimps
                  or night watchmen."
Blond Seyfettin (the mayor of the Circassian village)
                    disagreed.
"I don't know about the Germans,
but thugs don't end up pimps."
The driver Selim almost screamed:
"They end worse!
Huseyin Agha of Zindankapi
was a pretty big man.
He held all of Eskishehir at knifepoint.
Had gold to burn, too.
And what happened to him?
When a two-bit punk,
          the drunk Sherif,
flattened his nose at a whorehouse,
he was finished.
He couldn't show his face anywhere.
Then we heard they found his body in a ditch.
He'd been living off what fish he could catch.
He was trying to catch his supper
              when he got nailed in a ditch."
The owner of the carpetbag spoke,
his voice soft and puffy
              like fluffed cotton.
"The Germans will win.
I heard from high up.
They said this heathen called Hitler

is really a Muslim:
        he has a secret religion.
No wonder all those countries together still can't beat him."
Stunned, the driver Selim
        wanted to say something.
Blond Seyfettin,
as if seizing a chance to get even
        for a personal insult, glared at Selim,
                triumphant:
"Thugs can't be pimps!" he said.
The owner of the carpetbag continued:
"There's this pasha,
one of the old pashas.
In the Great War, he alone could beat the heathen English.
Now he's retired.
He's in business and writes for the papers, too.
We should either join with the Germans, he says,
        or let them pass through the Straits.
This is a big pasha,
        and he writes for the papers, too.
In the Great War, he alone could beat the heathen English.
My grocer, Haji Nuri Bey, knows him.
Haji Nuri Bey told me
        the Germans drove into the Balkans
                and made short work of the English and Greeks.
But, thank God, we're Muslims:
        the man respects us.
If we join the Germans
        and jump the English,
we can get Damascus
        back in one day."

Kazim from Kartal
        or Kazim Agha from the village of Yayalar
            or Kazim Effendi of Istanbul
        (about 45, he looked like a wolf)
said to Shakir: "Have a smoke."
Shakir from Sakarya
        (the one they took ten buckets of water from)
        sucked on the cigarette

as if rubbing salt and tobacco on an open wound.
How awful the desire
    to die in a bed with springs!
Shakir from Sakarya knew it.
Kazim from Kartal
leaned his head back against the wood.
His yellow wolf-eyes narrowed.
He watched Shakir,
    his head swaying from side to side,
rocking with the car:
        "Mehmets," he thinks,
            "Mehmets, poor Mehmets."
And one after another
the wheels clack away on the tracks, repeating
    (faster and faster, louder and louder):
            "Mehmets, poor Mehmets.
            Mehmets, poor Mehmets."
And the years of the Great War and the Mehmets' faces,
wrenched out of the darkness
and torn to shreds on the black brambles, pass
before Kazim in one endless troop movement.
Why does the comfort of today come so easy?
Why is remembering past disaster so hard?
Kazim was a brakeman in Pozanti,
        the year 1917...
Day and night troops on the move to the front.
Where does it start, where does it end?
Trains with wood-burning engines.
The smell of burnt pine the length of the tracks.
The army has the deed to the length of the tracks.
            Mehmets, poor Mehmets,
            Mehmets, poor Mehmets.
      Doomsday on four fronts...
The cars are made for forty people each,
but each holds eighty, a hundred Mehmets.
The doors of the cars are all locked.
The trains roll on, packed with Mehmets.
            Mehmets, poor Mehmets,
            Mehmets, poor Mehmets.
      The locked cars pitiless...

Back then, Pozanti was the last stop.
Brakeman Kazim undresses,
squats down facing the sun, and picks his lice.
Mehmets everywhere, everywhere troops on the move.
They leave hungry and thirsty, they come back crippled.
Death is God's will, but hunger...
If hunger doesn't drive men to attack like wolves,
it's sure to make them less than dogs.

Mehmets, poor Mehmets,
Mehmets, poor Mehmets.
The paymaster pitiless...

Pozanti is a stream burning up the sun.
Brakeman Kazim looks:
the Mehmets are skin and bones,
their mustaches droop.
The shoes on their feet are tattered and torn.
The Mehmets get down on their bellies, delirious.
The Mehmets pick horse dung for barley.
They wash the barley in the stream.
They'll dry it in the sun and eat it.
Mehmets everywhere, everywhere troops on the move.
Death is God's will, but hunger...

Mehmets, poor Mehmets,
Mehmets, poor Mehmets.
At most a handful of barley it gives,
the horse dung pitiless...

A siding branches off to the left of the switch.
A car is pulled off on the siding.
Six Germans sit in the car.
Faces red, asses fat.
Sitting at a table, they eat spaghetti.
Maybe they aren't so fat,
but Kazim sees them like that.

Mehmets, poor Mehmets,
Mehmets, poor Mehmets.
What is the magic of being a German?

The Germans' dog is tied to the car:
roan coat, clipped ears, fat rump.
The Germans are full and feed the dog their spaghetti.
Even the Germans' dog eats spaghetti.

Maybe it doesn't always eat spaghetti,
but that's how Kazim sees it.

> Mehmets, poor Mehmets,
> Mehmets, poor Mehmets.

A Mehmet walks along the siding.
He walks toward the dog.
Down on all fours, crawling,
he stops from time to time,
lowering his head as if scared he'll be stoned.

> Mehmets, poor Mehmets,
> Mehmets, poor Mehmets.

The Mehmet snatches the spaghetti from the dog and takes off.
He runs and doesn't look back.
If hunger doesn't drive men to attack like wolves,
it's sure to make them less than dogs.
The six Germans applaud the Mehmet.
The Germans have enjoyed the show.

> Mehmets, poor Mehmets,
> Mehmets, poor Mehmets.

A partridge flits from hilltop to hilltop,
but when he takes a hit,

> he drops on the spot.

He's had it—

> he'll never fly again, even if he has the strength . . .

The hub of the troop movement was the Selimiyé Barracks,
the blasted barracks full of Mehmets back from leave.
The wounds in their flesh have healed, their leaves are over,
but the Mehmets have had it:

> a wound has opened in their hearts.

It's almost the end of the war,

> the year 1918.

Hey, the blasted
Selimiyé Barracks . . .
In the barracks yard
> the earth swarms
> > with lice.
They crackle and squish underfoot as you walk:
you tread on the Mehmets' sucked blood.

This blood has glutted lice.
This blood is dead and black.
In the Selimiyé Barracks,
              the Mehmets' flesh isn't covered with skin or hair:
                    it's crawling with lice.
In the yard they call roll
                    for shipment to the front.
The Mehmets scratch, stare at their feet,
                    and do not answer.
The Mehmets have given up hope,
and they are stubborn.
Each day a hundred Mehmets turn up dead,
              their flesh fed to hunger and lice.
Master sergeant, call your roll through the night,
              yell all you like—
the Mehmets won't go through that door alive.
But the government is stronger than the Mehmets.
One morning
Mehmets filled the yard again like grains of sand.
Maybe ten thousand,
                    maybe more.
A solid stream of Mehmets
scratching and silent.
Man upon man.
Climbed up on a table, a fresh sergeant
                    (tall,
                    with a black mustache
                          and spotless headgear)
              calls roll with no response.
One hour, two hours.
If the Mehmets are stubborn, so is the sergeant.
Two hours, three hours.
No one answers.
The sergeant can't stand it:
he swears at them, starting with their mothers.
If he's hopeful,
              even if he's alone
                    on a mountaintop, it's dangerous to swear at a Mehmet.
It's worse to curse ten thousand hopeless Mehmets in a barracks.
The Mehmets' hands reach for the legs of the table,

and the sergeant falls from the sky on his face.
The Mehmets bend down, and when they stand up,
nothing is left of the sergeant—
no flesh, no bones, no clean headgear.
A battalion of MP's is called in.
The MP Mehmets arrive.
They have bayonets, no lice, and they're well-fed.
It's as if wolves got into the flock.
The roar is like Doomsday.
Mehmets chasing Mehmets.
A couple thousand sheep are torn from the flock.
Straight to Haydar Pasha Station, the cars locked.
The cars are made for forty people each,
but each holds eighty, a hundred Mehmets.
The cars roll on, packed with Mehmets.

Mehmets, poor Mehmets,
Mehmets, poor Mehmets.

I think I killed a Mehmet
one afternoon
on the stone steps
of the Selimiyé Barracks.
The Mehmet had bread in his hand.
Who knows
    where he got it . . .
The Mehmet's mustache was blond,
   the bread black.
I untied my red sash
   (four fathoms long,
     pure light,
       silk woven into wool)
and said: "You cut me a slice,
  I'll cut you a fathom."
He shook his head.
"Two fathoms?"
He shook his head.
"Three fathoms?"
The Mehmet wanted all of my silk sash.
His mustache was blond.
I looked at the bread.
My sash lit up his eyes.

40

I kicked him in the groin.
The Mehmet rolled backward.
Like a knot popping out of a pine board,
    a bone shot out of his head.
The bread was in my hand,
but the blood shed on the stones
      —live, red—
          ran on and on
    like my silk sash.

              Mehmets, poor Mehmets,
              Mehmets, poor Mehmets.
        When hunger rears its head,
        Mehmet to Mehmet pitiless...

Rocking with the car,
Kazim's head sways from side to side.
His yellow wolf-eyes widen and narrow.
Across him, Shakir from Sakarya
      looms closer,
         recedes,
            then comes close again.
And Kazim from Kartal,
now here, now back behind the years,
hears the voices in the car
through the manifest shapes of days past.
The voice belongs to the carpetbag owner:
"We can't fight the Germans anyway.
What should we fight them with?
The couple bum weapons the English dole out?
We'll wake one morning
      and see the man has lined up his planes overhead.
They're not birds you can shoot with a shotgun;
they aren't martens you can catch in a trap."

Kazim from Kartal
sees a Mehmet life-sized before him:
barefoot,
shotgun on his shoulder,
    Martini bullets in his cartridge,
      in his hand an axe...

The year is 1919.
Mehmet is a guerrilla in the Liberation Army.
The sky behind him,
he stands guard in the Izmit mountains.
Neither hopeful nor hopeless,
                    he's in a state apart.
And in his hazel eyes, fight to the death.

Kazim woke with a start
                and stepped into the corridor.
The Tartar-faced man followed him:
"Got a light?"
"Here."

Through the open door
                came the voice of the carpetbag:
"The Germans are strong beyond description . . . "

The Tartar-face swore:
"That pig must be a paratrooper—
should we call the train police?"
Kazim laughed
                (half his teeth were missing,
                        but he laughed so much like a child
                                his mouth wasn't ugly).
"Worse," he said,
                "worse than a paratrooper.
Looks like some small-town merchant
or maybe a rich shopkeeper . . . "

"The war will end this year.
This year the Germans will beat the English."

Nuri Ozturk
        (the nursing-home accountant)
                nudged the student:
"Hear that?
The pigs are talking politics.
Except I'm for the English, of course,
but I wonder sometimes.

What do you think?"
"Those who'll win the war
                aren't in it yet."
"I don't get it.
Oh, but I see now.
Sure!
You mean us.
But you're right.
Except we'll want the Caucuses."

The student wasn't listening.
He kept his eyes on the first section, where the prisoners sat.
Voices came from inside:
the prisoner Suleyman burst out laughing.
Kazim's eyes
        lit up, happy.
From the corridor you could hear
                Suleyman's every word:
"Right on, Halil!
Our economists must be poets, too.
You know what Engels said—
                something like 'Poets see the future.'
So it came to you as a couplet?
It even sounds good.
Seriously.
Maybe a bit poetic, but not bad:
                'This is the final battle death will fight;
                victory belongs to love and life . . .'"

The train stopped at the Yarimja station.
Yarimja is famous for its cherries.
The fruit orchards go on forever,
the branches bent with cherries sweet and sour.
The reds and greens
        —the colors of the sun, birth, and fertility—
sang a joyful song of revolution
                in the orchards of Yarimja.

The prisoner Halil
closed his book.

He breathed on his glasses, wiped them clean,
                gazed out at the orchards,
                and said:
"I don't know if you're like me,
                Suleyman.
But coming down the Bosporus on the ferry, say,
                making the turn at Kandilli,
                and suddenly seeing Istanbul there,
or one of those sparkling nights
                of Kalamish Bay,
                the stars and the rustle of water,
or the boundless daylight
                in the fields outside Topkapi
or a woman's sweet face glimpsed on a streetcar
or even the yellow geranium I grew in a tin can
                in the Sivas prison—
I mean, whenever I meet
                with natural beauty,
I know once again
                human life today
                must and will be
                changed . . . "

The train left Yarimja.
Third-class car number 510.
Third section.
Basri Shener.
Big, dark-lined, glass-green eyes
and wrinkled olive skin.
Small mouth, long nose.
He was born in Florina, Macedonia, in 1897.
His grandfather was well-born,
                his father was a forester.
                And knew the Koran by heart.
Basri studied up to high school.
From school, only a march stayed with him:
"You rose, like the sun, wearing the crown of freedom."
Greeting the Sultan at the Florina Station,
the children sang this march in their thin voices,
and Sultan Reshat still shines

like a bright toy in Basri's memory.
He sees him in the decorated station:
a likeable old man,
frock coat and pants drooping on short bow-legs,
red fez,
        cotton-white beard . . .
During the Balkan War, Basri's family emigrated.
They settled in Edremit.
His father died.
His mother cashed in the gold around her neck
          and bought long-lashed camels for Basri.
In "The Tale of the Severed Head," it says
camels are angels,
they wait at heaven's gate.
And their wool cures all pain,
for this wool is sacred:
who sleeps on it
        is cleansed of sin.
Basri carted olives on the camels till he was 19.
He met with bandits in the mountains
          and gave them bread.
He gambled at the inns,
then sold the long-lashed camels
and shut himself up for three months
        in the Kemeralti brothels of Izmir.
In 1916 Basri was drafted.
Chanakkalé, Onion Creek.
One midnight, Basri entered the trenches.
Bombardments.
More bullets than stars burned in the night.
He buried his face in the dirt
and shut his eyes tight.
When he opened them, it was dawn,
and he was the only man alive in the trench.
Basri wasn't used to bodies blown to pieces.
And cunning like fear,
        undaunted like fear,
he ran from the front, driven by fear.
His Mauser hanging from his neck, Basri walked
a road as long

and safe as fear.
Tekirdagh, Silivri,
sleeping in forges under the bellows,
then rented vehicles,
and then one nightfall, at prayer time, Istanbul.
Burnt-out buildings in Fatih.
He ditched his Mauser and cartridge belt in a cellar.
And the next day,
a sunny Wednesday,
he paid eleven silver coins
                 in Yenijami and bought civilian clothes.
Fear is stupid.
Basri moved around constantly.
If he stopped to sit somewhere in broad day,
he thought they'd grab him by the neck and take him away.
Night fell.
Back to the ruins in Fatih.
In the cellar of a burnt-out building
he spied a candle burning,
           papers and stamps,
                      and five men.
Fear is stronger than suspicion.
They agreed.
And for six months, in the doorman's cubicle of a well-known office
     building,
Basri sold medical reports and leave papers
                   and, for 25 kurush,
                         red war medals.
Fear is smart,
smart enough to make Basri forge
      his own discharge papers.
Goodbye, Istanbul.
And hello, Willows Village in Akhisar.
There's sure to be a Hasan in the village,
      and Hasan will have a mother for sure.
And when the disabled veteran Basri
         brings word from Hasan
               at the front,
Hasan's widowed mother, black-browed but blind in one eye,
will surely ask Basri to be her guest

(especially at tobacco-hoeing time).
And no matter how tired widows are,
they still want their bellies tired
                    by nights with men.
And being blind in one eye
          doesn't make the wanting less.
Basri got used to his black-browed, one-eyed, widowed love
              —but not to the tobacco fields
                              or fear—
and lived in Willows till the Armistice.
The day he got the good news,
without thinking of the tears
              in a widowed woman's eyes
                    —one good, one blind—
he sold his fear at the bazaar
          along with her oxen and ox cart.
O my black-browed, widowed love
          and the damn tobacco fields
                  and Willows Village—goodbye . . .
Izmir.
Old memories of Izmir.
The Greeks had entered Izmir,
          and the guerrillas were fighting in the hills,
when Basri's money ran out in Kemeralti's brothels.
Farewell, heathen Izmir, goodbye.
Basri joined Ethem the Circassian's gang at Bloody Gulch.
Night raids on villages.
Men hanged from plane trees.
Basri favored big five-in-one gold coins
and filled his belt only with those.
Then one dark rainy night
goodbye, Ethem the Circassian, goodbye.
Uludagh,
        Bursa.
Even if Bursa is in enemy hands,
a coffeehouse for hashish and gambling
                  is not unprofitable.
Some people smoke more hash
          and gamble more desperately
                    the more they're beaten down.

Basri opened a coffeehouse.
Married.
Had a son.
Divorced.
And the day Bursa was liberated,
Basri passed out free hash for twenty-four hours.
To celebrate.
And hugging his son,
        he cried for joy.
Now his son is 19.
He studies in Izmir
        at the Vocational School.
Basri has two houses in Bursa
and olive groves in Edremit.
The coffeehouse is still in business
        but it's due to close.
For Basri is down to three hours of sleep again,
and once more a strange fear is his companion—
        fear of his son.

Basri Shener sniffled.
He looked out the window.
The pine poles speedily falling away
        suddenly bored him.
He was tired of things speeding by
        one after another.

Across from Basri in the car
        sat a little hunchback.
But this tiny man
        bore his hunch bravely.
His thin wrists ended
        in big, bony hands.
His pointed knees stuck out
        under his navy-blue pants.
For some reason
        he looked like an old maid:
sad
    lovable
        fragile.

Like the one in "The Loyal Child,"
          who didn't marry but took care
               of her sick old father.
And under his big heavy lids
          he had the eyes of a well-behaved child.
          Those eyes
          could think no evil.
          But his full-lipped mouth
          hid an awful curse.
          A curse that wasn't voiced
               and couldn't be.
Hunchback Kerim came from Adapazari.
His father, a carpenter, died in the Great War.
The words "Great War" bring back to Kerim
a black-bearded dead face on a snow-white pillow,
          herding geese and digging potatoes on Fahri Bey's farm,
          schoolbooks,
              and, with her golden hair
              and lined forehead,
               his mother.
In 1919 Kerim went to Eskishehir,
          to his aunts and uncle, for school.
His uncle was a train engineer.
The enemy held Eskishehir.
Kerim was 14.
He didn't have a hunchback;
     straight as a sapling,
          he was a boy curious about the world.
On the days his uncle drove the train,
his aunts didn't feed Kerim
(they were two long-haired old women),
     so he made friends with the Indian soldiers.
These men who
    —amazingly—
          didn't speak Turkish,
who had black beards, shiny black eyes,
and dark hands with light palms,
threw Kerim boxfuls of cookies
over the barbed-wire fence.
They had a huge warehouse

Kerim would play inside.
It stored sacks of chickpeas, fava beans, and raisins
                    —amazingly,
                              for their mules to eat—
          plus crates of ammunition and guns.
One day his engineer uncle told Kerim:
"Steal me some guns from the warehouse.
I'll send them to the guerrillas fighting the enemy."
And Kerim stole guns from the warehouse:
                    one

                    one more
                         five
                              ten.
He betrayed his Indian friends
                         because he loved the guerrillas more.
The men with shiny black beards soon left anyway.
Kerim saw them off at the train station.
The next day, when the guerrillas
threw up the Lefké bridge
                    and entered Eskishehir,
Kerim's uncle took him by the hand
          and delivered him to them.
And from that day
      to this,
          Kerim's life has been a heroic song.
They took him from Eskishehir
to the pasha of the "Kojaeli Group."
He was a stern, unsmiling pasha.
Kerim quickly learned how to ride a horse,
herd animals
          (he already knew something about it),
scamper down rocks like a young goat,
and hide out in the woods.
And with all his accomplishments,
coming within a bullet's range of death
and surprised by the words "close call,"
Kerim delivered messages
                    across enemy lines.
The guerrillas respected him like a famed "Captain";
he loved them like playmates.

And the boy, as straight
                    brave
        and promising as a sapling,
played this terrible game with joy
                till 1921 . . .

The Kojaeli forest is hornbeam and oak,
tall
and dense.
You can't see the sky.
The night was calm.
A light rain had fallen.
But the leaves on the ground were dry
and crackled under Kerim's horse in the dark.
Ahead
        on the left,
        a fire burned in the foothills—
probably the heathen gang known as "The Sailors."
Raindrops from the branches hit Kerim's face.
The horse's head plunged deeper into the dark.
Kerim is on his way back from Loose Rejep.
He's given him papers
        and taken papers in return.
Suddenly the horse froze
like a statue
—it must have seen the Sailors' fire—
then suddenly reared.
Kerim was stunned.
He dropped the reins
and hugged the horse's neck.
The animal ran like mad.
The trees lashed the child one after another.
The forest with its hornbeams and oaks
blew past on both sides like a dark wind.
Who knows how many hours they rode that way?
Then suddenly they emerged from the forest
—the moon must have risen, because it was light—
and when Kerim rode at the same speed
            to Mill Center below Armasha,
                the horse suddenly fell on its face,

                                 and Kerim was thrown off, head over heels.
He straightened up.
The first thing he thought was to check his watch.
The glass was smashed.
He got back on the horse.
The animal limped.
They rode slowly.
Kerim's left ear bled.
They came to Kirezjé
                (between Sapanja and Arifiyé);
Kerim stopped.
He couldn't breathe.
The following night he entered Geyvé.
His back hurt so much
                        he couldn't get off the horse—
                                they had to help him down.
They put him on a carriage.
Adapazari.
Then maybe ten days, maybe fifteen,
        on ox carts and horse carriages,
his chest tighter and tighter.
Yahshihan
     Konya
        Silé township
            (where they made artificial limbs
                    for crippled veterans)
and finally
        the bonesetter Master Hasan from Hatchehan Village.
Kerim still dreams
                of this man's pockmarked face
                        riding down the thin path on a donkey
                                and leaning over him.
The master rubbed Kerim's back till he passed out,
then packed in tar this child's body snapped like a branch.
Twenty days passed.
And late one afternoon they took Kerim out of the tar
                                        a hunchback . . .

Kerim might have had an Independence Medal;
he doesn't.

He might not have had a hunchback;
he does.
And now in 1941,
as spring comes through the car window,
                    Kerim thinks:
"Before this month is out
            I'll probably have a prison record."
For years
        Kerim worked at the telegraph office.
Six months ago
            he embezzled 180 liras.
Even if it's given
        to a sick and dying friend
            one hopeless night,
                those who embezzle government money
                    must do time in prison.

The train approaches Derinjé.

Basri Shener
looks at Kerim
and smiles, his mustache short and trim
            under his long nose.
"Fate," he thinks,
            "cruel, hunchbacked Fate—
who knows what mischief caused
God to make him this way?"
Hunchback Kerim looks at Basri Shener.
"What a nice smile," he thinks,
                "what a nice man!
If I came up before a judge like him,
        maybe I wouldn't get too bad a sentence."

The door opened.
Nuri Ozturk stepped in
            (the nursing-home accountant)
and stopped.
He called out to the corridor:
"There's room here.
And the window's not closed.

Please, come in.
Except they're all clean people here."
The student answered from the corridor:
"You go ahead.
I'll come later."
Nuri Ozturk
        looked at hunchback Kerim.
Hunchback Kerim understood:
        he got up from his seat,
                the window seat on the left.
For years, Kerim had dealt
with others in a strange exchange—
to want nothing from them
        and give them everything they wanted.
And since he embezzled the money,
        the curse
                on his lips
                    grows
                        more terrible
                            by the day.
A curse that hasn't been
        and can't be voiced.

The corridor.
The prisoner Suleyman
        entered the corridor
                with the prisoner Melahat.
Melahat was olive-skinned.
Her long neck was as delicate
        as a bird's.
Her lips were red without lipstick.
But her feet were big,
and her hands looked like a man's.
The student stepped aside, smiling—
                probably at Melahat.
Melahat passed by.
Suleyman spoke to the young man
                    dark and hard:
"You mistake the lady for someone?"
"No.

But I . . .
I wanted to ask you something.
One of your friends is Halil Bey
                              the writer, isn't he?"
"Yeah, it's him—
        so what?
        You know Halil?"
"Just from his books
                and photographs.
If I could talk with him . . . "
Suleyman thought:
        "He's either a cop
        or a damn slick womanizer."
Then he made his diagnosis
                (with a man's intuition
                        and the instincts of an underground fighter):
"Neither a cop
nor a womanizer.
Merely curious about the famous.
May even be a sympathizer."
"We'll talk," he said.
"Drop by later.
Except when you come in
—now don't forget, it's all-important—
after you say hello,
sit right down by the sergeant
and, starting with him,
                offer everyone cigarettes.
Peasant guardsmen only hassle peasants.
They're suspicious of city people,
but they think only peasants are sneaky."

Melahat returned.
Suleyman parted with the student
and exchanged looks with Kazim from Kartal.

The train stopped.
Derinjé.
A young officer in the second section got off.
A pregnant woman got on in the third.

Bells.
Whistles.
Departure.

Third-class car number 510.
The corridor.
A man
looks down at the ground from the first window:
                    earth rushing up
                              and disappearing nonstop.
Thoughts race through his mind
                    at the same speed
                    as the earth:
"How fast the earth passes!
The poplar at the village spring,
          would it make a telegraph pole?
The trolley poles in Istanbul were iron.
If a man went around the world,
          would he find a city to match Istanbul?
She asked 25, but I gave 30—
          would she have dreamed of that?
She wore silk slips.
I could eat her.
Should have gone once more.
Hey, look at that rider—
          nice horse, too.
Could it do a day's trip in five hours?
A horse can't keep up with a train.
If a train raced a car,
          would the car fall behind?
The doctor can still drive his car;
          they let him,
                    because he's a doctor.
If the doctor came to our village,
          could he change Tahsin Hodja's mind?
How fast the earth passes!
The poplar at the village spring,
          would it make a telegraph pole?
About now the doctor's mother, Grand Hanum,
          will be walking the villa gardens.

Will frost kill the pumpkins I planted?
The doctor said: 'I'm pleased with you.
            Stop by when you get back,
                    and I'll give you more work.'
I wonder if he will?
Tomorrow's another day—
who knows what it'll bring?
That's a lot of sheep there.
Lots of goats, too.
Look at that dog—like a wolf!
He's attacking us!
Now there's two of 'em.
Get away, boy, git . . . "

He spun around, looking for a stone.
Then he caught himself and smiled.
His smooth temples crinkled when he smiled,
and his sparse white teeth gleamed
            as if a light flashed in his dark mouth.
This man has syphilis.
A sore no bigger than a quarter-kurush
            opened and closed—
                    painless,
                            bloodless, and insidious.
This man has syphilis.
But he doesn't know it.
Smiling, he watches a bird glide
            lazy and content across the deep-blue sky.
Working a doctor's garden
can't teach Chankiri Durmush
he got syphilis in Istanbul for thirty kurush . . .

The dogs drop way behind, still giving chase.
The train rounds a bend.
The rest of the cars appear
                    one by one,
                        all tied to one another
                                far into the distance.
It comes as a surprise
to be tied to things so far back.

Third-class car 510.
The corridor.
Behind Chankiri Durmush off in the deep-blue sky,
a man sits on the steps of the platform.
Squatting,
he leans back against the door
        as if against the village mosque.
He's resting,
lost in thought.
His mustache droops in an entreating smile.
White lines crease his dark thin neck.
He may have to kill a man.
He isn't sure.
They didn't say in the letter.
But his land "with such-and-such boundaries
            and of such-and-such dimensions"
—as the public records will show—
has been encroached upon by Ahmet's son Bekir from the same
    village.
There's a chance he'll kill Bekir with an axe.
But, for now, there's no chance
                he'll understand why
                        he'll kill Bekir . . .

The conductor came by.
Chankiri Durmush paid no attention,
but the man on the steps scrambled to his feet, flustered.
His smile grew more entreating.
Shy and unsure of himself,
he handed the uniformed conductor his ticket
as if handing an official his birth certificate.
The conductor—deliberate,
                dignified,
                    confident—
                        punched the ticket
and, as he left, said very distinctly:
"You can't sit there, brother.
                It's not allowed.
Go see.
        There must be

empty seats
        inside."

In the corridor, the Tartar-faced man
        (the *jura* player
            and watchman at the Merino factory)
        told Kazim from Kartal
        a story
           about Gallipoli:
"I was wounded the sixth night of May
        in eight places.
Two of the wounds haven't healed yet
        and still act up from time to time.
We're facing the English
at close range—
our hand grenades land in their trenches,
        theirs in ours.
We charged.
I got hit before I'd taken three steps.
The English Tommy gun
        raked my groin.
Time passed.
I raised my head:
stars in the sky.
Our men had retreated.
The English trench fires nonstop.
Bullets whiz
        overhead.
I started to crawl backward.
I claw the dirt with my hands,
        facing the enemy.
As I crawl back toward our trench,
I keep praying, 'Oh, God,
        don't let me get shot in the back!'
At a time like that,
      not much else comes to mind.
The dead keep rubbing against me—
I mean, I keep bumping into them.
Some lie on their backs,
        open mouths filled with blood,

and some on their faces;
some kneel,
        frozen,
                Mausers in hand.
'Oh, God,' I say to myself,
          'if you're going to kill me,
                you should have killed me like that—
                      gun in hand,
                            down on my knees,
                    facing the heathens . . . '
Anyway, morning came.
It got pretty light,
and I got to the trench.
They held out a Mauser.
I grabbed the end.
They pulled me in.
I figured out afterwards
          I'd crossed 25 meters
              in three hours.
I stayed in the trench for a while,
doubled over.
My wounds started to hurt.
They loaded me on a guy's back,
and we got to division headquarters.
Tents.
Stakes in the ground inside the tents,
straw covering the ground.
On the straw, all kinds of wounded.
Some crying,
        some cursing God.
They cut my clothes off with scissors.
I was naked as the day I was born.
They threw a coat over me.
There's no cloth for bandages.
My wounds are open.
Luckily,
        there's no blood—
        dirt stanched the wounds.
Time passed.
I drifted off

and woke when they grabbed me under the arms.
They took me outside.
It was evening,
the sun about to go any minute.
I'm cool on the outside, warm inside.
Horse carts stand lined up.
The medics load the wounded on the carts
one on top of another,
      like empty grain sacks.
Whoever ends up on the bottom, let him die.
Ten, fifteen wounded on a single cart.
Some screaming,
      some maybe dying then and there.
Anyway, we started moving.
The Bee Point road is rocky.
The carts shake.
Dark comes down.
I'm lying on my back.
A human body moves under me,
a pair of legs is on my chest,
        one intact.
We ride downhill.
The sky is all stars.
There's a soft breeze.
The carts roll on, one after another.
We got to Sandy Quay at dawn.
A tent.
Someone calls from the tent
      (without coming out):
"Where you from?"
"Such-and-such a place."
"Father's name?"
"So-and-so."
"Your name?"
"So-and-so."
"Throw him down, driver."
The driver picks up and throws him down.
My turn.
The pain is unbearable.
I swear at the driver, from his mother on down.

'Swear, brother,' he says
                —he's used to it—
                            'do your worst.'
They laid us on the sand.
The sea rustles in and out.
It got totally light.
Maybe a thousand wounded, maybe more,
                            are laid out on the sand.
We waited till late afternoon.
A ship came:
                    two smokestacks
                            the color of the sea.
They loaded us on the ship,
                    screaming and swearing,
                            again like empty wheat sacks.
On the boat it's like Judgment Day.
Sticky with blood
            steam
                        grease
                            sweat.
They took me down to steerage.
We started.
Seven days and seven nights.
My wounds got maggots.
I open my cape:
            little white worms
                    with black heads.
I bend over to look,
but the critters are smart:
                    when they see me,
they scurry back inside the wounds.
Seven days and seven nights.
If God doesn't want to kill you, He doesn't.
Turks are tough,
                    we can take a lot.
On the eighth day we arrived at Sirkeji.
The captain dropped anchor.
But
            they didn't want us: 'No room!' they said.
The captain raised anchor at evening prayers.

We crossed over to Haydar Pasha.
The Medical School was a hospital then.
They said, 'Okay.'
A crewman carried me up on deck.
                He limped a little,
                        but he was a Laz boy strong as steel.
I thanked God and looked around—
                the lights of Istanbul sparkled.
                Ah, my Istanbul!
Anyway, we got inside the hospital.
The walls pure white.
The electric lights like a vision.
The stone floors
                squeaky clean.
A bed with wheels is waiting.
They laid me on it.
Pure comfort.
God save the government!
At that hour I prayed for the government in gratitude . . . "

The Tartar-faced man fell quiet.
His forehead was deeply furrowed.
The sparse white beard
        on his pointed little chin needed shaving.
Kazim's wolf-eyes smiled strangely.
The student
        (who'd listened to the story from a distance)
                        was stunned and sad at first,
                then angry with pity.
Then he thought:
        "It's too bad
        how soon they forget."
And he followed his thought:
        "Like a species of fish
                        or tree
        or a type of metal,
        a kind of man lives in this country
        whose one memory worth telling
                        —the only thing he can't forget—
                                        is war."

And he kept thinking:
"Am I brave enough to face death
                    in a trench?
Most of those who did and died,
                    were they brave?
And today, those who face death and die,
                    are they all brave?
Most of the time, does this business
                    have anything to do with bravery?
Or do those in the trenches
                    follow the herdsmen
                              to the slaughterhouse?
                    Not just their bodies
                              but their minds captive . . .
Or am I wrong?
There could be such trenches
                    (for me, for example)
                    where I would gladly die.
I mean this now,
but if that day ever came,
          and I lived wounded a few hours
                    before I died,
                              wouldn't I regret it?"
The university student could think no further.
The conductor argued with the Tartar-faced man.
The student couldn't figure out why.
The Tartar-faced man seemed sorry already.
And the uniformed conductor
                    was dignified even in his rage.
Nuri Ozturk
          (the nursing-home accountant)
                    had hurried to the scene
and shouted above the others:
"Gentlemen, stop!
The conductor here counts as a government employee.
Except the government has been insulted.
We'll put it all in writing right away."
Kazim from Kartal said something to the conductor.
"Okay, I'll let it go," said the conductor.
The student grabbed Nuri Ozturk by the arm

and led him back to the third section.
The fight was quickly broken up,
but no one could ever explain
to the Tartar-faced man
               how he had insulted the government.

Third-class car 510.
The women's section.
Six passengers.
The oldest sat
               next to the window,
nothing but thick bones
               under her black cloak.
She was very tall
          and pale,
               with no eyebrows
and hollow cheeks.
Her wide mouth was wrinkled
               and shut tight,
               as if it had never opened.
The late Sherif Agha's wife sat thinking,
               thinking about Ratip and Yakup.
Her thoughts moved slow and dark,
               rustling wet rushes
               on a hot, starless night . . .
Ratip was her real son,
Yakup her stepson.
One was in the ground,
          the other in prison.
Yakup killed Ratip.
The late Sherif Agha's wife was thinking,
               Shahendé Hanum was thinking.
She didn't grieve for her dead son.
She'd never grieved for anything in her life,
               except once
               for the death of a long-spurred rooster.
And she'd never loved anyone in the world.
Her pale, bloodless flesh
               hadn't opened to love's easy warmth even a single night.
Like an abandoned ship sinking

under the weight of its terrible loneliness,
    she sank a little deeper each day.
She hated Ratip.
She hated Yakup.
She hated Ratip
  because his narrow shoulders stooped
      and his hands looked like a woman's,
      because he couldn't whip the drovers
      and loved people,
      and because he'd accepted without complaint
      to share with Yakup Sherif Agha's estate.
She hated Yakup
  because he looked like his father
      with his Mauser, whip, boots, and mustache,
      because the other one gave birth to him
      and the mill went to him . . .
Ratip was cowardly.
Yakup was brave.
Yakup killed Ratip
     in the coffeehouse
     under the plane tree,
     with a single bullet
     between the eyes . . .
It was late afternoon when they brought Ratip's body.
They laid him out on the divan.
His left arm flopped down
     and swung back and forth,
the sun glancing off his father's gold ring.
Thick-boned, erect,
her browless face all white,
    she stood at her son's head
    and asked: "Will they hang Yakup?"
With her own hands she had pushed Ratip
     on Yakup's red-haired wife:
either Yakup would be disgraced and leave,
or he would kill Ratip,
and they'd hang him for killing Ratip . . .
Either way, Sherif Agha's legacy
    —the land, the mill, the dairy—
      would remain intact.

But they didn't hang Yakup.
He served seven years.
He gets out in November.
For seven years the late Sherif Agha's wife,
        for seven years Shahendé Hanum worked,
as if embroidering an intricate design in colored silks,
to have Yakup killed in prison.
Yakup was shot three times and poisoned once.
Seven years of patience, cunning, hope, and determination
        to plot a single death.
And in the end
        she forgot why she had started the fight.
So much so that once, when they said,
        "Yakup is dead,"
        her embroidery needle slipped from her fingers,
        and for the first time in her life
        she fell to her knees and wept out loud.
For joy, they said.
But no, it was because Yakup's death
was her one tie to life.
Yakup will get out in November.
The battle goes on.
Thank God, only the dead can't be killed again.
The late Sherif Agha's wife sat thinking,
        thinking of death as if tracing a new embroidery pattern.
Under her broad chin
      the knot of her white scarf was tight and forbidding.
Shahendé Hanum must have been about sixty.
Her hands were hennaed.

A basket of cherries jiggled
            on the rack
          near the window.
The pregnant woman who'd gotten on at Derinjé
      sat with her round eyes glued to the basket.
The basket belonged to Shahendé Hanum.
Bayan Eminé, sitting on the pregnant woman's left,
           whispered boldly,
             almost demanding:
"Give her a bunch of cherries, grandma,

the girl's at the craving stage . . . "
The pregnant woman blushed to her tiny ear lobes
                    under her old hat.
But Shahendé Hanum didn't budge.
Bayan Eminé thought, "The old lady must be deaf,"
        and repeated her request—
                louder, bolder,
            and more demanding . . .
But Shahendé Hanum paid no attention.
The pregnant woman trembled with embarrassment.
Bayan Eminé,
now certain the old woman was deaf,
        poked Shahendé Hanum and shouted:
"Hey, grandma . . . "
Shahendé Hanum,
as if peeling her cloak from her thick bones,
                slowly stood up,
removed the basket from the rack with her hennaed hands,
                    and threw the cherries
                    out the open window.
Then she put the empty basket back
and sat down, retracting her thick bones into her black cloak.
The pregnant woman sobbed, her old hat shaking.
Bayan Eminé pushed back her silk scarf
                (it made her feel too close to Shahendé)
            and told her daughter: "Perihan,
            run and find those guardsmen up front
            with the prisoners.
            They just bought cherries.
            Ask them for some.
            If they don't have any, tell them to look around.
            Say your mother sent you."
Perihan was fourteen.
Cropped hair.
Short socks.
Long, thin, dark legs.
And patent-leather shoes.
Perihan leapt up
            and was gone.
Bayan Eminé praised her daughter to the pregnant woman:

"My girl is smart.
She'll finish middle school next year.
She's so good at French
        the colonel's wife couldn't believe it.
God willing, we'll make her a women's doctor.
Her father doesn't approve,
           but I'm determined.
She can do housework, too—
         cooking,
             embroidery.
She's washed my dishes since she was eight.
And she minds what I tell her.
I gave her a good licking the other day—
her father barely got her out of my hands.
As I told the colonel's wife:
         with girls, you should send them to school
         but keep an eye on them . . . "

Bayan Eminé came from a village near Aydin.
Her father was the son of a famous gang leader.
When the Greeks reached Aydin,
the gangs banded together against the enemy
but never missed a chance to kill one another
over power, fame, or the spoils.
And so they shot Eminé's father
              before her eyes
                early one morning
                   in the front yard . . .
Bayan Eminé was orphaned at eight.
Now she's thirty—
a woman with thick legs, big sagging breasts, and a potbelly.
But topping her heavy, ruined body
she has the delicate, silk-fine face
that tenth-century Persian paintings trace
and the Sheik's flute turns to melody—
the face praised in Ottoman poetry . . .

Perihan returned.
Her long thin hands overflowed with cherries.
Bayan Eminé gave them to the pregnant woman.

As the pregnant woman ate the cherries
with the sacred hunger of a young animal,
Bayan Eminé talked with Perihan:
"Did you tell the guardsmen who your father is?"
"I didn't, but they asked."
"The guardsmen?"
"No, a man with glasses
        reading a book—
            must be a prisoner."
"A prisoner?
        What did he say when he heard who your father is?"
"Nothing. Oh, he asked where we were from."
"Did you say Aydin?"
"I did.
        He asked if we came from the villages or the city."
"Did you say the villages?"
"I didn't."
"And why not? Are you ashamed of being a country girl?
You silly goose . . . "

Bayan Eminé laughed.
Then her beautiful face suddenly grew serious,
and as if to spite Perihan
                    she told the pregnant woman
                        for the whole section to hear:
"We're from Aydin.
From the country.
Perihan's father
        is a master sergeant in the National Guard.
He's also my cousin.
Sergeant Husnu.
We got married to keep the property in the family.
He had eyes for someone else,
            but his mother forced him.
Well, in fifteen years with Sergeant Husnu,
            I've been everywhere.
From among the Lazzes on the Black Sea
            to the Kurds in the east.
They say Kurds have tails—
                it's a lie.

They don't have tails.
But they're real hotheads, and very poor.
Some are rich,
             but not many—
                      just the chiefs.
For fifteen years I've gone around the world
             and I've seen it all:
movies, the theater, even a ball
             —I went just like this in my scarf—
                  in Diyarbakir.
And I played poker with the captains' wives
                  one whole winter in Giresun—
                  and won, thank goodness.
I even hit the lottery once:
                  three of us
                  got a thousand liras each.
I can't complain about my life.
Sergeant Husnu is nearing retirement.
Perihan will go off to boarding school,
the sergeant and I will go back to the village.
The sergeant says he can't work the land now.
                  He wants to open a store.
He can.
I'll work the land."

Next to the door sat a tiny woman.
She wasn't a dwarf
       (you can tell a dwarf),
                  which is why her size
                  was so surprising.
Her big azure eyes looked sad,
and she had wrinkled, freckled little hands.
Suddenly she asked Bayan Eminé:
"So your husband is in the army?"
"Sure is—
       a master sergeant in the National Guard."
"My two sons are in the army, too—
                  privates,
                  artillerymen
                  in Gallipoli . . .

Well,
I wanted to ask if we'll enter the war.
My sons say we will.
They're foolish young boys,
        they don't really understand . . .
Anyway, they probably want to fight.
Your husband must know what's going on.
He must have told you something . . . "
"From what Sergeant Husnu says,
                we'll enter the war . . . "
The woman's tiny freckled hands shook:
"So the boys weren't wrong—
                oh, my God . . . "
Bayan Eminé interrupted her:
"No,
        Sergeant Husnu says we'll go to war,
                but I say we won't.
The colonel also says we'll go,
but his wife says no.
Why go to war?
Anyone can see we're doing just fine without fighting . . . "
Uncertain at first,
then sure of herself, Perihan disagreed:
"But, Mother,
        our country?
If the enemy treads on our soil?
My teacher said:
                'Every hand's-span of our country
                        we'll water with our blood.
                Turks would sooner die than surrender.'
And remember
        what the radio said on Independence Day?
                        Was that wrong?"
The tiny woman looked at Perihan sadly:
"Girl," she said, "you're young—
grow up,
        marry,
                bear sons,
then I'll ask you
        what war is."

Perihan started to answer
when a voice like sky-blue satin
                              broke in:
"Now women are soldiers, too.
War's not just for men.
And what about all the kids killed by airplanes?"
The speaker was Shadiyé.
She sat opposite Shahendé Hanum.
There's a heartsick lover
              in an old Istanbul song,
his fez a little long,
his fez a little black.
And his soul is melancholy, ah . . .
Gold are his glasses, and gold his mustache.
He's crossed the parched desert, restless with longing,
and now impatiently he waits,
              on the shores of the Islands, for Shadiyé there to haste.
And he says: "Where have the sweet-smelling lilacs gone?"
And he says: "The autumn leaves turn and wither."
And he says: "When the earth becomes my home,
              Shadiyé, rejoice for me, for your sake . . . "
How strange that
          the Shadiyé in the pointed hat
          in third-class car 510,
                    discussing planes
                    that kill children,
            should sadly bring to mind
            the Shadiyé awaited on the shores of the Islands.
She was all delicacy and grace.
It was as if a frilly parasol cast shadows on her face.
And the parasol is tilted slightly to the left,
              casually pointing
              in the direction of the heart.

The train approached Izmit.
On the right, waterwheels:
          blindfolded horses going in circles
                as if they weren't alive,
                    as if they had springs
                        and were wound up.

And then the sea beyond.
Out on the sea
    —between Goljuk and Millstream—
        the warship *Yavuz:*
shapely,
    maybe freshly painted,
        sparkling,
but from a distance
surprisingly unimposing.
It looked like it had been picked up by its masts
        and placed on the water.
Nothing about it, not even its smokestacks,
    resembled its color lithographs
    in coffeehouses.
On the left, a paper factory.
High up, a plane.
A child running barefoot down the street.
A sailor.
A woman in a black cloak.
A man with a green flag.
Semaphores,
    a water tank,
        switches,
boxcars waiting to take something somewhere,
and official signs announcing the Izmit station.
The train slowed down.
Kazim from Kartal went into the corridor with the Tartar-faced man.
The train stopped,
and they stepped off.

Just beyond the station,
    straight ahead, was a bridge.
Men stood on it,
leaning over
to look at the stopped train.
They waited for the train to leave,
    to pass below them
        almost between their legs.

Kazim showed the Tartar-faced man

a tree near the bridge:
"See that tree at the foot of the bridge?
Like an animal
                up on its hind legs?
That big one
        to the left there.
Look.
With its branches arching over the bridge.
They hung Ali Kemal's body from one of those branches.
They snuck him out of Istanbul
                in broad daylight—
                he was getting a shave
                in a barbershop in Beyoghlu—
                                in 1922 . . ."

"Who was Ali Kemal?"
"A journalist.
In the pay of the English.
He was the Caliph's man.
Fat,
        wore glasses.
His pen dripped blood,
                but dirty,
                        stinking blood.
Sometimes
                enemy pens open
                        bigger, deeper wounds
                                than Mausers."
"Did we have Izmit then?"
"We'd just taken it.
The English still held Istanbul.
Ali Kemal was snatched right under the blue eyes of the English.
The rumor 'He's coming!' started here
        six or seven hours before he arrived.
People thronged the quay.
Maybe three-fourths of Izmit,
                even the women.
I was up near the Grand Mosque,
                watching through binoculars.
The boat finally appeared,
                tossing on the waves.

I ran down.
They'd taken Ali Kemal out of the boat
        by the time I got to the quay.
Up there
        on that hill
                is the government building in Palace Square,
                                the army office:
                        they took him there.
Outside the building,
        the square
                and the streets
                        were mobbed,
teeming with people like ants.
But seething,
        pitiless.
Many were laughing, too—
        Izmit was like a fairgrounds.
And it was hot,
not a cloud in the sky.
Ali Kemal was inside barely 20 minutes
                when they led him out.
He stepped forward.
Officers and police surrounded him.
His face like chalk.
Blond.
Suddenly the crowd began shouting:
                'Damn you, Artin Kemal! . . . '
He stopped,
turned around,
and looked back
        toward the door of the building,
        as if to turn around and go back in.
But they slowly closed the door in his face.
He staggered forward about ten steps.
The crowd kept shouting.
A stone from behind
        hit him in the head.
Another stone,
        this time in the face.
His glasses broke—

I saw the blood run down into his mustache.
Someone yelled: 'Get him!'
It rained sticks,
stones,
and rotten vegetables.
The guards stepped back.
The crowd fell on him like a black cloud
                    and knocked him down.
There they did what they did.
Then the crowd opened up a bit.
I saw him lying face-down
in just his underwear—
            short pants.
His bare flesh was like gelatin, plump and white.
He seemed to be still breathing.
They tied a rope around his left foot.
I'll never forget it:
his left foot didn't have a shoe or sock or anything,
            but the garter was still on his right leg.
They started to drag the dead man by the leg—
downhill, his head hitting the rocks,
and everyone following.
Once, the rope broke.
They tied a new one.
It was quite a lesson:
don't get the people mad.
They'll put up with it once, maybe a couple of times . . .
Anyway,
Ali Kemal went all over Izmit like that.
Then,
like I said,
they hung his body from a branch over that bridge.
Later they took him down,
        but his undershirt or pants,
        some piece of his underwear,
            dangled from another branch a couple months.
Later they auctioned off his watch and other things,
                        but much later . . .

I know someone
        who bought his sock for five liras as a souvenir."

The Tartar-faced man asked:
"Was his watch gold?"
"Gold."
"They didn't do right—
whoever bought the watch
        or the sock, they didn't do right.
It's supposed to bring good luck,
        but don't believe it.
A hanged man's stuff is unlucky.
They didn't do right.
And the Izmit people did wrong, too.
If the man is guilty,
        the government hands him his sentence
                and hangs him.
To lynch the man
        means to defy the government.
When I got wounded in Chanakkalé
        and lay in Haydar Pasha Hospital . . . "
Kazim from Kartal laughed.
"Yes," he said,
        "but you just insulted the government yourself."
"Me?"
"You."
"That's a lie.
I would never defy the government."
"You defied its employee."
"I argued with the conductor."
"The railway belongs to the government, and the conductor works for it."
This time the Tartar-faced man laughed:
"Then am I a government man, too,
        since I'm a watchman at the Merino factory?"
"For sure
        you are . . . "
"God forbid.
I'm not.
Not me or the conductor.
How can conductors and watchmen be government men?
I don't even count cops as the government.
Now the chief of police is different.
He's a government man . . . "

The conversation would have continued,
but the bell rang for departure.
Kazim and the Tartar-faced man ran for their car.
The train pulled out...

The train passed
          through downtown Izmit.
It grew less serious
          and more like a streetcar.
The people, shops, and houses
          didn't even turn to look at it.
And for all its racket,
          it couldn't wake the carriage horses
                         from their dreams.
But once it left Izmit behind
                this May afternoon
                and entered the isolate countryside,
                the train regained its gravity
                and became once more a "bridge of longings."

In third-class car 510,
forehead against the glass,
a man sat with a lost world flitting
                through his heart.
Kiryos Trastellis was an "Old Greek."
He was from the port of Missolonghi
                across from Patras
                on the Corinth Canal.
He didn't care for Phidias, Homer, or Aristotle.
He liked the sea, sun, and people.
And, for Mikhail Trastellis, the true wonders of this world
were lobsters and eight-footed octopuses.
Steerage bunks on fishing boats,
                a one-story house in Missolonghi, and his friends
                were Greece in his heart.
What's happened to Greece?
Kiryos Dimitryos Mikhail Trastellis,
here in the month of May
                in the year 1941,
                where are you headed now,

packing the sea, your home, and Greece
into a cardboard suitcase?
How did you end up all alone in the world,
how did things fall apart?
Your friends were killed.
The fishing boats lie at the bottom of the Corinth Canal,
like corpses in glass coffins.
This year Hitler's officers will dine on the lobsters.
Your father's in Athens,
your mother's on Chios,
your sister's in Alexandria,
and you're in third-class car 510.

The train crossed the Izmit plain.
When it's spring in the country
on afternoons like this,
as the light softens like a love song,
as the shadows of trees
stretch out on the ground,
cool and at ease,
as the grass with its birds, horned animals, and insects
looks younger,
more sensual,
and greener,
as the ponds sway
like lazy, contented goldfish,
the happy heart grieves
with the sorrow of being in the world today.

As Mikhail Trastellis looks out the window,
this earth says nothing to him.
But not because it doesn't know his language.
On spring afternoons like this,
the earth doesn't speak Turkish or Greek
but its own tongue.
But Mikhail's sorrow was so deep
he couldn't hear the earth
or think of other people and the world.
Yet in this car on this afternoon, his grief
was shared by others and the world today.

The train crossed the Izmit plain.
Third-class car 510.
First section.
The prisoners chatted with the guardsmen.
The prisoner Melahat asked Guardsman Haydar:
"Do you like kids?"
"Who doesn't?
When they asked the man, 'Is anything greater than God?,'
          he said, 'A child.'
It's true.
Can a child know fear of God?
                              No.
The one who doesn't fear the other is greater.
Do you have any kids, sister?"
"Yes.
I left her with my mother.
She just turned three.
I'll bring her out next year."
"To prison?"
"Yes."
"Why not?
It's all the same to kids.
To kids and cats,
prison or paradise—it's all the same . . .
Where's her father?"
"He's in prison, too."
"What was his work?"
"Tobacco.
I work in tobacco, too."
"In the warehouses?"
"Yes."
"I know about the warehouses.
We had an Ibrahim in our village.
Went to Samsun and worked in tobacco.
Three years later he died of consumption.
Is your husband where you're going?"
"No.
He's in another prison."
"God pity you, sister.
What can I say?

Don't worry—it'll all work out."

The prisoner Halil talked with Guardsman Hasan.
Guardsman Hasan asked:
"Think the government will start rationing bread?"
"Probably."
Guardsman Hasan thought a minute,
sniffled, and said:
"And it should."
"Why?"
"Bread must be respected.
People have lost all respect for bread.
City people eat one slice and throw one to their dogs.
Bread is the staff of life.
But I wish the village taxes would come down a bit,
along with the price of black cattle.
I've got all the land I could want,
but I don't even have a cat to pet."

Guardsman Haydar told Melahat about Hoyukler:
"An hour from our village
                is an Alevi village.
They're hard-working people, but they worship roosters.
This Hoyukler is in their village.
You dig,
        and up come giant stone statues,
                earthenware pots, gold stags.
Now the government's getting into it.
They take what's found to Ankara,
                to the museum.
Ever been to a museum, sister?"
Melahat laughed:
"No."
"I have. In Istanbul once."
"The military museum?"
"No,
the other one.
It's worth seeing.
Lots of heathen sultans carved in stone.
I guess iron didn't exist back then;

82

if it did, they'd be cast iron like Ataturk's.
And most of them are naked.
There are some women, too.
I even saw their tombs.
They were alive once, too;
now they stand in stone in the museum."

The sergeant discussed the war with the prisoner Fuat.
The prisoner Suleyman stared out the window,
reciting one of Fikret's poems to himself:
"'Dine, effendis, dine; this lavish table is all yours . . . '"

The train crossed the Izmit plain.
In the fifth section of third-class car 510,
the owner of the carpetbag, Halim Agha,
                              dozed off.
He'd withdrawn into his black beard
        and white wool socks
like an animal asleep in its warm, dank lair.
The train suddenly stopped.
Halim Agha peered out the window.
The lights in the car hadn't been turned on,
                but it was night outside.
They'd come to a station,
                a station bigger than any
                    Halim Agha had ever seen.
The station building was dark:
            its lights weren't turned on, either.
A dense crowd spread as far as he could see.
Drums beat,
and men carried torches blazing in the night.
Everybody clamoring and shouting.
In the spotty red light of the torches
        everything loomed larger—
                the drums, the station, the dark.
Suddenly it started snowing:
big heavy flakes.
The drums beat louder.
Flags unfurled—
                not red

but green.
A man had climbed up on the roof of the station,
a fur hat on his head,
        a saber on his gold-thread belt.
It was the columnist pasha who beat the English in the Great War.
Halim Agha recognized him,
although he'd never seen him before tonight.
He took a closer look
        and almost cried out loud.
The grocer Haji Nuri Bey stood next to the pasha,
motioning to Halim Agha from the roof:
        "Come here, come on up!"
Halim Agha went up
                and kissed the pasha's skirts.
Then they rode together in a car
                bigger than the Chankiri governor's.
It was raining.
The car flew like a bird down the slick highway.
Halim Agha sat facing the pasha,
his carpetbag up next to the driver.
The pasha leaned toward Halim Agha's beard:
"Thank God, it's done," he said, "nice and quick.
We've joined the Germans and entered the war.
Act fast.
Don't say anything to anyone, not even Haji Nuri Bey.
Bread will be rationed.
Do you have flour?"
"I do, pasha."
"Did you stock up on sugar?"
"I did, pasha."
"Kerosene?"
"Got it.
        Plus olives, bulgur, rice, chickpeas, beans—
                everything's set."
"Very good.
You'll be richer than Haji Nuri Bey."
"All thanks to you, pasha."
"Tomorrow everyone will know—keep it quiet today.
We'll say the first Friday prayers together in Damascus."
"God willing, pasha."

84

"You'll be richer than Haji Nuri Bey,
          richer than Haji Nuri Bey,
                    than Haji Nuri Bey."
He sat with the pasha under a trellis
          on a snow-white, silk-fine Egyptian mat.
He asked the pasha:
"Is this heathen Hitler really a Muslim?"
"He is.
I saw him in the baths with my own eyes
—heathens don't cover their private parts there—
he's circumcised."

A cat shot between Halim Agha's legs,
                    long hair flaring
                              bright orange.
Halim Agha started after the cat.
The cat ran,
          he chased;
                    the cat ran faster,
                              he chased harder.
They reached the downtown baths.
The cat went in.
The weighmaster's daughter Sherifé walked out
          and sashayed down the street,
                    her bath things bundled under her arm.
Her full cheeks flushed scarlet,
her black hair wet under her scarf.
She was about fifteen.
Halim Agha wrapped Sherifé's hair around his fist.
He laid her on the sugar sacks
and opened her blouse.
He bit her left cheek.
Blood from his teeth marks trickled down her white throat.
The pasha tapped Halim on the shoulder.
Sitting at the governor's table,
          the pasha ate falafel.
Halim Agha said:
"Pasha,
          God has willed up to four wives.
Give leave

so religious law rules."
The pasha smiled.
"That will come, too, Halim Agha,
                    but all in due time.
Have the imam marry you to the girl."
"Her father won't stand for it."
"Then divorce your wife."
"I'll lose the land and the two stores."
"Then you know what to do . . . "
Halim Agha's wife was washing clothes in the kitchen.
She didn't hear her husband come in.
She'd squatted down,
back to the door.
As her arms moved in the wooden tub,
her shoulder blades rose and fell under her black dress.
Halim Agha looked at his wife in the kitchen.
The kitchen ceiling had vanished—
stars showed above.
Halim Agha walked on tiptoes.
His sneakers didn't make a sound anyway.
He got up real close to his wife.
With his right hand he grasped the axe he'd hidden in his coat.
The axe lip was chipped in three places.
He raised it and brought it down on the woman's neck.
No blood came out.
The head didn't drop.
It stayed tied to the neck by a piece of skin.
And hanging there,
                    it stared at Halim Agha:
"Agha, what have you done?" it said.
                    "You struck once—strike again!"
Halim Agha knew
—he remembered reading it in a fairy tale—
you should only strike once.
If you strike twice, it'll come back to life.
So he didn't strike again.
The head frowned,
            knitted its blond eyebrows,
        then snapped from its dark thin neck,
                    and fell to the ground.

As the head snapped and fell,
            the neck skin ripped away,
            peeling like a willow branch.
Some school kids took the head for a ball
and started playing in the army office yard.
As the agha passed with his axe,
the captain's son kicked
        the head
                into the agha's arms.
The agha looked at what had landed in his hands:
it wasn't his wife's head
but the severed head of the prophet Ali.
Halim Agha started to cry.
And he was terrified.
The pasha asked why.
"Pasha," he said, "I killed my wife."
"No problem—
she's dead, you're alive.
We'll say she died in an air raid," the pasha said.
"You go off to Istanbul and have yourself some fun.
Now you're a bigger man than Haji Nuri Bey.
And come see me at the paper—
                        we'll have coffee."
Halim Agha rented a third-class rail car,
one without section divisions.
All for his very own . . .
He covered the car with kilims.
Then he took off his socks
        and stretched out in his underpants at the very center.
He lit the brazier
and put on the coffee.
The coffee foamed in the pot.
He saw the weighmaster's daughter Sherifé sitting across from him.
Her thick white calves and orange nipples
        were so close to his beard
that when he leaned across to embrace her waist
the train suddenly stopped.
The owner of the carpetbag
        flew into the air
        without wings or tail

all the way up to the clouds.
Then suddenly hitting his head on a star,
        he fell into the sea
        and sank to the bottom like lead—
        and shook himself awake.

The train had really stopped.
The people in the section had flocked to the window.
They were all excited.
There were shouts
                and whistles.
Halim Agha held his throbbing head
                        and asked:
"What is it—what happened?
Make room for me, too."
They didn't make room at the window.
But the Tartar-faced man explained:
"You were sleeping—the train screeched to a halt.
We fell all over one another.
There's no station or anything.
It's the middle of nowhere.
The conductors got down,
        they're shouting and running around."
Halim Agha didn't listen further.
He shot into the corridor in his wool socks, crying:
"I knew it, I knew it—
        I saw it in my dream!"

Down on the ground
the engineer Aladdin stood next to the locomotive.
He looked like he'd suddenly stopped his horse
                in the middle of a race and dismounted,
        still holding the reins.
The engine was sweating.
It gasped and wheezed,
panting white clouds of steam.
The fireman Ismail called down:
"Boss, which car pulled the emergency brake?"
"I don't know—
                we'll check."

Alongside the cars, the conductor shouted:
"Gentlemen, don't panic.
Ladies, please remain on the train."
Aladdin went up to the head conductor;
they talked;
he walked back.
On the road they'd just crossed,
        some people appeared, carrying things.
The fireman Ismail asked:
"Is the man dead, boss?"
"Can't tell."
"Why did he jump?"
"I don't know."
"What do you say, boss—
        was it for love?
He asked for the girl,
        but they wouldn't give her.
Or his wife cheated on him."
"I don't think so."
"If it wasn't love, it had to be money.
He couldn't see any way out."
"Maybe."
"Or one of his friends had shafted him something awful."
"Who knows . . . "
"Or the real truth, boss,
        is that the poor man didn't have a ticket."
"It's possible."
"Look, I just thought of something else:
he had a son or brother or someone abroad;
the airplanes bombed,
        and he got killed."
"God, Ismail, I don't know!"
"Yeah, but what do you think?"
"What I think is,
the door to the steps was open,
the man didn't notice,
he leaned back
and fell . . . "
"Boss, that won't do."
"Why not?"

"Because it can't be."
"Why can't it be?"
"I don't know why not,
                but it can't."
The engineer Aladdin thought a minute
and then said with a strange, sad smile:
"You're right, Ismail,
that's true—
it can't be.
There are so many reasons in the world today
to go crazy enough to want to die,
and people are beaten down so easily,
that you can't accept it was just an accident—
that the door to the steps had been left open."
Ismail understood only part of this long sentence
and agreed with just that:
"I can't accept it, boss . . . "

They put the body in the baggage car.
It was a man about fifty.
The engineer Aladdin climbed back on the locomotive.
The head conductor signaled,
and as the train started,
in the fifth section of car 510
the owner of the carpetbag,
        peeved that his dream hadn't come true,
puffed away on his cigarette
        like a black-bearded water pipe.
The time
        was 6:38 p.m.

BOOK TWO

I

Spring comes to the Haydar Pasha Station café
with Arnavutkoy strawberries smelling sweeter than roses
                    and grilled red mullets wrapped in grape leaves.
Yet
Hasan Shevket
drank his raki with a single slice of cheese.
The time
was 6:38 p.m.
His hands shaking on the checked
                    tablecloth, Hasan Shevket
                              stared into his glass
        and thought of a title by Anatole France:
        Le Crime de Sylvestre Bonnard.
He thought:
"Should translate it."
He thought:
"Has it been translated?
                    And when?"
He didn't know, because
since becoming one of our famous authors
he hadn't read anything in Turkish except his own works.
"Le Crime de Sylvestre Bonnard.
The Crime of Sylvester Bonnard.
Nice title.
But what was his crime?
And who *was* Sylvester Bonnard?
Isn't there a thumb-size man in that book,
                              or even smaller?
Doesn't he talk to Sylvester Bonnard
by candlelight,
perched on the red-leather binding
              of a handwritten Latin book?
But maybe that's another novel . . . "

Hasan Shevket stared into his glass
        and thought:
"The thumb-size man—

which is to say
your conscience, who talks to you by candlelight
or when you're alone
with your drink.
And here's a thumb-size man of my own
(fair and stocky,
just like me):
he sits on the rim of my glass, dangling his legs.
If my hands didn't shake so,
if I could tip him over
with the point of my fork,
he might fall into the raki and drown.
His teeth are all rotten.
His voice is just a croak.
He whimpers like a sleeping child dreaming his mother's dead
and says: 'Hasan Shevket,
Hasan Shevket,
you're a wreck.
How did you get this way?
Who did this to you?
How long have you been like this?
And some of the others have gone so far!
Now they shake your hand like you're a distant memory,
and look at you with barefaced pity.
Sure, Hasan Shevket, they've long forgotten
those Armenian and White Russian
rooming houses stinking
of burnt olive oil and urine.
How high and mighty they act now with women!
They've long forgotten the humiliation
of patched underpants.
The world is all theirs, with all its blessings.
They don't still have to write literary columns
for students and young officers
at two liras apiece—
at fifty.

But why, Hasan Shevket,
why?
Were they smarter than you?
No.

More knowledgeable?
No.
Any less malicious?
        Less deceitful?
                Less arrogant?
No, more!
Even the painter Mahmut gets five thousand for a portrait.
He's lazier than you,
                and more of a drunk.
Are you envious?
Maybe a little.
Confess.
Yes:
you'd like to see them all die
                        suddenly,
                                in one day—
                in a flu epidemic, say.
But you'll die before them.
One of your kidneys is long rotted.
Spring has come, Hasan Shevket,
                the sap runs in the branches.
And the birds have built their nests—
                you couldn't even do that . . .'"

The platform was crowded.
The Anatolia Express would leave at seven sharp.

Hasan Shevket looked beyond his glass
and saw Nuri Jemil on the platform:
he had stopped at the portable bookstand
                                to read something.
"Look," Hasan Shevket said
                to his thumb-size man,
                "look at Nuri Jemil.
He's rented a summer house in Suadiyé.
He makes at least five hundred a month.
And maybe he gets a little something from the German Consulate,
    too.
More power to you, Nuri Jemil,
                        more power to you!

You, too, have long forgotten
that desperate
        wretched night
we shared our loneliness
        with the stars above
and passed out under the bank sign
                at the corner of Galatasaray—
                        me from raki,
                                you from cocaine.

You damn
cripple . . . ”

Nuri Jemil was lame.
Unaware of Hasan Shevket
conversing with his thumb-size man,
Nuri Jemil solemnly lit a cigarette.
He returned the book to the stand
and saw Tahsin
        climb aboard the sleeper.
Suddenly, as if he'd smelled something bad, he made a face,
                deliberate
                        and exaggerated.
Tahsin
(a doctor and member of Parliament)
—a tall, portly man
with the brightest hazel eyes
and a jetblack mustache
        drooping over his still-full cherry lips—
disappeared into the sleeper,
        unaware of Nuri Jemil's exaggerated display.

Hasan Shevket
        picked up his glass, turned it around
        and around in his hands,
        and held it up to his eyes.
He spoke as if someone really sat on the rim
                of his glass, listening to him:
“My thumb-size man, did you see?
Nuri Jemil is green with envy.
He's jealous of Tahsin.

The lousy cripple.
He has his eyes on Parliament
             or maybe the Cabinet.
And I know how he plans
                         to go about it.
Not from reading his columns
—thank God, I'm not guilty of that—
but from the way he holds his cigarette, for instance.
At each German victory
          his heart pounds
                        like the drums of a Prussian regiment.
What I can't forgive about Hitler
is how he grants the likes
          of Nuri Jemil the chance to sell out,
                how he feeds them with grand designs.
So grand
they can't stand it.
That's why they show it
                    in such stupid,
                            impudent ways.
What's the pure Turkish for 'impudent'?
No doubt they'll come up with something from Chaghatai.
What if I said in my Turkish 'brazen' or 'bold'?
No,
there's something more naked about 'impudent,'
                             more shameless.

It's a pity
I never stroked
        a smooth, firm, impudent
             pair of breasts
                    that filled my hands;
mine were all withered and dead . . .
My thumb-size man,
let's be frank:
Could you be bought?
No.
For five hundred a month?
Impossible.
Seven hundred?
Without taking any risks

or compromising your honor?
For little scholarly articles,
little neutral columns?
Yes.
It's possible.
No.
That's being a collaborator.
Why think in such horrid terms?
But you're right.
Money is filthy.
Proudhon said: 'Property is theft.'
One of our Communist literati told me:
        'You're a petit-bourgeois anarchist.'
Why?
I'm no anarchist.
Money?
Money's filthy.
What about a position of power?
A government post?
A chance to give orders, be in charge?
Especially if there is no choice?
After all, it's clear now
                the Germans will win.
And anyway, I still have scores to settle
with certain people.
Certain people?
The whole lot of them!
Then there's no problem?
Don't push me—
what about my principles?
Can't your principles change, my thumb-size man?
They can.
Hasan Shevket,
        you don't understand politics.
What's so hard to understand?
Nuri Jemil was a lowly writer,
                and now...
True.
It's not so hard.
Except..."

Thus, little by little,
Hasan Shevket
tried to cajole
his thumb-size man
when suddenly the thumb-size man
        stood up on the rim of the glass
                and shouted at the top of his voice:
"You're worse than Nuri Jemil, you pimp!
        You don't even have the guts to be corrupt . . . "
Hasan Shevket turned beet-red.
He took a sip of his drink.
The glass shook.
The thumb-size man fell into the glass.
With his rotten teeth
and croaking voice,
he drowned in the raki.
Hasan Shevket felt a sharp pain,
                as if someone had stepped on his corn.
And a single tear rolled down his left cheek . . .

The platform was crowded.
Nuri Jemil entered
        a first-class car
                of the commuter train.
The red-velvet car was empty.
Only a few
        such cars remained.
They were all ancient,
        relics of another era.
(Fortunately, times change fast in my country these days.)
The new ones had imitation-leather oilcloth.
Nuri Jemil was pleased
        he'd run into a velvet car.

Nuri Jemil grew up
                without a father,
                                sickly
                                and poor,
in poverty that hurt him like a burn
        —poverty that only kids can feel

(not those born into it
              but those who become poor)—
and made him envious of all he lacked.
Partly that
        (and partly his later years)
                may explain his lifelong hatred of the poor
                                and respect for the rich:
his respect was dark
            but fearful,
                hidden,
                    wary that it would show,
and sometimes full of rage,
as if he wanted to retaliate
        for a personal insult.

One rainy holiday morning
                is Nuri Jemil's worst childhood memory.
The colors of his outfit bought at the Covered Bazaar had all run
    together,
and the grandson of the big villa in Goztepé
(a plump eight-year-old)
had come down the stairs in the uniform of a sultan's aide
carrying a little sword with a gold-inlaid handle,
                and made him cry.
That's partly why Nuri Jemil was pleased
                he'd run into a velvet car.
Because in the late-afternoon light,
            when he sank into the soft, worn-smooth red glow,
        he would inhale the old sweat in the velvet
        with a sad air of triumph and feel,
            on his narrow shoulders,
                the pure-gold braided epaulets
                of a sultan's aide.

To make it to a velvet car,
        Nuri Jemil had fought for fifteen years
                surrounded by people just like himself—
people like cats,
        porcupines,
                peacocks,

100

like packs of jackals roaming the steppe
                    with lowered heads.
Their hostility was two-faced,
and their friendship always stood
                    ready for betrayal.
Like Nuri Jemil,
        they each thought they alone were right,
                    they alone brave,
                            they alone unlucky...
And just like him, they all
        were convinced their genius
                    wasn't being recognized
in a world full
            of unseen
                    evil forces.
And like Nuri Jemil, they all
        lived by selling their brains and fed
on one another's heart, flesh,
                    and self-respect.
The sight of people battling
                others just like themselves
is as pathetic as the sight of a swamp
                in noonday heat.
Maybe Nuri Jemil felt
            this pathos, maybe not.
But for fifteen years he fought—
            friendless,
                    tired,
                            drunk, and sleepless.
Sometimes he couldn't even afford a whore.
Sometimes he'd talk to himself,
                especially when listening to old songs
(then he'd become
        more childish than he was as a child):
"I've written a goodly number of books,
even some best-sellers.
At least half of those readers were women,
and half of those women were young,
and half of those were beautiful.
And of the beautiful, there's got to be

one who can love me.
Where is she?"

On his big drinking binges
       Nuri Jemil would accost women on streetcars
                    at the top of his voice,
          especially women with men.
Or, choking with grief, he would dream
          of another world.
In his sad, drunken world
       he was a superman
          all alone,
              dominating,
              distant and unapproachable,
              proud, cruel, and full of disdain.
And in that world, people died just as in this,
but not him.
He never passed out of this endless drunk.
He lived with the stars,
      never feeling the fear of the great dark.

Nuri Jemil never read a book to the end.
And he never said, "I haven't read it."

Nuri Jemil was a liberal democrat and an individualist—
          until 1935.
He banked on "the individual's absolute right to liberty"
          as the road to success—
until 1935.
Nuri Jemil opposed the regime
      until 1935
          for being undemocratic.
Then, one spring afternoon in 1935,
      Nuri Jemil stood in the copy room
of a magazine (involved, he vaguely sensed, with the police chief,
      blackmail, and the Intelligence Service)
and stared at the cracked glass:
the glass glinted,
and the hungry man with a growth of beard
      —the crack like a whiplash across his face—

was him.
One spring afternoon in 1935
Pan-Turkists broke into the room
                and almost beat him up
                for being a "democratic extremist."
But the man in the cracked glass had only wanted to eat,
he was so hungry...
To fight for fifteen years to get somewhere,
then be crushed one spring afternoon...
Nuri Jemil found in himself the strength for a fresh start
(those were his words),
dropped democracy like an old hat
(those were also his words),
and offered his services
                to Rifat Bey and his sons.
They owned the newspaper
with the largest circulation.
They created a hero every twenty-four hours.
They were involved with mills, kerosene,
        the Krupp factory, and the best-paying embassies.
Nuri Jemil knew all this
(but these are not his words).

Now Nuri Jemil has an account
with the bank where he'd passed out
                years back.
He's married now,
less drunk
and more famous.
Now he's our leading foe of democracy.
And, together with the First District prosecutor Mumtaz of Uskudar,
he passes out thirty-year sentences for Marxism daily.
Now he opposes the regime
        for not joining the totalitarian front.

The platform was crowded.
Nuri Jemil looked out the window of the velvet car.
A soldier stood below—
                Corporal Ahmet.
Nuri Jemil thought of a column subject:

"War is an ironsmith's forge,"

                        he would write;
"nations must be steeled in it . . . "
Not that he'd been steeled in this forge

                            or would be.
Because—he smiled—he was lame, thank God.

Across the way, Tahsin
      (the doctor-Representative
            with the brightest hazel eyes)
emerged from the sleeper.
Nuri Jemil
saw him beyond
      Corporal Ahmet
           (the veteran of the Balkan War,
               the Great War,
                  and the Greek War).
His smile suddenly vanished:
"Tahsin knew why I was smiling—
      now the whole world will know . . . "
And with the speed of a dream,
—neither thinking nor unthinking,
both logical and illogical—
      he was overcome with dread.
He looked at his leg as at incriminating evidence . . .
He jumped up and stepped down hard
as if to hide it.
His rancor now turned on himself.
He stood at the window
for Tahsin and the whole world to see.
He leaned out
and tapped Corporal Ahmet on the shoulder:
"Have a cigarette on me, soldier."
Corporal Ahmet wasn't surprised by the offer.
He was tired.
He looked
      at the man in the window and took
the cigarette:
"Thank you, sir," he said.
Nuri Jemil,

          his face green
                    and drawn,
                              sank back into the red velvet.
Suddenly bored
and weary,
he closed his eyes.

In the station café, Hasan Shevket
sat at the same table with the same slice of cheese
          on his plate like a leftover of a wasted moonlight party.
Well,
it's his sixth raki.
But the same slice of cheese.
You only live once.
If there was an open road
          lined with poplars,
                    straight and endless.
If you were young, unimaginably young, and ran as fast as you could,
and worlds went flying past.
Well,
a seventh glass.
The same slice of cheese.
Where do these voices come from?
Where do they go?
Once, somewhere, moonlight went to waste.
It won't come back.
To sit in a train station and watch life pass by
          as the cheese on your plate goes untouched, untasted.
Hasan Shevket
sipped his seventh glass with the same slice of cheese,
and the station clock read
          6:48.

Nuri Jemil slept,
                    a bedbug in the middle of his sallow forehead . . .
The car was dead-quiet.
The old red velvet was a stinking dreamland,
with the look of a locked butcher shop
          and something like the smell of blood in the air.
Nuri Jemil slept,

dwarfed
and shrunken.

A friend came up to Hasan Shevket
—one of those friends you can't remember when or where you met
or when you last talked or about what
or even his name.
All Hasan Shevket could remember about him
were his big toes in patent-leather shoes.
Hasan Shevket's friend
said:
"I say God,
you say Nature.
There's a higher justice,
a moral power.
Europe was founded with blood, sweat, and tears;
now it's coming down with blood, sweat, and tears.
No good can come of a house
built of mortar mixed with tears.
The son pays for the father's sins.
For instance, the descendants
of our Iznik lords
are now bums living on the street.
God—you say Nature—took the minds of some
along with their money.
Ali Pasha's son:
they had a farm
it took ten hours on horseback to cross from end to end.
Baths in Bursa.
Ali Pasha ruled over eighty villages.
They say he forced Abdul Hamid to make him a pasha.
His picture still hangs
in some old kebab joints in Bursa:
collarless shirt,
short wolfskin jacket,
boots,
rough homespun pants
but not riding breeches.
He stands like a giant,
leaning on his hunting rifle,

eyes open wide like he wants to devour you.
But his grandeur survives only in photos.
And soon they'll vanish, too,
          like Ali Pasha's glory, wealth, and fame.
His youngest daughter turned whore after the Armistice.
She walked Beyoghlu with Greek officers.
As I said, only one son still lives
               in the last remaining mansion.
The mansion has maybe forty rooms,
               but it's in ruins,
                         everything falling apart.
He inhabits those ruins like an owl, all alone,
palsied,
          his whole body quaking,
                    sitting on a lambskin rug, waiting.
If the neighbors didn't throw him some bread
                         from time to time, he'd be dead.
There's a moral power—
I say God,
          you say Nature."
Hasan Shevket interrupted his friend:
"I say no God,
               no moral power,
                         no Nature.
I say nothing.
I don't even eat
               the slice of cheese on this plate,
                         I mean, I can't . . .
I can't afford a second slice.
And my father was no lord or tyrant.
And I don't give a damn for the fall of Europe.
We should fall, too,
          and the sooner the better,
                    along with Europe.
I had such beautiful things to tell people.
They didn't let me say a single thing.
All of you, the best and the worst, descend from the same shit.
Here, I offer you
          my single slice of cheese.
Please,

eat it ... "

And Hasan Shevket shoved the plate of cheese
                    in front of his friend ...

The platform.
A uniformed police chief crossed the platform
                    toward the entrance,
                              almost running
                                   but very erect.
Whenever a policeman runs somewhere,
                    grave matters come to mind.
And only a cop can keep his authority
                    while running and jumping.

A lieutenant whispered something to a major.
The major walked over to the entrance.
The lieutenant stayed put,
gleaming like a freshly oiled pistol barrel.

The platform suddenly filled with plainclothesmen,
          hats and ears all cut from the same mold.
They tried so hard not to be noticed
                    they stood out all the more.

The stationmaster spoke with the traffic manager,
                         both of them excited.

The man standing to the left of the entrance
                              crossed to the right.
He was short and fat.
He removed his hat,
buttoned his jacket,
folded his hands over his stomach,
and bowed his head.
He waited.

Corporal Ahmet
          (the veteran of three wars
                    who was famous for saying,

"Hang in there, brother, the end's in sight")
still stood by the commuter train,
                 still smoking Nuri Jemil's cigarette.
Giving his old friend fatigue a rest,
he watched the comings and goings,
                 his chestnut eyes amused.
And Corporal Ahmet, who in solid darkness could detect
        the slightest movement beyond barbed wire,
                 sensed something was afoot.

Suddenly the crowd stirred.
Starting at the entrance,
        the men took off their hats,
                 like bottles being uncorked,
                         and bowed.
It was a sad sight.
A man led the way into the station,
not as if he'd walked through a door
        but as if descending a marble staircase
                 to the bared heads.
Yet up close
        he looked like a decent man—
not pompous,
        possibly courageous,
                 even a little weak.
He had a round nose,
        slightly red
                 from too much drinking.
His cheeks were full,
        lined,
                 and white.
And he had the colorless eyes
        of patient, old Nordic women.
He walked in silence.
And he listened with polite indifference
                 to the words whispered
                         up to him from those below.

"So that's why all the excitement," thought Corporal Ahmet.
"He's got quite a retinue—

wonder who he is?
Must be a big shot."
He thought of something funny
and smiled to himself:
"Think of the hicks back home:
if Ali saw this,
he'd figure it was the county supervisor.
Fact is, this guy is bigger than a governor.
He's no Representative—
a governor beats a Representative.
He must be a Cabinet member.
They're really kowtowing to him.
If you ask me,
       nobody should bow down that way
                    except to pray.
But you can tell the guy hasn't served in the army.
Or if he has, he must have been a reservist.
Is this any way for a commander to march at an inspection?
These reserves, they can't even slap right.
When you're talking army,
      it's one, two, three—
          march,
             slap,
                guts—
    it's all got to be tough.
But guts aren't just for war.
This one's about over.
Hang in there, brother, the end's in sight."
Corporal Ahmet smiled to himself again.
But suddenly he spotted a three-bars-and-two-stars
          about a hundred paces off.
He'd come out of nowhere
and went up to the dignitary.
Corporal Ahmet's smile
shattered like glass.
He snapped to attention
and saluted.
And following standard operating procedure,
          he stopped thinking altogether.

The dignitary being seen off
        stood by the sleeper,
                surrounded by people
                        and insulated in his polite indifference.

Burhan Ozedar
said something to the dignitary.
Burhan Ozedar's long, thick, spread legs
were planted firmly
        under his body,
and his hairy hands moved slow and easy.
Now and then his left eye winked,
but nothing about it was playful:
maybe it was a disease.
Burhan Ozedar
was born in Sivas about 1884.
He was known as Kemankeshzadé
        before last names came in.
His father was the trader Osman Agha:
        he had land in Black Fort,
            two stores in Sivas,
                and 150 mules.
Burhan finished high school in 1904.
During the Great War, the army commandeered the mules.
From '14 to '18, he bought his way out of the service three times.
His father died at seventy.
The Armistice and occupied Istanbul.
Burhan owned 25 gold pieces,
and Greeks made the cigarette paper
                for all Anatolia.
Long live the Nationalists:
Burhan petitioned the National Assembly,
and soon the rolling papers
                had stars and crescents.
It was still Greek capital,
but Burhan was a partner now.
The first shipment of goods:
                1921.
First apartment building:
                1924.

Restoration of the Ahmet Pasha Mosque in Sivas:
                                    1925.
(This pasha from Sivas had captured who-knows-what fort from the
    Austrians
                        during the reign of who-knows-what sultan.)
In 1926 Burhan
              endowed a ten-bed hospital wing.
The same year, his second apartment building.
Then railroads:
              800 kilometers between 1925 and 1934.
In '35, the idea for a movie
          about Ahmet Pasha from Sivas.
In '36, a cast-iron stove factory.
The same year, the publication of the first volume
                        of Ahmet Pasha's biography.
In '37, prospecting in the Erzurum mountains.
A rail-car factory in '38.
In '39 his son returned from Berlin
          a civil engineer.
The women were sent back to Sivas the next year:
              Sivas is far away
                        and safe.
Burhan does not drink, and never
          has he unbuttoned for illicit pleasure.
When he goes out socially, his family stays home.
He sent his daughter to the American Girls' School,
but a beret is the only hat he'll wear.
Burhan Ozadar is a millionaire
                        in American dollars.
And in his will
          revised this year,
              half his wealth goes to his family
                    and half to charity.
But in his old will
      (drawn up in 1931)
          three-quarters went to charity.

Sometimes he's so open
          and frank
              that he surprises even those closest to him.

That's when he winks
        his left eye faster, as if fighting back tears.
One morning
he walked into his chief engineer's room
and blurted out:
"I've changed my will.
I don't have to explain.
It's my own business.
Nobody can demand an explanation
                                except God Almighty.

But people are strange,
or I am.
Something's caught in my throat—
if I don't tell it, I'll choke.
You can't make big money from the sweat of your brow.
I don't know about anybody else,
but no sweat's behind mine.
It was very clear to me early on,
then I slowly forgot
or wanted to forget.
That's life—
a man gets ahead, climbs the hill,
and reaches the point
where he never looks back to where he started.
As the phoenix bird lifts us from the depths of hell,
we feed him flesh cut off our thighs.
But when we reach the summit of the mountain,
                        we forget the bird
            and say our own sweat got us there.
Our own sweat: the flesh cut from our thighs?
But the bird didn't even eat it;
        he starved himself to raise you up.
He gave you your piece of flesh back.
That's how it is.
Oh, yes, two master fitters came to see me yesterday,
and I sent them to you.
Check them out carefully before you hire them.
And oh, increase the work day in the shops
                            five minutes at a time.
Take care now."

And all that day
    Burhan's teary left eye
        winked
           nonstop.

They climbed aboard the Anatolia Express:
    the dignitary,
        the three-bars-and-two-stars,
           Tahsin (the doctor-Representative),
             and Burhan Ozedar.
The crowd bowed a little lower.
And Corporal Ahmet
        still stood at attention.
But he'd started thinking again:
"Hang in there, brother, the end's in sight . . . "

It was 6:58 by the station clock.
A woman stood right under it:
(neither beautiful nor ugly)
        growing more beautiful,
(neither young nor old)
        growing younger.
(A faraway look in her eyes.)
The faraway look in her eyes is the sacred desire of flesh.
(Her lips are closed tight.)
Her tight lips part.
(She looks like she's made a momentous decision.)
She watches the young porter
    who's been loading the baggage car
        and stands wiping his sweat.
He's naked from the waist up.
He just took off his shirt.
His thick, muscular arms are dark.
His broad chest is hairy.
His lips are full,
and his nose is magnificent.
As he grabs the heavy bundles and heaves them into the air,
his taut long legs and narrow hips strain and flex.
To sleep with this porter just once
and bear him,

     screaming,
         one, ten,
             a hundred,
                 a thousand kids—
                 dark, fair, red-haired, blond.

It was 7 by the station clock.
The Anatolia Express pulled out.

II

Night falls in the mountains.
Distances disappear,
but love stays in the heart.
Night falls, my lamp's not lit.
The sky and mountains turn violet.
Why won't you come?
Night falls, the sun is gone.
Night falls, I'm all alone.
What am I to do?
Darkness closes in again:
the day is done.

The Anatolia Express streaked past . . .

The moon rises and climbs the sky,
seeking her lover.
The full-blown moon rises,
enameled with light.
The moon rises with the wind,
and everything goes white.

Everything was white.
The Anatolia Express raced under the moon,
its windows masked.
Seen from outside,
it was dark
         like blue glass.

But it was the color of orange sherbet inside the dining car.
The dignitary sat next to the three-bars-and-two-stars
at the first table,
across from Tahsin and Burhan.
Burhan said:
"The peasants should all wear the same clothing,
        cheap
         and durable.
Because, in the first place, they're practically naked.
I drew up a proposal
    for your—
      I mean, the government's—textile factories . . .
If this idea proves too much for your directors and advisers
—the government always makes camels out of fleas—
give me the contract
and I will handle it myself.
But I want a tough law.
Those lunkheads must be forced
      to clothe themselves."

Tahsin
  (the doctor-Representative)
        reached for the wine.
The Poplar Creek wine came in a tall, slender bottle.
Made by a Hungarian in Ankara,
it resembled Rhine wine.
Its color was pale yellow, a very pale gold,
      something like molten platinum.
It had a light,
   delicate taste
    somewhere between dry and semi-dry.
Tahsin watched the wine fill the crystal glass
  like dawn breaking
     on a clear day.
And with a mocking edge to his soft voice, he said,
"My dear Burhan Bey,
I believe this clothing business was already started
by Sumer Bank,
    one of our—
      I mean, one of the government's—agencies."

"Sumer Bank's stuff isn't worth a dime.
The peasants won't buy them.
Anyway, what I'm saying is . . . "
"I understand, Burhan Bey:
you want something like a uniform."
"Yes.
Durable and compulsory like a uniform."

The three-bars-and-two-stars broke in
        (a man about sixty, he was short
        and worked to lower his high voice):
"One thing we have to remember, effendis.
Clothing was issued to some janitors
                                I saw.
You couldn't tell them from our officers
                                        at fifty paces.
We must avoid such blunders in the future."

Tahsin took a sip from his glass:
"Our state monopolies can't produce wine of this quality yet,
                                but they will.
We'll produce finer wines than Chateau d'Yquem.
[He turned to Burhan.]
Sumer Bank's clothing may not be perfect yet,
                        but it will be.
But to make the peasants all wear the same clothes
                                by force—
                                        can't be."
Burhan Ozedar asked, without winking his left eye:
"Why not?
Weren't we forced to wear hats instead of fezzes?"
"In that case, force was revolutionary;
in this case, it would be reactionary.
And for some reason, our businessmen
lack confidence in statism.
Yet the state supports you."
"And we support it."
As Tahsin prepared to answer,
the dignitary softly said:
"Then there's no problem."

He said it as if offended.
Tahsin saddened
as he remembered another man,
                    now dead.
Another table,
            now broken up.
Tahsin thought:
"The dead man was a hero:
a high-roller and a winner,
            he trusted no one but himself.
He was derisive, belligerent, cunning, domineering.
Even though he put me where I am,
                he could be so cutting
                    that more than once I wished him dead.
I thought my prison walls would come down
                if his table did.
He died.
His table was broken up.
But his guests buried with him
            anything heroic in them.
I knew how old I'd grown
            the day he died."

He helped himself to filet mignon with mushroom sauce.
As he cut the meat on toast,
                he looked at the dignitary and thought:
"Why isn't he like him?
They were friends.
They started out together.
But this one can't fill his shoes.
I see how he suffers.
He sulks at the whole world.
He no longer wants to help or hurt anyone.
His indifference is scary.
A black worm turns
        inside his plump, pink body.
And the pain is his alone.
                What do we care?
But why can't he be a winner?
What does he lack?

Maybe he's not a big enough bastard."

Suddenly Tahsin flashes back to a night twenty-five years ago:
"A man takes a woman in his arms.
She lies back on a plush rug, he's on top.
Shadows cover her bare shoulders;
                                        her skin is hot.
The lamp goes out.
The woman flips over like a fish,
and as she gives herself, she reaches up to the man's ear
                                and whispers, full of hate:
                                                    'YOU BASTARD'...
The woman's heart beats under the man like another body entirely.
And in the next room,
                        her husband
                                    lies on his deathbed.
The bastard was me.
The dying man was my best friend.
Three days later he died.
But why all this now?
Damned memory works in mysterious ways..."
Tahsin winced:
some mushroom sauce got in his bad tooth.

Burhan Ozedar turned to the three-bars-and-two-stars:
"Have you read the biography of Ahmet Pasha—
our Ahmet Pasha from Sivas?"
"No, I haven't."
"I'll present you with a copy, then.
But you're familiar with Ahmet Pasha, aren't you?"
Absorbed in the foam on his beer, the three-bars-and-two-stars
was caught unawares:
"No, I can't say I know him—which Ahmet Pasha is this?
We had an Ahmet Sivas in our class
        who died in the Balkan War when he was a captain..."
Burhan was stunned.
His huge body shrank and recoiled.
The dignitary scratched his nose
(he'd done it since childhood
                whenever he felt embarrassed for someone).

Tahsin's black mustache grinned:
"This pasha from Sivas must be one of the old Ottomans,
from the days of Sultan Selim or so . . . "
Burhan sat up straight:
"What Sultan Selim, Tahsin Bey?
He was one of Sultan Suleyman the Magnificent's bravest soldiers.
And no foreign recruit, either, but a Turk through and through.
                    Like me, he was pure Sivas—
                    a lion of a commander."
This time the three-bars-and-two-stars spoke with certainty,
seeing no reason to lower his high voice:
"I don't know him.
There's no such general in our military history."
Tahsin stared at the three-bars-and-two-stars, thinking:
"Why doesn't he just make a joke of it
                            and back down?
Or is his courage only military?"

Burhan spoke as if his lips were bleeding:
"General, I hear our new military histories
        are like the history books our kids read these days.
Pretty soon we'll be denying the Fatihs, the Selims, the Suleymans.
Our kids are clueless about the vast Ottoman Empire.
When they hear 'sultan,' they think it's the bogeyman.
I think we've destroyed all we could,
and we should stop now:
                    it's gone far enough.
There's no reason to outdo the English in democracy.
Just look at their sense of tradition.
And we've forgotten how to read the Prophet's Nativity Hymn.
We've had a revolution, but it's enough.
Now let's own up to our past and our roots.
Sultan Selim must live on in our children's dreams
                    in all his imperial glory."
The three-bars-and-two-stars got excited:
"My sentiments exactly,
                    you're right . . . "
The dignitary said:
"Then there's no problem . . . "

Tahsin thought:
"We've entered a new era,
              we're all exhausted . . . "
Overcome with sadness again,
he started to spoon his compote
and squinted at the table
in front of him:
three people—
Monsieur Duval
                    Jazibé Hanum
                              and Osman Nejip.
Tahsin knew all three.
Osman Nejip was a leading intellectual.
He caught Tahsin looking at him
and smiled imperceptibly.
His arm reached out as if he were yawning,
        and he languidly picked up the bottle
                of mineral water in front of Jazibé
and filled the lady's glass.
Nejip had very long limbs.
No matter where he was,
        he always appeared to be underwater—
languid, limp,
              barely stirring,
                        like a lazy sea-creature.
Sometimes his movements were so liquid and drawn-out
that watching him
you'd feel some cold,
                  slimy,
                        bloodless thing curl around your flesh,
and you'd want to slap him
                just to make him move a little faster,
                              a bit more humanly.
On the days when Osman Nejip went to work
(which wasn't often—he rarely worked),
he cast a sad, boneless shadow
        over the whole building.
Locking himself in his office,
he'd lean back in his chair and rest

his long legs on the crystal-topped desk.
Signed photographs hung on the walls:
                              Gokalp,
                              Talat Pasha,
                              Ataturk, and Inonu.
Nejip would sit that way for hours—motionless,
eyes half-closed,
                  staring at the walls.
Ziya Gokalp, who first told him about Durkheim,
was his mentor.
Talat Pasha got him his first government grant.
Ataturk put him where he was,
and Inonu watched out for him.
Osman Nejip was respectful and polite toward them all,
but secretly he laughed at them all.
According to Osman Nejip, Gokalp was too clumsy,
Talat Pasha too ignorant and crude,
Ataturk much too active,
and Inonu too stiff and rigid.
And all four
              (so Osman Nejip thought)
              really seriously believed in and fought
                              for something.
But (for Osman Nejip) nothing
              in this world
                  was really worth
                      seriously believing.
To get angry or jealous, fight or persevere,
to roar with laughter or burst into tears
              was (according to Osman Nejip)
                  hollow and ridiculous.
Money that comes easy
              without effort or fuss,
                  women who come and go easy
                              without hassles,
                  cars, central heating,
                  and smiling eyes that disguised their mockery
                      more than sufficed
                              (for Osman Nejip)
                                  for sixty years of life.

The rest was empty talk
        (so Osman Nejip thought).
We only live once.
We can avoid thinking about death as much as we like,
                but we'll still die.

Osman Nejip's wife cheated on him constantly.
Osman Nejip knew it.
The lovers would sit openly at Osman's table.
After dinner, as Osman Nejip sat languorously smoking his pipe,
his now-aging wife
        (although her legs were still exceptional)
        would quarrel with her lover in another room.
And Osman Nejip's mocking eyes
        would smile
            without showing their mockery.
Osman Nejip has mistresses.
Each year the old one leaves,
        and a new one arrives from Europe.
Osman Nejip prefers Swiss goods.
They come beautiful, healthy, and without passion
and work like easy-to-wind clocks.

The dining car had heated up
        because the windows couldn't be opened.
The air smelled of alcohol,
                French cooking,
              face powder, and steam.
The little red lamps belonged on the set
              of an operetta—
                gay
                    artificial
                        lyrical.
Monsieur Duval and Jazibé Hanum conversed in French.
For the last ten minutes Osman Nejip had been peeling
              a little orange and listening.
Rich Ottomans
        had ivory back-scratchers
      shaped like long, thin, carved spoons
          and topped with tiny hands.

Jazibé Hanum resembled those spoons:
off-white like ivory,
flat-chested, tall, and thin like a spoon handle,
she had a small head just like those tiny hands.
The daughter of the painter Omer Pasha,
Jazibé Hanum was born in 1894
in Kandilli, the Bosporus, Istanbul.
At one she was presented to the Sultan.
Her father painted her portrait at three.
In 1902 she started piano lessons.
She could speak French at ten.
And between fifteen and twenty:
  "As the lights of Kandilli floated in sleep,
  She drifted with the moonlight on the sea."
She got married (1915).
Her husband, Mufit Bey, was in the Foreign Service.
1916: Vienna.
In '19 they returned to Istanbul.
1920: Paris.
'22: visit to Ankara.
The same year: Berlin.
Four years in Berlin.
1926: Tokyo.
Visit to Ankara
   (1928).
1929: off to Rome.
The Mediterranean,
Lloyd Triestino.
En route, Mufit Bey died of a stroke.
Return to Istanbul.
The funeral ceremony
   (tears and white-gloved police).
Memories
  till the end of 1930.
Early in 1931 she married
  Shefik Bey, a bank officer.
Her husband was a little younger than her.

Osman Nejip had finally peeled his orange.

He was pleased with his orange,
                    himself,
                              and the world.
The naked orange—proper and blond like his Swiss mistresses—
rested
        on the tips of his long, bony fingers
about to go limp.
Osman Nejip smiled imperceptibly.
Jazibé Hanum told Monsieur Duval
        about one of the Duchesse de Rohan's luncheons in Nice.
The names of the foods
        and the words struck him like notes
                    picked out on a piano:
"... *Langouste à la Mornay* ...
Chevreuil à la Saint-Hubert ...
... *c'est une bonheur* ...
... *délice* ... *causé* ...
Sauce grand veneur ...
            Champagne rosé ... "
Monsieur Duval listened
politely, lost
            in thought.
He was tall,
fair-haired,
and handsome.

III

A white night flew by outside the blue windows.
There was a moon outside, and a sea,
and the earth under the moon was happy.
Those inside the blue windows of the dining car didn't notice.

Two men in black suits
sat at the last table.
One was blond, the other dark.
The dark one pointed out Monsieur Duval:

"That Frenchman . . ."

There was a moon outside, and a sea, and a dream sailboat on the sea.

". . . do you know who he is?"
"What Frenchman?"
"The man at Osman Nejip's table—
Monsieur Duval de Thor.
He's a multimillionaire.
He's got quite a chateau on the Loire,
                    a real medieval castle."
"The Germans must be enjoying it now."
"Possibly—but so what?
The guy telegraphed from here the contract
to supply a German army corps with milk."
"Is he buying the milk from us?"
"No, no.
It's from his farms in France."
"So he feeds milk to his enemy?"
"No, no.
He's just making money."

Outside, the earth under the moon was happy.

"How long has this guy been here?"
"He's been coming and going fifteen years.
He heads a firm that does business in the Near and Middle East.
Here they've been involved in cement, cotton, and gunpowder.
They wanted to generate electricity from the Sakarya River
        and raise Merino sheep on the Dalaman Ranch.
They own the biggest hotel in Ankara.
But the government
                    nationalized gunpowder
and took over the Merino wool business:
        it has a big, yellow factory with a black roof in Bursa.
Electricity from the Sakarya
        is still at the talking stage.
And cotton was turned over to the Bank of Agriculture."
"What's left for them?"
"Cement and the hotel.

They're doing a brisk business.
The war is at our door:
fortifications need cement,
and the hotel is needed for diplomats."

There was a moon outside, and a sea, and a dream sailboat on the sea,
      calling to mind
           only big, beautiful,
                loving thoughts.
Outside, the world of fields and trees
      stretched out along the coastline.

"This Monsieur Duval, is he Osman Nejip's friend?"
"Osman Nejip has no friends:
      he just takes money from Duval's firm."
"Do Tahsin and Duval know each other?"
"Tahsin got the cement
for his Bosporus villa from Duval without paying a cent—
                          as a sort of tax."

Outside is a tree
      heavy with birds and leaves
           under the moon by the sea.

"Your Monsieur Duval looks a little thoughtful."
"He must be thinking of his unborn child again.
His wife is barren.
The guy's a devout Catholic,
so he can't divorce his wife.
It must be sad to die
      and leave millions behind
           but not a single child."

A white night flew by outside the blue windows.
Those inside the blue windows didn't notice.

The dark man in the black suit had a strange smile,
his pointed nose crinkling,
as he asked his friend:
"How many people are at Monsieur Duval's table?"

"Three."
"No, four.
Duval is one,
      Jazibé two,
            Osman Nejip three.
And Shinasi Bey makes four.
But you can't see Shinasi Bey
            because he's deceased.
He died by his own hand,
            squeezing a bullet into his snow-white temple.
He was sixty.
The suicide of someone old
      is like someone old crying:
           they're both disgraceful.
Shinasi Bey had been a member of the privy council.
He was also a former ambassador.
Duval made him a director of the gunpowder business
            (a miscalculation—
              he didn't realize new people were in power);
then the government took over gunpowder.
Duval dropped Shinasi Bey
            (calculating correctly
             and realizing new people were in power).
But this correct calculation didn't seem quite right to Shinasi Bey.
And early one morning,
          at dawn,
             boom . . .
Shinasi Bey was gone.
The night before, they say, the deceased had locked himself in his room
        and played *Aida* on the gramophone
           till dawn."

A train flew by under the moon,
a train dark
except for sparks,
        fire-flecks,
            flying between the wheels of the engine.

The blond man in the black suit asked the dark:
"Who's the short, fat, hairy one?

With eyes like oily olives?
He's so animated when he talks."
"I see him.
That's Kasim Ahmedoff.
A refugee, one of our Azerbaijani brothers.
But if truth be told,
even if I were a Pan-Turkist fresh from Berlin,
        I couldn't call that man my brother."
"Is he that awful?"
"No, no—
        he's sharp.
Smart enough to understand business and high finance.
And a bit of a con man.
One night about twenty years ago
he boarded Captain Vassilieff's freighter
        in a hail of machine-gun fire
                and escaped the Bolsheviks in Batum.
(Apparently, Bolsheviks don't appreciate certain talents.)
The captain died in the middle of the Black Sea.
He was a fork-bearded old man anyway.
And when the freighter docked in Istanbul,
Ahmedoff—the somewhat flustered passenger
                who'd left Batum without baggage—
        stepped onto the Galata pier
                with the title to the ship
                        in his pocket.
Istanbul was occupied.
So the title had to be certified
        by the English superintendent of police.
Two months later the Italians bought the freighter,
and Ahmedoff and the pipe-smoker split the proceeds."
"Scandalous."
"No, no.
Just business.
And I'll tell you something else."
"Don't tell me—I know.
How many people are at his table?
                        Four—
                no, you'll say five.
The dead captain is the fifth."

"Very perceptive.
But your vision isn't perfect at this distance.
True, there is
        another dead man,
                another suicide.
In fact, he's hunched over Ahmedoff's Scotch.
But take a closer look:
        is he anything like a fork-bearded old captain?
He's not.
This dead man is young, thin,
tall, and clean-shaven.
In order to die, he had to cross three seas in secrecy:
                        an ocean
                                an open sea
                                        an inland sea.
He was an engineer for an American oil company.
He'd worked in an office in Chicago.
He may have thought of becoming a gangster,
but he hadn't thought of death
                till he set foot in a Bosporus hotel.
The years would have passed without a trace,
like a razor across his clean-shaven face,
        if they hadn't struck oil in Gallipoli.
When the oil company got news of this discovery,
together with officially stamped papers
        and bottled samples of the product,
                they dispatched him to Istanbul.
It was Kasim Ahmedoff who'd struck oil.
They all drove out to Gallipoli in secret.
(Oil secrets are like state secrets.)
They drilled a test well that night.
The product came up plentiful and pure.
(You have to act fast in the oil business.)
The engineer rushed off a telegram:
'Wire $300,000. Stop. End.'
He may have been a little drunk when he sent the telegram,
                maybe even during the drilling.
Liquor was outlawed in America back then,
and Ahmedoff had stocked his car with Johnnie Walker.
You can see where the story's going.

Ahmedoff took the $300,000
(again split fifty-fifty with the right parties).
The engineer could bring up only about eight hundred kilos of oil:
although Ahmedoff had poured in a thousand kilos
when he dug up the ground,
fifty kilos had probably surfaced in the drilling,
and the earth must have absorbed a hundred-fifty."
"And the engineer?"
"Like I said:
a hotel on the Bosporus.
Dawn.
Good-bye, America.
Boom . . .
It's strange how
dawn and the light
waking up all colors
                              pushes those on the edge over to death."
"This Ahmedoff is a scary guy."
"Yes, but his bald head doesn't work like it did.
Check out the young girl with him.
A nice piece, no?
She must taste as sweet as a slice of mandarin orange.
But Ahmedoff is taking her to Ankara for nothing.
Ankara has aged."

A hearty laugh rose from one of the tables.
The black suits looked toward the sound.
It was Hikmet Alpersoy laughing—
a handsome, virile,
fifty-five-year-old man.
His broad shoulders shook,
and his green eyes sparkled with laughter.

The blond man in the black suit said to the dark:
"Isn't he the picture of health?
You can tell he hasn't been sick a day in his life."
"No, no.
He's got chronic gonorrhea.
But maybe that doesn't count as an illness."
"You're bad."

"Did I ever say I was good?"
"Don't get mad."
"I never do."

Across from them, Hikmet Alpersoy laughed again.
The blond black suit told the dark:
"I like that guy's laugh—
open
      free
          and easy.
He must have a light heart."
"Well, not too dark.
A heart is like a light bulb:
it gives off light if it gets the current.
Without the juice, the best bulb in the world
          won't shine
             or be seen."
"Don't mock."
"I'm not."
"Who is this man?"
"Hikmet Alpersoy.
A contractor.
And a manufacturer.
He's quite the ladies' man.
As the French say,
    'Bon enfant, bon viveur.'
During the Great War, he worked in the War Ministry.
But his sister got too friendly with the German officers,
      and he was let go
(by Enver Pasha,
a bit of a fanatic
    when it came to Muslim womanhood).
But the Armistice saved Hikmet Alpersoy,
and soon afterward the Anatolian Independence Movement
    made him half a million liras in two years."
"How?"
"Hikmet trafficked in guns and old army boots.
He'd ship them to the Anatolian government—
         as a service to his country.
He'd buy them low and sell them high—

business."
"You make it sound ugly."
"A bedbug by any other name
would be as ugly.
But I admit
I'm a bit of a wise guy."
"No, just one-sided."
"So there are many sides to things?
Which is mine?"
"You were talking about Hikmet Alpersoy."
"Yes.
Except there's not much left to tell . . .
After the Independence, Hikmet did business with France and Italy.
Then he finally settled on Germany.
Once more he sold Ankara arms.
Only now it wasn't patriotic smuggling
                            or service to his country
but strictly business,
                  one-sided
                        and perfectly legal.
Hikmet likes cars.
He has a nice apartment in Berlin
and a bachelor's pad in Paris.
He even
toured Europe with the governor of Istanbul
                  in his own Chevrolet.
Although now and then
Hikmet has his bouts of depression,
he spends his cheer and money with equal generosity.
But unfortunately
a Jewish girl has captured this great womanizer
                              the past two years.
His green eyes see no one but her."
"Interesting man."
"That he is.
Did I tell you about his canning factory?"
"No."
"About five or six years ago
he and a Bulgarian opened a cannery."
"So what?"

"Nothing . . .
Except the dead seem to have invaded this car tonight."
"Are you starting that again?"
"Don't interrupt—
        I'll show him to you."
"He's sitting at Hikmet's table, right?"
"Yes,
but he can't get near the table."
"Did this one kill himself, too?"
"No.
Even though the doctors ruled it suicide,
        I'd call it out-and-out murder."
"You're a funny man."
"Thank you."
"This suicide or murder victim,
is he young or old?"
"Young.
But you're right.
It's hard to tell.
You can't tell the age of the dead from a distance,
especially if their legs are broken,
        their ribs smashed,
                and their brains dashed out."
"So he fell from a high place."
"That he did.
The dead man worked in the cannery,
        Hikmet Alpersoy and the Bulgarian's cannery.
The pay was twenty-five kurush
for a fourteen-hour day."
"That's a disgrace."
"No, no.
It's just a question of 'surplus value.'"
"I don't understand."
"You wouldn't, even if I said it in Turkish.
But to return to my story.
Selim
        (the dead man)
        couldn't take fourteen hours for twenty-five kurush.
Fifty kurush and ten hours, he said.
The other workers agreed.

Now this was hardly a deep, philosophical idea.
But it was a dangerous one.
And so Hikmet and the Bulgarian
     immediately reported it to the police,
and right away they made some arrests.
Ten people were brought before the commissioner:
     four women, six men
          (the ringleaders)
          and Selim—a Communist.
But Selim was no Communist.
He didn't even know what communism was.
He was just eighteen years old
and wanted fifty kurush instead of twenty-five
     and ten hours instead of fourteen.
But the cops thought different.
They laid Selim on the floor.
And when Selim got up,
     he couldn't step on his feet.
They laid Selim on the floor.
And when Selim got up,
     he couldn't see.
They laid Selim on the floor,
     and when he got up, he collapsed.
They grabbed Selim under the arms
     and took him to a dark room.
They hung him by his hair from a nail
     so his toes
          just brushed the floor.
A streetcar screeched past below.
Somewhere nearby, evening prayers were read.
They took Selim down.
They laid Selim on the floor.
And when Selim got up,
     he saw a window
          far off in the distance,
             a bare dark window.
He ran for it.
The glass shattered.
First his head disappeared,
     then his two feet."

"That's frightening;
        it's like a nightmare."
"Be thankful it's not your nightmare."
"But how did you find out all this, Faik Bey?
You said your name was Faik, didn't you?"
The dark man in the black suit smiled:
"Yes, I'm Faik.
As for the information,
it was a combination of curiosity,
        a love of gossip,
                and my job.
I was a doctor for the police.
I'm not any more:
I've agreed to be chief of staff at a hospital on the steppe.
So I won't betray
        a professional confidence
                if I tell you something else.
Now, look at the third table on this side.
See it?
A man and a woman.
White, blond, and blue.
Young Nordic gods
                couldn't be better built."
"That's true.
But they aren't Turks."
"No.
They're Germans."
"From the embassy?"
"No."
"Is he a commission agent or something?"
"No."
"They're not show people, are they?"
"No, no."
"Tourists?"
"Nope."
"Well, what are they doing here?"
"Look closely at their table, and you'll see."
"You mean we'll see another dead man there?"
"Not one but a thousand,
                two thousand,

three thousand dead.
But as the numbers of the dead increase,
        their atrocity value decreases.
Especially if they died in an air raid."
"I don't understand."
"It's really quite simple.
This dead child, that dead woman, that dead old man
        joining hands in a circle
                around the table of the two Nordic gods
are products of the Rotterdam bombings.
And those two blue-eyed white gods
        guided the birds of death
                straight to their prey."
"You sound like a poet."
"Yes, unfortunately.
When poetry's brought into this business,
                        it's truly disgusting.
Especially this kind of poetry.
But what can you do?
These awful things build up inside you;
you're sickened, horrified,
enraged,
and then you look and find your hands are tied.
You can't do anything.
Then come the words,
        the poeticizing,
                with a little irony
                        and a touch of the lyrical-romantic.
And of the worst kind.
There's a dead man here at our table, too.
Neither a suicide nor a murder or an air-raid victim.
He's talking away
and lapping up the wine.
And in spite of it all
he's pleased with himself."
"You mean me?"
"No, me . . . "

In the moonlight
a dark train

pulled into a dark station.

The blond man in the dark suit glanced out the window:
through the blue glass, the dark station
                        and the shadowy people
                              looked twice as sad, twice as desperate.
They seemed to be whispering
        about death, separation, and nights without dawns.
And though the moon was bright,
the rails were dark on the ground,
        visible for just five or ten steps before they vanished.
Only two arc lights burned—
over open cars pulled off on a siding
(you could tell from their canvas covers
                they were loaded with munitions).
The station and its annexes
were plunged so deep in darkness
        the passengers scurried around on the platform,
                losing their cars and one another.
A woman's cry floated all the way up to the dining car:
"Hatijé,
        where are you,
                    girl?"

The blond man in the black suit asked the dark:
"Where are we going, Faik Bey?"
"I'm headed for the steppe,
        and you're on your way to Eskishehir, I believe."
"That's not what I meant."
"Ah, yes.
'Quo vadis, domine?'"
"Isn't that the title of a novel, Dr. Faik Bey?"
"It is."
"Don't joke."
"I wouldn't."
"What I mean, Dr. Faik Bey,
is that all you've been telling me,
and now this dark station,
made something inside me suddenly give way:
I felt disillusioned

and strangely sad,
as if I'd die tonight for sure.
No,
as if we'd all die tonight—
you,
me,
all these people,
this dark station.
I mean,
      I grieved for myself
and everyone else.
This has never happened to me before.
I mean, for the first time I know
     —really and truly know,
         in a physical way—
         that people besides me live on this earth.
Not just to say it
         or because it's a fact
but suddenly to feel it under my skin,
             to know
                and understand . . .
What do you think?"
"Sure, you feel it,
     maybe you know it,
        but I doubt you understand it.
Anyway, what's the difference?
You'll forget even if you understand.
It was a passing thought that's come and gone,
       or just about.
And if it doesn't go away, you'll get used to it.
And once you do, there's no problem.
Habit restores the comfort
     of never having felt
        or known
       or understood anything.
It may be a poorer comfort than the first,
but it's a comfort nonetheless."
"You're right, Faik Bey.
And yet . . . "
"And yet, where are we going, right?"

"Yes, where are we going?
Where is the world headed?
          Where are people going?"
"To understand that, Mister..."
"Shekip Aytuna..."
"To understand that, Mr. Shekip Aytuna...
Did you choose the last name 'Moon River' yourself?"
"No, my boss did."
"It was a good choice.
To understand that,
          we have to know where we've come from and where we are."
"Absolutely..."
"Absolutely—but you
                    and I,
                              what do we do once we understand?"
"Yes."
"Yes."
"Yes,
it's a dead end,
          it's a..."
"Have you noticed, Mr. Shekip Aytuna?
I noticed it before when you were talking:
all of us enlightened people sound alike—
          the same shades of meaning,
                    the same intonations.
Isn't it strange?"
"I don't know..."
"Is your grief gone, Mr. Shekip Aytuna?"
"Just about."
"Wonderful.
Are you married?"
"I'm single."
"Ah, a sultan's life!"
"I'm engaged, Dr. Faik Bey."
"Congratulations.
Wine?"
"No thanks, I..."
"You don't care much for alcohol."
"No.
It doesn't agree with me."
"Moderation in all things is best..."

IV

The Anatolia Express pulled out of the dark station,
     the engine blowing clouds of steam in the moonlight.

The dining car.
The kitchen.
The chef spoke with the waiter Mustafa.
The chef, Mahmut Asher,
was the "neoclassic" type of our new reformed cuisine,
which is to say he looked like a cook on a freighter
          bound for Singapore in an American movie—
fat and jolly,
his white hat slightly askew,
and clean-shaven:
"The Ankara Palace, my boy,
the Ankara Palace got its apples from California.
[The waiter Mustafa
               listened.]
Apples, my boy, from the land of California!
Flown by plane to Paris
     and from Paris to us.
Have you ever seen California apples?"
"No."
"California apples, my boy,
     are big and red.
And they're all the same size,
all alike as if turned on a lathe."
"So you wouldn't stoop to ours?"
"God forbid—
               no.
Monsieur Fernand wouldn't let in the door
even the choicest of Amasya apples."
"And who was he?"
"What do you mean who was he?
Haven't you ever heard of him?"
"Never."
"So much the worse for you.
And you call yourself a waiter?"
"I wish I didn't."

"Why?"
"Oh, nothing.
Tell me about the guy.
Who was he?"
"Monsieur Fernand was a master.
If he weren't a heathen, I could call him my patron saint.
They brought him from Paris.
He was the prime minister,
the chief of staff, of chefs.
He got eight hundred a month from the Ankara Palace—
eight hundred bills, my boy.
But he deserved it:
the man was deep,
an artist.
Once a week the French ambassador,
        the Comte de Chambrun,
                would come down to the kitchen to see him."
"What did they talk about?"
"Sauces, I think.
As you know, French cooking
                means sauces.
At the Ankara Palace, my boy, we used to make a sauce
            called *sauce grand veneur*—
        nothing like it anywhere in Turkey.
It took a kind of mushroom called truffles,
            a black mushroom.
They grow underground.
The French use pigs to sniff them out and root them up.
The pigs are trained just for this job.
The truffles came to us from Paris, my boy,
                    in boxes."
"So they don't grow here?"
"God forbid—
            not this kind.
I hear they tried growing them in Konya.
They even used dogs instead of pigs.
But it was no use:
        truffles have to be black,
        and the ones in Konya came up white."
"Is Monsieur Fernand still in Ankara?"

"He left three years ago
                    when his contract expired.
But we were trained.
We snatched the heathen's skills right out of his hands.
Ibrahim from Kastamonu
            even invented a new sauce for filet of wild boar.
Just let a Turk get a whiff of something,
            and he'll grasp the whole thing in a flash.
We're smart.
But we don't respect ourselves.
Now they're paying the Turkish chef at the Ankara Palace
            a hundred-fifty a month.
What does he lack that Monsieur Fernand had?
            Being a heathen?"

"Mustafa, the coffee's ready . . . "

Mustafa took the coffee from the busboy
                                and left.
He served the coffee.

"Waiter!"
Hikmet Alpersoy
            (the contractor-manufacturer
                    with the hearty laugh)
                            called the waiter Mustafa:
"Waiter, bring us three bottles of Poplar Creek wine."
Mardanapal objected:
"Three bottles are too much—
            one's enough."
"No, it's not—
we'll take three."
Mardanapal laughed
            (he laughed like an old frog):
"Still living hard, Hikmet Bey,
                and you've hit fifty."

Four of them sat at the table.
Mardanapal has represented a German firm for twenty years.
He's a Polish Jew.

Because, along with electrical supplies,
                    he so easily sold
the professional integrity of our officials, big and small, in contract bids,
the Nazis handed him
a "certificate of clean blood"
                    and kept him on.
Mardanapal's young wife is a wonder:
long, thin legs;
        a pair of breasts like firm, green figs;
big, dark, velvet eyes;
                    and a forehead like rose marble.

The waiter Mustafa brought the wine.

Mardanapal looked
        (sad eyes bulging under hairy eyebrows),
Mardanapal looked
at the dignitary's table.
"Hikmet Bey," he said,
        "I'd like to ask this guy one thing;
                I'd give a hundred thousand
                        for a straight answer."
"What are you going to ask him?"
"Will we go to war?"
"He won't tell; ask Tahsin."
"Tahsin won't tell, either."
"Because he doesn't know."
"I know what Tahsin will and won't tell.
He won't tell even if he knows."
Fehim spoke:
"Only one man in Turkey knows.
Don't listen to anyone else."

Fehim was an assistant D.A.,
                handsome and young,
                        with a slight lisp.
His father died in exile in Paris,
and his wife is the daughter of a Kurdish lord.
In three years the wife and husband ate up
                        an apartment building,

a mansion,
and sixty-five thousand in cash.
They still have a French *dame de compagnie* at home,
Fehim has a Ford,
a three-thousand gambling debt,
and fame—still not forgotten after five years—
for disturbing the peace
at a club in Current Point
and getting slapped for it in Dolmabahtché Palace.
The one in the palace
had the head guard slap him.
Fehim was stunned, scared, and angry at first,
but then he threw himself face-down
at the feet of the one in the palace
and cried
like a helpless child.
Yet that very day,
that morning
in court,
he had stood up, stately in his gold-striped black robe,
and called for a death sentence.

Hikmet Alpersoy asked:
"Why do you want to know whether we'll go to war, Mardanapal?"
"Just a matter of calculations, Hikmet Bey."
Fehim asked:
"Do you want Hitler to win?
What does your heart say?"
Hikmet Alpersoy laughed heartily:
"Mardanapal doesn't count as a Jew."
Mardanapal said softly:
"My passport doesn't say,
but Mardanapal is a Jew.
I'm a Jew, thank God."
"Don't let Hitler hear you."
"Let him.
I'm making him money."
"If they handed you Hitler, Mardanapal,
what would you do?"
"I'd make him a partner."

"In order to shaft him?"
"You wouldn't kill him?"
"Who isn't going to die in this world?"
"Man, aren't you the least bit mad at the Germans?"
Aziz Bey had asked this.
Mardanapal laughed
       but didn't answer.
Aziz Bey had his hands in his pockets.
Those pockets with long, slanted slits
             weren't on the sides of his pants
             but up front.
Even his tuxedos had those pockets
(a holdover from the days of the gangs.)
Aziz Bey was a Circassian.
His father was a forest ranger.
But today Aziz Bey
           owns forests the size of a colony:
       they supply Istanbul with wood and coal.
If you meet him in the summertime,
         on the steps of his chalet deep in the woods,
            he's a British governor in India,
            from the snow-white safari hat
               to the faint smile of an aristocrat.
And winter nights, when wolves prowl and the trees howl,
if you're a guest at his table
(his table is ten meters long),
you'll see him at the head, gold-yellow and blood-red,
serving roast game and wine to friends.
And around there, the wives of foresters and guard commanders
(almost all ugly women)
are up to their elbows in gold bracelets.
Only one township governor objected,
       and three days later his home was invaded
          and he was beaten unconscious.
Sometimes on the forest floor, on the red oak leaves,
       under the long, thick, knotty branches,
          you'll stumble on bodies with bullet holes in their heads:
villagers caught poaching wood.
Aziz Bey doesn't know how many people work his forests.
He doesn't have a clue about accounting.

His accounting department is the back of his cigarette package.
His relatives, who are his forest rangers and gunmen,
steal from him shamelessly.
Aziz Bey knows
    but says nothing.
Because his cigarette-package accounting
   steals from the workers ten or a hundred times more.
Sometimes they talk of a consumptive girl in the forest
who wandered under the trees like a ghost.
The girl died,
   leaving Aziz Bey a marble tomb under the reddest hornbeams
     and forest upon forest.
But fish
can never have too much water,
and Aziz Bey
can't get enough trees.
More and more trees,
more than anyone ever owned,
    more than any bird can see the end of.

Aziz Bey asked:
"Why did you laugh, Mardanapal?
I'll give you some good news anyway:
we'll reach an agreement with the Germans;
      you'll see.
Are you happy, Mardanapal?"
"We'll all be happy together, Aziz Bey.
And your half-finished business will be resolved."
"Huh, you heard about that, too?"
"We hear everything.
    We're Jews.
The Germans offered you a million, right?
Good money.
And they know how to do business.
You'll buy up the whole province in two years
    if they're partners in your trees.
C'est une bonne affaire, truly,
    worth every cent.
We'll reach an agreement,
   and we'll all be happy together."

Something was brewing outside the blue windows,
but those inside didn't notice.
Outside, a fine white mist
ringed the reddening moon.

Inside, three women and a man sat at the fifth table.
The man was young and plump.
The women were old and painted.
And the flesh under their chins sagged,
                              pale
                                    and wasted.
The third woman
(the one with false teeth)
extended her bejeweled, desperate hand
(under the table)
        and slipped it into the man's pants pocket.

Outside, clouds swelled in the east
        —moist, red, jetblack—
                and marched west,
                        bringing lightning, wind, and rain.
And over the earth rising to meet
the lowering clouds, telegraph poles raced
        a dark train:
                        the Anatolia Express.

The dining car had long finished with their fruit and coffee.
Chef Mahmut Asher,
        the maitre d', and the waiter
                met at their table
                        behind the glass partition.
From where they sat, they could see the length of the car.
The people inside kept talking
but without a sound,
        opening and closing their mouths
                        hopelessly like fish.

Outside, lightning flashed in the east.
A child squatted right down,
covered his ears with his wet hands, and counted:

148

"One, two, three, four, five, six, seven."
The thunder roared:
the lightning must have struck close by.

In the dining car, a very old man
—a part of this world—
jotted figures on a pink slip of paper
and then—apart from this world—
gazed out alone
at the rain hitting the blue glass.
The drops rolled down like beads,
rain lashing the window.
A dark train carried the men through the storm.

The waiter Mustafa wiped the table with his sleeve,
took a yellow-leaf notebook out of his pocket,
        and carefully opened it to the first page.
Chef Mahmut Asher asked:
"What's this supposed to be, son, this notebook?"
"I've got an epic copied here, Chef Mahmut."
"So you go for such stuff?"
"I do."
"Me, too.
Who wrote it?"
"A man in prison."
"Good.
I like prison epics, son."
"This isn't like that."
"Too bad.
Prison epics are sad.
When it comes to songs and love, sad is beautiful.
The man sings, you feel pity.
You must have pity in the heart, son—
                I mean, humanity.
Isn't there anything to pity in this one?"
"There is and there isn't.
It's a little like the Koroghlu epic."
"I like that, too.
God be with you—
        let's get started."

Outside, the storm raged at its height.
The wind carried the sound of the rails and the rain hours away
and brought back howls from kilometers off.
Not just in the east but all through the dark night,
                lightning flashed
at almost measured intervals . . .

Mustafa started the epic:
"'They who are numberless
                like ants in the earth
                        fish in the sea
                                birds in the air,
who are cowardly
                        brave
                                ignorant
                                        wise
                                                and childlike,
and who destroy
                and create,
my epic tells only of their adventures.

They who fall for the traitor's lie
                and drop their banner on the ground,
leave the field to the enemy
                and run for home,
and they who pull a knife on the renegade
and who laugh like a green tree
and cry without ceremony
and who swear like hell,
my epic tells only of their adventures.

The destiny
                of iron
                        coal
                                and sugar
and red copper
and textiles
and love and cruelty and life
and all the branches of industry
and the sky

150

                    and the desert
                              and the blue ocean,
of sad riverbeds
and plowed earth and cities
              will be changed one morning,
one sunrise when, at the edge of darkness,
        pushing against the earth with their heavy hands,
                                        they rise up.

It's they who inspire
the brightest shapes in the most knowing mirrors.
In this century, they were victorious, they were defeated.
Many things were said about them,
and about them
                  it was said
they have nothing to lose but their chains.'"

Mustafa stopped.
Mahmut was a little taken aback:
"That's a strange epic," he said,
        "this guy in prison has written a different kind of epic.
He's stirring up something.
But your voice is sad, son,
              and it reads like music:
                    it touches a man.
Is it over?"
"No, this is just the beginning."
"Then it's something like an overture.
Let's see how it ends."

Mustafa read on:
"'THE YEARS 1918 AND '19,
AND THE STORY OF BLACK SNAKE.'"
Mahmut asked:
"That's what the story's called?"
"Yes.
I'm reading."
"Okay, read."
"'We saw flames, we saw betrayal,
and with our eyes on fire

we survived.
Cities fell one after another:
Istanbul (October-November 1918),
Izmir (May 1919),
and Manisa, Menemen, Aydin, Akhisar
(between mid-May
                    and mid-June,
the time for cutting tobacco,
                    when the barley has been harvested
                        and the wheat lies ahead) . . .
Adana
        Antep
            Urfa
                and Marash
fell
        fighting . . .

. . . .
. . . .
. . . .

The people of Antep are fighters.
They can hit a flying crane in the eye,
a running hare in the hind leg.
And on their Arabian mares
they sit tall and slender, like green cypresses.

Antep is a hot
            hard place.
Antep people are fighters,
Antep people are brave.

Black Snake,
        before he became Black Snake,
worked in one of the Antep villages.
Maybe he had a good life,
                    maybe not.
(They didn't leave him time to think about it.)
He lived like a field mouse,
scared as a field mouse.

"Bravery" comes with land, guns, and horses.
He didn't have any horses, guns, or land.
Black Snake
had the same twig-thin neck
          and the same big head
                    before he became Black Snake . . .

When the heathens entered Antep,
the people of Antep
          flushed him out
                    of the pistachio tree
                              that hid his fear.
They put a horse under him
          and a Mauser
                    in his hand.

Antep is a hard place.
Green lizards
                    on red rocks.
And hot clouds pace the sky,
                              back and forth . . .

The heathens held the hills.
They had artillery.
The people of Antep
                    were surrounded on the flat plain.
The heathens' shrapnel fell like rain.
It dug up the earth by the roots.
The heathens held the hills.
The blood of Antep flowed.

A rosebush on the flat plain
was Black Snake's cover
          before he became Black Snake.
The bush was so scrawny,
and his head and his fear so big,
that he lay flat on his belly
          with his gun still empty . . .

Antep is a hot

hard place.
Antep people are fighters,
Antep people are brave.
But the heathens had artillery.
Nothing could be done, it was fate:
        the people of Antep would have to surrender
                        the flat plain to the heathens.

Before he became Black Snake,
        Black Snake didn't really care
                if the heathens held Antep till Doomsday.
Because he had never been taught to think.
He lived on the earth like a field mouse,
scared as a field mouse.

His cover was a rosebush.
He hid under it, flat on his belly,
when behind a white rock
a black snake
                raised its head—
skin all spangles,
        eyes fire-red,
                tongue forked.
Suddenly a bullet
                tore off its head.
The snake collapsed.

Black Snake,
before he became Black Snake,
saw the black snake's end
and yelled
                the first thought of his life:
"Take heed, wild heart—
death found the black snake behind a white rock
and will find you even in a steel box . . . "

And when he who had lived like a field mouse,
scared as a field mouse,
sprang forward,
the people of Antep, awed,

154

quickly fell in behind him.
They made mincemeat of the heathens in the hills.
And he who'd lived like a field mouse,
scared as a field mouse,
became "Black Snake."

This is how I heard it.
And I put the story of Black Snake,
                    who headed a guerrilla band for years,
                        and the people of Antep
                        and the city of Antep
                in the first book of my epic
                        exactly as I heard it . . . ' "

"Bravo, Black Snake!
                That's the way, Antep!
            Now this I like—he wrote it well."
Mahmut Asher had a lot more to say,
but someone called from inside:
"Waiter!"
It was Hikmet Alpersoy
            (the cannery owner
                    and arms dealer
                        with the hearty laugh).
"Bring me some mineral water.
Your Poplar Creek wine must be fake—
            it did quite a number on my stomach . . . "
"No, sir,
        our wines . . . "
"Save it.
Just bring me some mineral water fast."
The waiter Mustafa's lips trembled,
his dark cheekbones flushed red,
and he could barely keep from swearing.
Besides, for the past year
(since the day he visited the man in prison),
being a waiter had felt like wearing a sticky, dirty undershirt.
He'd seen the man inside through iron bars and a wire fence.
The man had the face of a child.
When he realized Mustafa was a waiter,

something like pity
            or disappointment
                        or even disapproval had crossed his face.
Or maybe not—
maybe a bar had cast a shadow on his face
                        at that moment.
Whatever it was,
Mustafa no longer considered waiting on tables respectable.
It was like being a servant.

Mustafa told the maitre d' in an angry voice:
"That gentleman over there didn't like the wine—
it upset the pimp's sensitive stomach.
He wants mineral water.
Here, take it to him."
The maitre d',
a proud man in a Pullman uniform,
was so amazed at so many things at once
                        that he actually took the mineral water.
But as he left, he said:
"Mustafa, don't read any more of that thing until I get back . . . "

Outside, the darkness was like moist earth.
Driven by the wind and rain, the Anatolia Express
rushed along the rails at an incredible speed.

The maitre d' returned.
Mustafa continued his epic:
"'THE YEAR 1920 AND THE STORY OF ISMAIL FROM ARHAVE . . .
We saw flames, we saw betrayal.
The enemy forces were on the march again.
Akhisar, Karacabey,
Bursa, and Whitewater east of Bursa:
            we retreated, fighting.
On August 29
      of 1920
            Ushak fell.
Wounded
      and burning with rage
                  but standing our ground,

we're in the Dumlupinar hills.
Nazilli fell . . .

We saw flames, we saw betrayal.
We held out
      we're holding out.
1920: February, April, May,
Bolu, Duzjé, Geyvé, Adapazari:
infiltration by the Caliph's forces, treason.

And the same in Konya
on the 3rd of October.
One morning
Delibash entered the city
      with his green flag and five hundred deserters.
They held Aladdin Peak for three days and nights.
And as they fled toward Manavgat
               to their deaths,
severed heads hung from their saddles . . .

And on the 29th of December in Kutahya.

One night
a traitor
      with four cannons and eighteen hundred horsemen
              —Ethem the Circassian, by name—
went over to the enemy,
with his mule train loaded with rugs and kilims
and his droves of cattle and sheep.
Their hearts were dark,
their belts and whips silver-studded,
they and their horses well-fed . . .

We saw flames, we saw betrayal.
Our spirits raged, our flesh endured.
Those who held out were not giants,
bereft of love and passion, but human beings
with their unbelievable weaknesses, scary power,
guns, and horses.
The horses were ugly,

uncared-for,
no taller than stunted brush.
But they were patient and could run full speed
on the steppes without neighing or foaming.
The men wore long coats
                    and went barefoot . . .
They had fur hats on their heads
                    and in their hearts, grief
                    and boundless hope . . .

Men were defeated, ungrieving and hopeless.
With bullet wounds in their flesh,
they were abandoned in village rooms.
And there they lay on their backs, side by side,
all bandages
              skin
                    and combat boots.
And their fingers were gnarled
              as if torn at their roots,
their stiff hands caked with earth and blood . . .

And deserters
passed beyond the villages in the dark
with their fear and Mausers and bare dead feet.
Starved,
they were pitiless
in their misery.
They came down to the lonely white road
and stopped the horseman riding with the stars,
and because they were starving in the Bolu mountains,
                    they pushed off steep cliffs
the carts loaded with homespun cloth, cigarette papers, salt, and soap . . .

And far away
              —far, far away in the Istanbul harbor—
this late at night
the Laz boats loading smuggled arms and uniforms
        are freedom and hope,
                    water and wind.
They've plied water and wind since the first seafarers.

The boats were chestnut wood,
ranging from three to ten tons,
and under lateen sails
      they brought tobacco and hazelnuts
         and took back sugar and olive oil.
Now they harbored their great secret.
Now, putting behind them the sadness of human voices at sea,
freighters at anchor,
and flaring lanterns of rowboats
      swaying below Kabatash,
they slipped past the enemy turrets in the dark water
           and, small

             cunning
              and proud,
       headed for the Black Sea.
At the helm and in steerage are such men
—with long, hooked noses
and a passion for talk—
who, as easily as singing a song, can die
for corn bread and dark-blue anchovies,
without expecting anything from anyone . . .

. . . .
. . . .

The straight-stemmed lead-gray vessel
      glowing red in the dark
         is an enemy torpedo boat.
And the flaring fire
      rocking
         on the waves
is Captain Shaban's five-ton boat.
Twenty miles from the Kerempé lighthouse
in the dark night,
the waves were tall as minarets,
their crests crashing and shattering white . . .

The wind:
      a northeaster.
The enemy torpedo boat disappeared

with its captives on board.
Captain Shaban's boat
        sank with its burning mast.

Ismail from Arhavé
        was on this doomed boat.
And now
off the Rocky Point lighthouse,
in the dinghy of the sunken hull,
he's all by himself with his charge,
but he's not alone:
        crowds of winds
                and clouds
                        and waves
are all abuzz around Ismail.

Ismail from Arhavé
        asked himself:
"Will we get there with our charge?"
He answered himself:
"Can't be we won't."
One night on the Tophané wharf
the machinist Master Bekir said,
"Ismail, son, this package
is for your safekeeping,
        not for anyone else."
And, at the Rocky Point lighthouse,
when the enemy spotlight played on the boat's sails,
Ismail asked his captain's permission:
        "Captain Shaban," he said,
        "we must deliver our charge,"
                and he jumped in the boat's dinghy
                and rowed away.

God is great
but the boat is small, said the Jew.
Ismail took a hit to the stern,
                then another,
                        then a third.
If he didn't know the sea as well as he knew how to throw knives,

                              he'd have capsized.

The wind switches to the north.
Way in the distance is a tiny red light,
the starboard lantern of a ship
          bound for Sebastopol.
His hands bleeding,
          Ismail pulls on the oars.
He's at ease.
He's beyond everything
          but his struggle and charge.
Ismail is in his element.
The charge:
          a heavy machine gun.
And if the harbormasters don't look quite right to him,
                    he'll go all the way to Ankara
                         and hand-deliver it.

The wind keeps changing.
It may turn to the northwest.
The closest land is at least fifteen miles off.
But Ismail
          trusts his hands.
They're equally confident
handling bread, oar-stems, or the tiller of a rudder
          or Fotika's breasts in Kemeralti.

The wind didn't shift to the northwest.
Suddenly, as if all its ropes were cut with a knife,
it pulled a one-eighty
                    and dropped.

Ismail wasn't expecting it.
The waves rolled under his boat a bit longer,
then the sea went
          completely flat
                    and jetblack.
Stunned, Ismail dropped the oars.
How awful to give up the struggle!
Ismail shivered inside.

And, jumpy like a fish,
he saw his isolation
     in the shape of a rowboat
        a pair of oars
           and a dead-
              still sea.
And suddenly
     he felt so crushed by loneliness
that his hands lost their touch:
he leaned too hard on the oars.
They snapped.

The water dragged his boat farther out.
Nothing could be done now.
Ismail drifted on a dead sea
with bleeding hands and his charge.
First, he swore.
Then he felt like praying.
Then he smiled,
     bent down, and stroked his sacred charge.
Then—
Ismail's fate
     is unknown . . . ' "

The cook Mahmut Asher
rubbed his eyes with the backs of his huge fists,
and his voice cracked.
"I know this Ismail, son," he said.
The maitre d' laughed:
"Come on now, master,
there's not really a man named Ismail—
no one like that ever lived.
What you heard is a story . . . "
This objection almost angered Mahmut Asher:
"Son, how can you say it's a story?
God forbid!
It's an epic, didn't you hear?
Didn't Koroghlu live?
And are Tahir and Zuhré lies?
Plus, I told you—I know Ismail from Arhavé.

But I haven't seen him in twenty years.
So he died back then?
It's too bad—
he was a real man."
Mahmut Asher fell quiet.
The waiter Mustafa looked at those in the dining car
beyond the glass partition,
the rage in his heart rising to his throat.
Mahmut Asher spoke again
as if to himself:
"You're right, son.
Ismail from Arhavé is now a story.
All the days past are now just stories.
Those days were different, these days are different.
Today, son, men are a different breed—
        a different breed, son, the men of today.
Look here, Mustafa,
does this guy write about any battles?"
"He does."
"So he tells about the Inonu battle, too?"
"He does."
"I was in that one.
Later they called it the First Inonu Battle."
The waiter Mustafa asked with amazement:
"So you were in the war, too?"
"Sure was.
The Inonu battlefield, son—
the wind and cold
stung like bees.
It was after the dead of winter,
        right around the equinox.
The fighting lasted five days and five nights,
a real bloodbath.
When it was over,
the heathens left gun carriages,
        cases and cases of cognac,
                and six trucks behind in the snow.
And as they ran away, my boy
        —of course, it wasn't all that clear who was running—
but as they ran away,

they burned bridges and villages."

Chef Mahmut Asher,
          the "neoclassic" type of our new reformed cuisine,
suddenly appeared completely different to Mustafa,
down to the shape of his nose.
And his white hat vanished.
The maitre d' asked Mustafa:
"Where did you get these writings?"
"From my brother."
"Does your brother know the prisoner who wrote this poem?"
"They're friends.
I went to visit him once."
"Who? The poet in prison?"
"Yes."
"What does your brother do?"
"He's a worker . . . "

The dark train carried the men through the storm.
Rain lashed the blue windows,
beading the glass.
Mustafa continued his epic:
"'The First Inonu Battle,
then the Second.
On the 23rd of March in 1921
the enemy's Bursa and Ushak forces attack us.
Their artillery and infantry
          are three times ours.
We have lots of cavalry.
But horses don't have bolts,
          cartridges,
               or barrels,
and swords
     are cheap bare metal.
March 26.
Night.
Their right wing closed in.
27 March:
contact on all fronts.
28, 29, 30:

continued fighting.
And on the night of March 31
    (I don't know if there was moonlight)
sounds and sparks filled the Inonu dark.
And the next day,
   April 1st,
     Trench Hill lit up.
It's six-thirty:
Brown Hill is burning.
The enemy has left the field to our forces.
Then from April 8 to 11:
Dumlupinar.
Then June.
A summer night.
Only sparkles of light
    and the buzz of bugs.
We're crossing the Sakarya at three points
    on rafts.
We took Adapazari
   in a surprise attack.
And, circling the rushes of Sapanja Lake,
approached the textile mill east of Iznik.
The enemy
—partly by sea,
    boarding ships,
and partly by land,
   pulling back to Bursa
    via Karamursel—
evacuated Izmit in the night.

Then the 23rd of August
and the great battle of the Sakarya
that lasts until the 13th of September.
We have 40,000 foot soldiers
   and 4,500 horsemen.
The enemy has 88,000 infantry
   and 300 pieces of artillery.
The battlefield is bordered on the north
   by the Sakarya River
    and mountains.

Mountains
     —Mandrake Mountain,
       Sky Mountain—
with sharp
steep sides,
chalky soil,
    and gritty pines
growing far apart on the rocks,
     isolate like hermits.
Here only cloven-hoofed deer
can drink from the Sakarya.
The Sakarya runs through sheer cliffs
from where the Ankara waters join it
to the northwest of Eskishehir.
To the south
      and southwest
           lies the Jihanbeyli plain:
             a waste land
             so leafless and sad,
             so endless and vast,
it makes you want to die, with no regrets
           for anything left behind.
Facing that desert,
    those mountains,
      that river, and us,
the enemy fought nonstop for twenty-two days and nights
and had to retreat.

Still,
the year was 1922,
and fifteen provinces and their flags
      and nine big cities
          were in enemy hands.
Which meant their holdings
        were unbelievable:
eleven rivers, seven lakes,
and two-and-a-half million acres
       of forests—ours, with their fires
               and axe wounds at their roots—
one navy yard, two munitions plants,
and nineteen bays and harbors

—maybe many of them without
    a wharf
        or breakwater
            or red and green lights,
with maybe nothing to light up their waters
                but the lanterns of rowboats—
but ours,
with their wooden docks and sad fishermen.
Plus three seas
    and six railroad lines;
and then roads as far as the eye can see—
the roads that take us home
and away from home,
the roads we take into the desert
      or to Gallipoli and our deaths, never
    asking why or
        what for—
and then the land
and the people of this land:
the rug weavers of Ushak at their looms,
the leather workers of Manisa famous
      for gold-stitched saddles,
the poor starving on roadsides and in stations,
and the smart,
    serious, dashing
         workers of Izmir
          and Istanbul,
            young bloods all,
and grain merchants and weighmasters and town fathers
and the nomads of Aydin with their haircloth tents
and then day-laborers
         sharecroppers
           subsistence workers
and peasants,
with or without livestock,
in sheepskin boots
    and rawhide shoes.
Fifteen provinces and their flags
     and nine big cities
       were in enemy hands . . .'"

V

The Anatolia Express approached Sapanja.
The blond man in the black suit
said to the dark man in the black suit:
"I've been watching quite a while, Faik Bey—
the cook, the maitre d', and the waiter
          are reading something over there behind the glass."
"You haven't looked closely:
the waiter reads, and the others listen."
"Yes.
I wonder what they're reading."
"'What can that waiter possibly read?' you think.
A waiter reading!
And you find it strange that a cook
          would listen to something read."
"That's right.
And they don't seem to be reading Karagoz stories."
"What made you think of the shadow play?"
"I don't know.
But it could be something else."
"Why not the poems of Ahmet Hashim?"
"Impossible.
No way.
The cook couldn't understand Hashim."
"You're right, Mr. Shekip Aytuna:
Ahmet Hashim doesn't have a single word—
                              open,
                                        amazing,
                                                  brave,
          just, or hopeful—to say to the cook."
"Is that what poetry is about, doctor?"
"Poetry is about the world.
And in today's world, those are the only things worth saying."
"You have such strange ideas."
"Strange, yes,
and even ridiculous,
hypocritical, affected, despicable even,
because they're just a lot of talk—

because they don't fight, and can't . . . "

Outside, the rain had quit,
but the wind still blew hard.
Sapanja Lake glistened in the pitch-dark.
The Anatolia Express slowed down
past soaking-wet, jetblack trees.
And as the noise of the train let up,
a new sound broke through the roaring wind:
                    the rustle
                        of water and rushes . . .

The train stopped.
Shouts came from outside.
The wet hands of women and children holding up things
        pounded on the blue windows of the dining car.
The people inside looked at the grasping blue hands.
But the Anatolia Express left Sapanja
        without buying a single apple.
It was 9:57 p.m.

And 108 kilometers south of the Anatolia Express,
        the 3:45 train out of Haydar Pasha Station
        pulled into Bilejik.
No rain or wind there—
            moonlight sparkled like snow.
And because third-class car number 510
        had masked its lights
        instead of its windows,
            two passengers gazed at the moon
            from an open window in the corridor—
                Nuri Ozturk (the nursing-home accountant)
                and Kazim from Kartal.

The moon sailed across the white expanse of the sky
                        like a sleigh.

The university student sat in the prisoners' section.
The prisoner Halil explained the socio-economic causes of the last war.
Although he spoke in round numbers and abstractions,

he was all wound up, as if he were fighting.
And his nearsighted eyes shone through his glasses.
And despite the numbers of people dead and cities razed,
the student felt those eyes on his forehead like two hopeful hands.
But the sergeant despaired.
He mumbled to himself:
"They rebelled,
        they went against God.
And what a war it will be now—
what pandemonium,
                what days of weeping and wailing—
the war between the earth and sky!
                    Life itself is at stake."
Then he turned to the prisoner Suleyman:
"Suleyman Bey," he said,
                "Suleyman Bey,
the dove lamented to the end of time:
'Better not to be born!'
Because it was born and saw death first—
                    eternity, I mean.
Alas, it's fate
how the world turns.
First comes a rise,
then the sure fall follows.
The world belongs to no one but the wind.
Before you know it, you have turned to dust..."

The prisoner Fuat,
Istanbul in his heart,
                watched the night outside the open window.
The prisoner Melahat thought of her daughter:
"She has two dresses and four pairs of socks,
                but her shoes are worn out,
                    and if it's winter, she'll need a wool scarf."
Guardsman Haydar dozed.
Guardsman Hasan listened to the prisoner Halil.

The moon sailed across the sky like a sleigh,
        getting no nearer or farther away
        but keeping its distance,

round and bright—
moving with the train,
slowing down with the train,
and stopping with it at Bilejik Station.

Nuri Ozturk took three deep breaths in the corridor
and spoke as if singing a sad song:
"I can't see the moon but think of my love."
The moon lit up Kazim's yellow wolf-eyes.
Kazim from Kartal said:
"I think of years past,
                the years of the Liberation Army."
He stopped, then quickly went on:
"How many years have passed since
a moonlit night just like this!
Just like now, I'm in a silver box—
                the same strange light, the same silence.
Moonlit nights are either noisy
                        or perfectly still.
I'm alone, face-down on the ground,
                behind my carbine—
                        a virgin Ottoman carbine.
The front sight gleams
                at the end of the barrel,
a hundred years away,
                        minuscule at a distance.
We got orders from headquarters that day:
'Take out the translator of the English commander in Gebzé.'
The translator Mansur had organized the villages
                        and was selling us out . . .
I'd figured right where he would pass.
He appeared across the way.
On horseback.
A big
        English artillery horse.
The animal trots on its own
                down the middle of the train tracks,
                        slow and easy.
The translator must have let the reins drop,
                and his head nods—

                    maybe he's asleep on the horse.
The man looms larger as he nears.
People always appear bigger in moonlight.
He's about four hundred paces away.
I raised the barrel just a bit and aimed
at Mansur's nodding head.
A rock rolled down the cliff on the left.
A bird flew from the tree on my right
            —a plane tree—
                    the bird must have scared.
I turned to look at the bird
                    and came face to face with the moon:
                            it was huge, just like now,
                                    full
                                        and white.
It almost blinded me.
So by the time I'd aligned the front and rear sights
again and aimed and fired,
the first bullet hit his shoulder
                    instead of his head.
The man grunted, 'Unh'—
I heard his voice right at my ear.
He turned the horse's head
                    and took off at full gallop.
I fired a second bullet.
He slumped to his left on the horse.
A third.
He fell off the horse.
But one foot caught in the stirrup,
                    and he was dragged behind the running horse.
Then his foot shook loose
            and Mansur dropped on the spot;
                    the horse went around the bend.
I stood up
and walked toward the guy.
I'm going to take the papers on him
                    with the names of his spies.
Four telegraph poles stand between us—
                    at fifty each, that's two hundred meters.
Suddenly the translator straightened up,

lurched to the left,
                        and ran downhill.
I shouldered the carbine.
A fourth bullet:
the guy dropped.
I started running.
He straightened up again
at a hundred paces.
Mansur walks ahead of me, swaying like a drunk—
                              not running now
                                    but walking.

I stopped running, too.
We came to the sea.
An empty factory.
And a white house
        with a wooden pier.
I saw the guy start into the water.
The papers would get wet.
I fired a fifth bullet.
He fell into the water and got up.
As I reloaded,
a light came on in the house,
        a window opened,
                and I think a woman looked out.
The translator screamed as if being strangled.
The window shut.
The light went out.
The translator grabbed at the pier.
He climbs up, dragging himself like an animal with broken hind
    legs.
I can still see him.
What a mess.
And moonlight strikes the sea,
coming and going,
                going and coming.
Anyway,
to make a long story short,
I finished off Mansur with a knife.
His papers got all bloody,
but blood doesn't blot out words . . . "

Kazim from Kartal suddenly stopped,
then quickly went on:
"The guy was scum,
            that's for sure.
He was a traitor,
            that's a fact.
How many loyal brothers' blood
            was on his hands, I know.
But even so
the man rode sleeping on his horse in the moonlight.
What I mean is,
to kill a man like that in that way, even in those days,
and not suffer when you look at the moon
            years after everything's settled,
you'd need to have a heart of stone
            or be the soul of justice.
Mine isn't stone, thank God,
            but it's just.
If you ask me how I know for sure,
I fought out of love, expecting nothing,
got wounded several times,
            and so on.
And when the fighting ended,
I didn't get any land or apartments.
I was a farmer in Kartal before the war,
            and I'm a farmer in Kartal after it.
Only, well, now and then
            I talk about it . . . "

Nuri Ozturk almost said out loud:
"Except you don't just talk about it—you brag away."
Actually, Nuri Ozturk couldn't stand
            Liberation Army stories
            because he hadn't gone out to Anatolia at the time . . .

Third-class car number 510.
The fifth section slept in the half dark.
Only Shakir from Sakarya (the man with cirrhosis)
            was awake,
his big head erect

on his twig-thin neck
                    (like a mistake in logic).
His hands were folded on his belly.
If those gnarled hands
could have thought and talked,
they might have said: "Shakir,
the water in your belly grows by the minute.
Death's sleep is upon you—
                    how can you close your eyes?"
But they didn't say anything,
because Shakir no longer deigned to think.
And he no longer felt
        even the desire to die in a bed with springs.

Third-class car number 510.
The corridor.
Two passengers gazed at the moon.
The moon shuddered and started moving,
        and soon it sailed across the sky
                        like a sleigh.
The train left Bilejik Station behind.
And about ninety kilometers to the north,
        another train
                —the Anatolia Express—
raced south through the wind-blown dark.

The dining car was half empty.
The waiter Mustafa had read more of his epic:
"THE STORY OF THE MUNITIONS PLANT,"
"THE STORY OF HASAN,"
"THE STORY OF THREE MEN,"
and
"THE STORY OF MUSTAFA SUPHI AND HIS COMRADES."
The maitre d' had frowned the most during this last story,
and he looked gloomy inside his uniform.
"Mustafa, my boy," said Chef Mahmut Asher,
"you're tired.
You can read the rest later when we're alone . . . "

And Mustafa stuck his yellow-leaf notebook in his pocket.

10:36 p.m.
The dignitary
                    rose from the table.
The others stood up, too.
"If you don't mind, I'm going to bed—
                    please don't get up."
Tahsin (the doctor-Representative)
                    thought:
"Intelligence goes to sleep this early?"

10:36 p.m.
Monsieur Duval talked with Jazibé Hanum:
"I like your peasants—
                    they're patient and don't make demands.
Your merchants aren't bad, either,
and your government men are harmless.
Above all, you need to develop your agriculture.
And you need to get rid of statism . . . "

10:36 p.m.
Emin Ulvi Achikalin, the Izmir merchant, sat with his head full of figures
for about a hundred thousand in currants, raisins, and figs.

Kasim Ahmedoff belched,
and the lips of the girl sweet as a mandarin orange
                                        trembled.

Hikmet Alpersoy concluded:
"350,000."
Mardanapal began:
"Make that 400,000, but there's one thing."
Assistant D.A. Fehim thought:
"I could ask Mardanapal to lend me 500."

10:36 p.m.
And on the Anatolia Express,
a young man stood on the platform of the first-class car.
He was a medical student.
His father used to be just a village agha,
but in the last fifteen years he'd acquired

two rice mills and three farms.
The medical student stood on the platform, looking sad.
He wasn't thinking of the Altai Mountains,
the mountains he dreamed of reclaiming one day
with a naked sword in his hand
and a steel helmet on his head,
alongside horsemen sporting seven plumes.
Now his heart only mourned
another uneventful train trip.
Yet such beautiful women traveled on trains!

10:36 p.m.
On the Anatolia Express
two women sat talking in a second-class section.
They were fifty,
and both showed
their fifty years.
The one on the left was a professor's wife.
Her hat off
and her long, broad face red from crying,
her wrinkled hands rubbed her white temples.
The woman on the right talked nonstop:
"You've put up with the man all these years.
You've raised two kids tall as he is.
Why divorce him?
He has to take care of you.
Let him.
Even if you catch him in the act,
don't you divorce him.
He'd like nothing better.
But just expose the man for what he is,
then sit back and have some fun yourself."

10:36 p.m.
Nimet Hanum sat in the same section.
A young woman,
she works at a ministry.
She isn't beautiful,
but she has something else—
a certain warmth.

She's beautiful because she's not.
Everyone close to her calls her "darling."
She sat reading a letter.
She'd written it to someone far away
                and would mail it in Ankara,
                        or maybe not—
                                no, she would for sure.
The letter opened:
"Orhan,
yesterday I started writing you a really dirty letter
but changed my mind.
But why tell you this now?
Who knows?
Must be the bitch in me.
But if I could have finished it,
you'd have been pissed
                        and happy,
                                turned on
                                        and so on.
I'll say this much:
I needed you yesterday—
yesterday I wanted you so badly.
And despite all you screw up,
                I missed your cocky self.
This physical hunger was something new.
It was a crisis, and it passed.
But what's the use—
I'm sure these crises
will recur whenever you're away.
This physical hunger was something new.
And I can't stand this kind of thing to start.
It mustn't.
My mind must overcome my flesh.
But in certain private moments
                I become a mindless body.
At those times, desire rules.
But not for just any man.
I'm not that far gone.
I only wanted you.
But what a craving—

so pathetic
                        so awful
                                    so helpless and so all alone.
But not to be laughed at.
And that scares me.
Pray for me, my love, since you're not here.
Yesterday I broke a glass in my hand in my fury.
What a shitty, hysterical fit!
Why are you so far away?
But don't come—
                        you can't anyway,
                                    and I don't want it—
                                                stay there the rest of your life . . . "
Nimet Hanum put the letter in its envelope.
She leaned her head against the window
and looked out through the painted glass.
The Anatolia Express sped past a village.
And it was 10:36 p.m.
In the village, on the second floor of an adobe house,
                        a woman lay on a thin mattress
                                    in a dark room.
Hatijé heard the train roar:
the tracks could have run through the house.
Below, the piebald ox bellowed.
Hatijé's husband rolled over on the mattress.
She thought,
            sly
                        and happy:
"After the harvest, my husband will marry
                                    Pockmarked Ekrem's daughter.
They'll have a Muslim marriage.
The girl is full of life, a purebred Ottoman.
She can play the new bride until November;
                        then we'll put her to work."
Under the quilt
        Hatijé's tired legs melted with pleasure.
And Hatijé thought:
"Then I won't get dead-tired hoeing."
And her heart beat as if it would burst from joy,
as if she'd lost her arms

and was freed forever of their aching.

10:36 p.m.
In the town ten kilometers beyond Hatijé's village
the coffeehouses were still open;
a gramophone played in one, a radio in the other.
And behind the lowered shutters of his shop
            the stove-maker Hakki
            sat cutting a tin pipe,
            careful and precise as if cutting a diamond.
He followed the thoughts running through his mind.
Hakki's thoughts
flickered and disappeared on his soft face.
Hakki had divorced his wife four years ago.
The woman had married the cobbler Rifat.
But now Hakki wanted his ex-wife back.
The woman appeared in his dreams a month ago,
            and it drove him crazy.
Finally, he and the woman agreed:
tonight they would strangle the cobbler Rifat in his bed
                                    with a rope,
                        throw him down the well,
and take off for Balikesir.
Hakki looked at the shelves in his shop.
There, next to the rope, sat an alarm clock,
and it read 10:36.

It was also 10:36
            by Ferit Bey's watch
            fifty kilometers away.
Ferit Bey, the governor of Green Pine Township,
            and Sergeant Seyfi, the local Guard commander,
            waited outside Sherifs Village.
They sat on their haunches,
cigarettes hidden in their cupped hands.
Taking deep breaths,
they sniffed the village through the dark:
no smell of burning wood or warm dung or even moist earth
                        (yet the rain had quit just an hour ago,
                            and the earth was soaked),

nor a lit window or anything moving,
     as if all the animals and people had abandoned the village,
and the only sound was the wind.
Sergeant Seyfi
         stuck his left index finger into the mud
             up to the knuckle.

Ferit Bey whispered:
"We're waiting for nothing—
       she won't come."
"She'll come.
She's waiting for her kids to fall asleep."
"How many does she have?"
"Three."
The men fell quiet.
Half an hour passed.
The sergeant's finger stayed buried in the mud.
Sergeant Seyfi was a peasant—
the kind who could squat down,
patiently sit like that for hours
       without saying a word to Ferit Bey,
and then just get up and walk away.
Ferit Bey, the township governor, said:
"I can't wait any longer, sergeant.
I'm leaving."
"As you wish."
"And you?"
"I'm staying.
     Since we came."
They were quiet.
Ferit Bey didn't leave.
He was afraid.
Time passed.
"So she stops by your station all the time?"
"She does.
The sergeant before me got her in the habit.
Once, the whole station went through her in a single night—
            didn't faze her a bit.
She even darned our socks in the morning.
We gave her five kurush each."
Sergeant Seyfi was dark-skinned,

and under his young bony nose
              his mouth was proud and confident.
Ferit Bey also had olive skin,
and he wore an ash-grey suit.

A dog barked in the village,
but the other dogs didn't join in—
              it barked once and fell quiet.
Sergeant Seyfi pulled his finger out of the mud
and said without getting up:
              "She's coming."
Ferit Bey stood right up
and instinctively
              straightened his tie.
Eminé appeared.
She was tall and thick-set.
She waded through the dark,
at ease
and not at all shy.
Sergeant Seyfi waited till she got closer,
              then he rose.
Bashful, Ferit Bey
              took in the woman.
Only her eyes were bare.
Her feet would be bare, too,
but Ferit Bey knew
    bare feet in peasant women
              had nothing to do with nakedness.
Eminé carried a felt mat under her arm,
    its corners flapping in the wind
              and beating against her rump.
They didn't speak to the woman.
Sergeant Seyfi took Ferit Bey by the arm and started walking.
Eminé followed
    fifteen steps behind
              with her felt mat under her arm.
They walked about a quarter of an hour,
the damp spring night blowing in their faces.
And when they reached the woods
(fragrant with stately pines),
Sergeant Seyfi stopped in a clearing

and said to Ferit Bey in a loud voice:
"I'll wait over there
if you want to go first."
Ferit Bey stammered:
"I—
I don't want anything."
Sergeant Seyfi laughed:
"Does the gentleman require silk sheets?
                    Then you step away..."
Ferit Bey walked off,
                    disappearing into the dark.
Then
and only then
            Sergeant Seyfi turned and looked back.
The woman stood there, thick-set and straight.
The sergeant motioned to her.
Eminé went up to him
and bent down.
She laid the mat under her arm on the moist earth
                            as if making a bed for her child,
and stretching out on her back on the mat,
she looked up at the sergeant standing over her...

Twenty minutes later they all emerged from the woods,
Sergeant Seyfi and the township governor in front
and Eminé behind.
They walked awhile.
When they got to the bend, the woman turned left
                    and headed for Sherifs Village,
                            her mat under her arm.
The men didn't even notice she was gone.
They walked toward the town,
the damp spring night blowing in their faces.
They heard the distant rumble of a train.
"The Express," said Ferit Bey.
"If we were on it now,
                    sitting back
                            relaxing in the dining car..."
Sergeant Seyfi mumbled:
"So it must be past midnight..."

It was 12:10 a.m. in the dining car of the Anatolia Express.
Three people were left in the car:
the waiter Mustafa, the maitre d', and Chef Mahmut Asher.
They sat at the first table,
where the dignitary had sat an hour ago.
The white tablecloths were gone,
and the red lights had been turned off—
now they were just old lamp shades.
It smelled like a deserted bar.
And the waiter Mustafa
                    read his epic:
"'AUGUST 1922'
        and
'THE STORY OF OUR WOMEN'
        and
THE ORDERS OF AUGUST 6 . . . '"
Chef Mahmut Asher asked:
"Is that where we quit?"
"Yes.
We read the story of Mustafa Suphi and his comrades last,
                            and this section is next."
"Okay, then, read."
"I'm reading:
'The ox carts rolled under the moon.
The ox carts rolled beyond Akshehir toward Afyon.
The land was so vast
and the mountains so far in the distance,
it seemed they'd never reach
                    their destination.
The ox carts advanced on solid oak wheels,
the first wheels that ever turned
under the moon.
The oxen belonged to a world
                    in miniature,
                            tiny and dwarfed
under the moon,
and the light played on their sickly broken horns

and the earth flowed
                    under their feet,
                              earth
                    and more earth.
The night was bright and warm,
and in their wooden beds on the ox carts
the dark-blue bombshells lay stark-naked.
And the women
hid their glances from one another
as they eyed the dead oxen
and wheels from past convoys . . .
And the women,
our women
with their awesome, sacred hands,
        pointed little chins, and big eyes,
                our mothers, lovers, wives,
who die without ever having lived,
who get fed at our tables
        after the oxen,
who we abduct and carry off to the hills
        and go to prison for,
who harvest grain, cut tobacco, chop wood, and barter in the markets,
who we harness to our plows,
who with their bells and undulant heavy hips
surrender to us in sheepfolds
in the gleam of knives stuck in the ground—
                              the women,
                                our women,
walked under the moon now
behind the ox carts and shells
with the same ease
and accustomed weariness of women
hauling amber-eared sheaves to the threshing floor.
And their scrawny-necked children
        slept on the steel of 15-cm. shrapnel shells.
And the ox carts advanced under the moon
beyond Akshehir toward Afyon.

The orders were issued on August 6.
The First and Second Armies, with their detachments,

ox carts, and cavalry regiments,
moved into position.
98,956 guns
       325 cannons
         5 airplanes
2,800+ machine guns
2,500+ swords
and 186,326 bright human hearts,
plus twice that many eyes, ears, arms, and legs,
                     were on the move in the night.
The earth in the night.
The wind in the night.
Remembering and beyond remembering
                 in the night,
              the people, machines, and animals
huddled together with their steel, wood, and flesh,
and finding a fearful safety
              in huddling together
                 in silence,
                       they marched with tired feet
                       and hands caked with dirt.
And among them,
in the Second Transport Battalion of the First Army,
      were the driver Ahmet of Istanbul
              and his pickup.
Truck No. 3 was a strange creature:
old
      brave
            stubborn and malicious.
Despite the knotty hornbeam log
under the chassis, tied to the axle
in place of the snapped left rear spring left in the mountains,
and despite having to stop and lean against the dark
to ease its heart pains
every ten kilometers,
and even as it lacked two of its four fan blades,
it knew full well its officially invested power,
and the orders of August 6 referenced it
and its comrades as ". . . a series of about 100 motor vehicles
with the total capability of 300 tons,

commandeered and organized . . . ”
Those commandeered and organized—
                Ahmet's pickup among them—
passed the people, weapons, and ox carts
descending to the Afyon-Stable Mountains region.

A distant city and a song were on Ahmet's mind.
The song is a stately melody.
And the city
                with white-tented rowboats, black barges,
                        and sun-struck watermelon rinds
                is by the sea.

"The fan seems
        to be losing rpm's.
The comrades have gone ahead.
The moon has set.
The view is just stars and mountains . . .

Ahmet, my boy, you're from Suleymaniyé.
Beat Shorty with two gammons under the plane tree,
get up,
walk down the row of coffeehouses,
pass the fountain,
the schoolyard, the seminaries,
and right there, behind the War Ministry,
a woman in a black cloak
will be squatting down and scattering
corn for the pigeons.
And the cardsharps
will be turning tricks on umbrellas.

The engine isn't cooperating—
the damn thing will strand me here . . .

What were you saying, Ahmet, my boy?
The foundries are on the right.
Then, as you turn off at Long Market,
the bookstall on the left corner:
                The Tale of the Crystal Palace,

the six-volume *History of Jevdet,*
and *Scientific Cuisine:*
Cuisine comes from *kitchen*—
that is, cooking.
And God, how I love stuffed mackerel!
You hold it by its gilded tail
and eat it like a grape cluster.

Up ahead is a cavalry troop;
                    it turned left...

Go straight down Long Market
—shops, chairs, backgammon pieces, prayer beads,
and you from Istanbul,
you take the skill of your own hands for granted
and marvel at the people of Istanbul:
you say how fine, how various their skills!
Rustem Pasha Mosque.
The rope shops.
Enough rope, cable, and cast bronze bells here to equip
a hundred sailing ships
and countless mule trains.
Zindankapi, Babajafer,
the Fish Market in the distance.
The dried-fruit stands.
We're at Fruit Wharf:
        the sea beyond is on my mind,
                with its white-tented rowboats, black barges,
                    and sun-struck watermelon rinds...

Is the left rear tire
losing air?
I should get down and look...

At Fruit Wharf
we took the 'beggar' packet
to the wishing well in Eyup.
Plump hands,
a bit bowlegged,

but eyes like green olives.
Eyebrows like crescents.
Just when we got to Kasimpasha, her white scarf . . .

The tire's losing air.
If I don't fix it . . .
You can wait, Babajafer."

Pickup No. 3 stopped.
Darkness.
The jack.
The pump.
His hands.
As his hands worked on the tire and the old wheel,
Ahmet—cursing and angry for cursing—
remembered:
one night, as he lugged his stricken grandmother
                  from one couch to another,
                                  the poor woman . . .

"The inner tube is torn from end to end.
Spare?
None.
To cry for help
              in the mountains?

You're from Suleymaniyé, my boy.
Pickup No. 3 was given to you alone.
And you know what they say—
        each lamb hangs by its own legs.
Driver Ahmet of Suleymaniyé,
                              strip . . ."

He took off his clothes.
His jacket, pants, underpants, shirt and fur hat
                          and red sash
went to stuff the tire,
leaving Ahmet naked
              in his combat boots . . .

The song is a stately melody.
        The city by the sea,
        the white scarf.
"We're doing fifty.
Hang in there, bane of my existence!
Hang in there so the mountains can see
           Driver Ahmet in his birthday suit.
Hang in there, my lion . . . "

Never
has any man
    loved a machine
with so much tender hope . . . ' "

Chef Mahmut Asher cackled with pleasure:
"Way to go, Driver Ahmet, my boy,
          way to go!
Istanbul people are smart,
and when they're brave-hearted, they really are.
I wonder what became of Driver Ahmet?
Maybe he drives a city bus in Ankara
or maybe a minibus between Mudanya and Bursa.
What if he's on this very train?
          In third class, of course . . . "

The waiter Mustafa was more pessimistic:
"If he's not dead . . . "
Mahmut Asher suddenly grew serious:
"God rest his soul.
You're right.
Maybe he died later,
maybe he fell in battle back then."
The waiter Mustafa repeated:
"Maybe he died back then,
            along with pickup No. 3 . . .
You know, Master Mahmut, there's this picture

they hang on coffeehouse walls:
it's sunset in the Arabian desert,
a wounded Bedouin lies in a pool of blood on the sand,
              and the man's gazelle of a horse stands
                    over him, sniffing and mourning its rider..."
"I know those."
"So you know them.
Master, I believe
if Driver Ahmet died back then and there,
pickup No. 3 stood over him, mourning
and guarding him from the birds and the beasts in the mountains..."
"You're right, son.
        It would've stood by him.
But a human body disappears fast.
If you went to those mountains now,
no sign of Driver Ahmet would remain,
but a scrap of metal, a wheel, or something of the pickup would last.
That's how it goes..."
Mahmut Asher quickly sniffled:
"Anyway,
read how this thing ends."
The maitre d' asked:
"Is there a lot left?"
"No.
Five or six pages.
I'm beginning."
And the waiter Mustafa began:
"'THE STORY OF THE HOURS 3:30 TO 5:30 A.M.
ON THE NIGHT OF AUGUST 26...
2:30 a.m.
Kojatepé is a burnt-out old hill
without trees, birdsong,
              or the smell of earth.
Under the day's sun and the night's stars,
                    it's just rocks.
And because it's night now,
and because the world seems more ours,
          closer,
                    and smaller in the dark,
and because in these hours

the earth and the heart
        speak of our homes, loves, and ourselves,
the guard in his homespun cap stood on the rocks
stroking his smiling mustache,
        watching the starriest dark in the world
                from Kojatepé.
The enemy is three hours away.
And if it weren't for Hidirlik Hill,
the lights of Afyon would be visible.
To the northwest lie the Beauty Mountains,
lit up here
        and there
                by fires.
Running Brook glitters in the valley,
and now the guard in his homespun cap
imagines only the water's journey.
Running Brook may be a rivulet
        or a stream
           or a small river.
Turning the mills at Streamford,
        it runs with its boneless eels
           in and out of the shadow of Seven Martyrs' Rock
and through the big
        head-high
           purple
                red
                  and white flowers
        of the hashish fields.
And before Afyon,
turning east under Six Eyes Bridge
and meeting up with the Konya train tracks on the way,
it leaves Great Shepherds Village on the left
        and Red Church on the right
                    and flows on.

The man on the rocks suddenly thought
        of all the riverheads and riverbeds in enemy hands:
who knows how wide they are,
                how long?
He didn't know the names of very many,

but before the Greeks and before the Great War,
when he worked as a day-laborer on the Selim Shah Farm in Manisa,
                  he'd get dizzy crossing the waters of the Gediz.

Fires lit up the mountains
                here
                     and there.
And the stars were so bright, so light and airy,
that the man in the homespun cap believed
in sweet and easy days of vindication,
without knowing how or when they would come,
and with his smiling mustache he stood by his Mauser
at the lookout point on Kojatepé.

3:30 a.m.
The squad is positioned
        on the Halimur-Ayvali line.
Corporal Ali from Izmir,
his eyes feeling their way in the dark,
looks at each of his squad members
as if he'll never see them again:
the first soldier on the right
                  is blond,
the second dark,
and the third stutters—
but no one in the company
          can sing like him.
The fourth is craving buckwheat soup again.
The fifth will shoot the man who shot his uncle
the night he gets back to Urfa after his discharge.
The sixth,
a man with incredibly big feet,
is being sued by his brothers
for leaving his land and his single ox
to an old refugee woman,
and the company calls him "Crazy Erzurum"
        because he does guard duty for his friends.
The seventh is Mehmet's son Osman.
He was wounded at Gallipoli, Inonu, and Sakarya,
and he can take a good many more wounds

without batting an eye
and still be standing.
The eighth,
        Ibrahim,
            wouldn't be so afraid
if his teeth didn't chatter so.
And Corporal Ali from Izmir knows
rabbits don't run because they're scared—
           they're scared because they run.

4:00 a.m.
The region of Black Mouth-Willow Creek.
The 12th Infantry Division.
All eyes are far away, in the dark,
all hands are close by, on the machines;
everyone is in place.
The division chaplain
—the only unarmed man there,
           the man of the dead—
has planted a broken willow branch in the direction of Mecca,
bowed his head,
        folded his hands,
           and started sunrise prayers.
Inside, he is at peace.
Heaven is eternal ease.
And whether they win or lose
to the mortal enemy on the battlefield of the Holy War,
he will hand-deliver the martyred souls
           to the Lord of the Universe.

4:45 a.m.
The environs of Sandikli.
The villages.
A cavalryman with a drooping black mustache
stands beside his horse under a plane tree.
His Chukurova horse
    foams at the bit,
        knees bleeding,
           tail lashing the dark.

The men, swords, and horses of the Fourth Company
of the Second Cavalry Division sniff the air.
Behind them, a cock crows in a village.
And the cavalryman with the drooping mustache
          covers his face with his hands.
There's another rooster in enemy territory beyond the mountains,
an axe-combed, milk-white Denizli rooster:
the heathens must have butchered it long ago
                    for soup . . .

4:50 a.m.
Dawn breaks
          in forty minutes.
"Never fear—our crimson flag will ever greet the dawn."

South of Coal Hill, across from Hay Peak:
two reservists of the Fifteenth Infantry Division.
The younger, taller one
—Nurettin Eshfak,
              a graduate of the Teachers' College—
          plays with the safety of his Mauser
                        as he talks:
"There's something off about our national anthem,
I don't know how to say it.
The poet Akif is a believer.
But I don't believe
everything he does.
What keeps me here
              is the joy of being a martyr?
                          I don't think so.

For instance, listen:
'The days God promised us will come.'
No.
No sign's descended from the sky
              about the days to come.
We've promised those days
              to ourselves.

I want a song
              about the days after we win . . .

'Who knows, maybe tomorrow...'"

4:55 a.m.
The mountains
              light up.
Something is burning somewhere.
The sun will rise any minute.
You can smell the Anatolian earth
                    waking up.
And at this moment, letting your heart soar like a falcon,
seeing the bright light,
and hearing voices call you far,
far away,
you're ready to fight to the death
on the very front line
in this highest and greatest of adventures.

Artilleryman First Lieutenant Hasan
                    was twenty-one.
He turned his blond head to the sky
                    and stood up.
He saw the vast dark and the fading stars.
He wanted now, in one mad dash,
        to do something so brilliant, so legendary,
that his whole life and all his memories
              and his 7.5 battery
              seemed, by comparison, pitiful and paltry.

The captain asked:
"What time is it?"
"Five."
"Half an hour, then ... "

98,956 guns
and from Driver Ahmet's pickup No.3
to 7.5 Schneiders and 15 cm. howitzers,
with all their machinery
and their ability
to die for their country
—that is, for their land and freedom—

the First and Second Armies
were ready to attack.

Under the plane tree in the half-dark, the cavalryman
with the drooping black mustache and short boots
mounted his horse.
Nurettin Eshfak
checked his watch:
5:30 . . .
And the final offensive began with dawn
and artillery fire . . .

And then.
Then all the enemy's forward defenses fell
50 kilometers south of Black Fort.
And then.
Then we completely surrounded the enemy forces
near Aslihanlar
by August 30.
And then.
Then on August 30 the enemy's armed forces were annihilated.
Then on 31 August 1922,
as our armies marched toward Izmir,
Crazy Erzurum
was hit by a stray bullet.
He dropped to the ground
and felt the earth between his shoulder blades.
He looked up
and away.
His eyes flashed with surprise,
and his shoes lay on their backs, side by side,
bigger than ever.
And for a long time
his shoes, left behind by friends who jumped over them and walked on,
gazed at the sunny sky,
thinking about a refugee woman.
And then.
Then they suddenly shuddered and jerked apart,
and as Crazy Erzurum died of grief,
they turned their faces to the earth.'"

The waiter Mustafa fell silent.
Chef Mahmut Asher asked:
"Is it over?"
"Yes."
"So it's really over?"
"It really is.
What more do you want him to write?"
"I don't know.
You're right, son.
What more could he write?
We beat the heathens and entered Izmir.
And then.
Then came the Republic.
And yet . . . "

The maitre d' said:
"What are you trying to say, chef?
Don't be afraid—spit it out."
"Who should I fear?
It's just that the epic ended
          a little sad
and brought me down.
It's like you're running freely on open ground
          and your foot gets caught in a trap."

The maitre d' smiled strangely.
The waiter Mustafa said nothing.
The train pulled into Bilejik Station.
And in the upper berth of the second section
     of the sleeper, Hikmet Alpersoy snored on.
In sleep, no sign remained of the man with the wonderful laugh.
Sleep had aged him, hiding
          the color of his eyes,
                    robbing his face of light.
Now he was just a sixty-year-old drunk
          snoring in silk pajamas.
And in the lower berth of the same section
          Burhan sat on the edge of his bed
          in his cotton nightshirt
                    (he couldn't part with it)

and read the biography
of Ahmet Pasha from Sivas, his head busy
        with plans to expand
           his rail-car factory.
When the train stayed too long in Bilejik, Burhan looked outside.
Under the window stood two blue men:
      the maitre d' spoke to the train police.

Meanwhile, about sixty kilometers south of Bilejik,
       the 3:45 out of Haydar Pasha
          had long passed Inonu
          and neared Eskishehir.

Third-class car number 510.
The corridor.
The prisoner Suleyman stepped into the corridor
and spotted Kazim from Kartal.
They were alone.
Kazim whispered:
"Hello, Suleyman."
"Hello, peasant."
"Let's go out on the platform, Suleyman, so we can talk freer."
"It's better here.
     We can make like we don't know each other,
         like we're just looking out the window together."
And so they did.
Suleyman asked:
"Where are you headed, peasant?"
"To Ankara. After that, wherever Halil goes—
him to the prison, me to a hotel."
"Is that what they told you to do?"
"Nobody told me anything—it was my idea.
Just in case.
I'll look the prison over from outside.
No harm in that, is there?"
"No, that's fine."
"Any news from our poet, Suleyman?"
"He was sent out five months ago."
"I know.
He went to D.

I wondered if he wrote you any letters."
"He did.
You mean you saw him off, too?"
"Sure,
        all the way to where he is.
The prison at D is pretty bad.
It has incredibly high walls.
But show me a wall that can't be scaled."
Suleyman laughed:
"If you could,
        who would you spring first?"
"Jelal first."
"So you like him better?"
"It's not a question of liking—
        the guy is a poet."
"And Halil is a scholar."
Kazim thought before answering:
"True—he'd be in the first bunch, too.
But Jelal first.
I told you, he writes poetry.
He doesn't just fiddle—he writes poems.
I don't see you writing any.
All you know is how to lap them up.
I saw how this thing's done:
it's worse than farming,
        harder even than growing vegetables out of season.
Did you ever notice when Jelal writes poems
he gets like a fifteen-year-old girl
                in bone-
                        cracking labor
                        and writhes in pain,
        as if creating the world all over again."
Suleyman got a little annoyed:
"Sounds like you all but worship Jelal, peasant.
But ever since Namik Kemal,
        we Turks have had a strange admiration for poets.
And I know another reason you like him:
he was going to put you in his Independence War epic.
But he didn't."
"So what?

He must have found something better and truer.
He hasn't finished the poem, has he?"
"He has."
"Is it good?"
"Sure.
We've got three copies with us.
I'll give you one.
Except you still haven't learned
          not to think like a peasant anarchist."
"Like a what?"
"You undertake things on your own, without checking with anyone.
If what you're thinking ever becomes necessary,
it won't be you or me
          but those in charge who'll decide where to start."
Kazim frowned.
His yellow eyes looked hurt:
"Okay, I understand.
Is it wrong to go out there with Halil, too?
Should I get off at Eskishehir and go back?"
"No, peasant—
                    you could even check out my prison,
                              and Fuat's as well."
A toothless, childlike smile spread across Kazim's face,
and he said, almost shouting:
"You 'Bulgur Pilaf' Suleyman, you!"
Suleyman was alarmed:
"Don't yell, peasant."
Then he quietly chuckled.

All their friends knew about the bulgur pilaf.
The story went back eight years:
one cloudless summer day,
Suleyman had been told to meet with Kazim.
Suleyman was tired and ravenous
by the time he got to Kazim's farm.
In the morning sun, the vegetable fields held the peace
          of green-bean poles as far as the eye could see,
and red tomatoes with still-moist little runnels in the ground.
Kazim sat under a trellis.
In the distance, a woman in a white scarf

bobbed up and down in the corn.
Blue smoke rose behind the trellis.
The air smelled of cooking meat
and a crisp green salad with lots of vinegar and olive oil.
They talked under the trellis for about an hour—
            Suleyman sly and cautious,
                Kazim ironic and bold.
And the smell of roasting meat still in the air
                whetted Suleyman's appetite more by the minute.
Finally, a barefoot little blue-eyed girl
brought a pot, two wooden spoons, and two onions.
"Help yourself," Kazim said, lifting the lid.
Suleyman met with such a plain-looking bulgur pilaf
        that his face fell in hopeless defeat,
                and he mumbled as if hurt:
"Thanks, Kazim Effendi, but I'm not hungry."
Kazim's wolf-eyes smiled
as Nasreddin Hodja
        must have smiled many times.
Kazim sent the bulgur back.
They brought roast meat, salad, helva,
                and two half-liter bottles.
Embarrassed but brave
        and ready for any and all attacks,
                Suleyman dug in
        as Kazim said softly:
"As you know, most of our peasants just eat bulgur,
and seeing as how you work for the poor peasants . . . "
Suleyman interrupted Kazim:
"You're right, Kazim Effendi," he said,
            "but I'm right, too:
roast meat beats plain bulgur.
But bring on the bulgur now, if you want,
                and I'll put it away before the helva . . . "
Which Suleyman proceeded to do,
though it didn't save him from being tagged
        "Bulgur Pilaf" Suleyman from that day on.
All their friends knew about the bulgur pilaf.

Kazim repeated:

"You 'Bulgur Pilaf' Suleyman, you!"
Suleyman was quiet.
He spat out the window into the night.
Then he leaned out and spoke
as if talking to someone walking
alongside the train:
"How are things between you and God, peasant?"
Kazim answered, a little irritated:
"You know how it is."
Suleyman was pleased with his counterattack.
Kazim continued:
"A man can live without God
or with.
Especially if He's like mine
        and doesn't meddle in things
or bother with politics.
It's like an amulet, Suleyman,
        like remembering my dead father."
Suleyman laughed:
"Since I saw you last,
        you've figured a way out with your peasant smarts."
Kazim didn't reply.
Despite everything,
he believed in God
and was no friend of the Bulgarians.
So much so that
whenever he heard a fiery story about Bulgarian revolutionaries,
he would sulk at the world
but quickly take consolation in saying,
"Either what they did to pregnant women in the Balkan War was a lie,
or those revolutionaries come from a different tribe of Bulgarians."

They heard footsteps.
Kazim and Suleyman turned to look.
Shakir from Sakarya appeared in the corridor.
Holding onto the section doors
        and dragging his water-logged body on his skinny legs,
                he went up to Kazim and Suleyman.
He wheezed:
"How far are we from Bilejik?"

Suleyman started.
Kazim smiled.
"We passed Bilejik long ago,"
Suleyman answered.
Kazim broke in:
"Were you asleep?"
"How can I sleep, brother?
So Bilejik came and went?
Now where will they drop me?
What'll I do now?
Where will I go . . . "

Kazim no longer smiled.

Shakir beat his bony head with his fists
      and kept repeating:
"What'll I do now?
I'll die on a train.
They'll throw me on the tracks:
I'll be dead meat for the birds and the beasts.
What'll I do now?
What'll I do now?"

Suleyman stared at the floor in silence.

And rocking Shakir away in the moonlight,
  never to bring him back
     ("This won't happen again, this is the end—
      now what'll I do?
        Now what'll I do?"),
  third-class car number 510 sadly rattled on . . .

VII

Dawn.
The sky an endless pane
    of frosted glass.
And the steppe parched, stone-hard.

Lime, clay, and rock salt.
And hills frozen in broad waves.
Like a fast-rising wind, the light
           drove the clouds over the steppe
                          red
                              blue
                                  and yellow.

Every sunrise
and sundown the clouds
turn the steppe
into another world . . .

The sun quickly rose half-a-spear high,
exposing the steppe:
the rawness of a new-born planet,
the sad waste land of valleys on the moon,
not a shed
           or a wheel rut
           or the happy call of a fruit reaching for a human hand,
no animals, no plants—
just the endless loneliness of giving nothing.
Looking at this insolent earth,
you hear the first battle cry of our species—
trap it under a rock
and together, screaming, attack
                and destroy it, as if killing a mammoth.

The clouds above dispersed.
The 3:45 train out of Haydar Pasha
crossed the steppe like a brave little toy.

Finally, a man appeared.
Alone, on a donkey.

A village appeared at last
(without trees or windows),
all dried mud and dung.

A little girl emerged from the earth,
unkempt but cute and dirty like a wild kitten.

She carried a clay jug bigger than herself.
She looked after the train.
Sniffed the air with her button nose.
Smiled.
Her cheeks dimpled.
Zehra didn't have a father.
Why?
Maybe he went off somewhere and didn't return.
Maybe he'll come back.
Who knows,
maybe today, this very afternoon,
            he'll emerge from the steppe.

Zehra's mother was inside, still asleep.
But here there is no "maybe" or "who knows":
it's certain
        she'll never wake up.
Under her coverless dark quilt,
        among the fleas jumping for joy,
            she lies naked, straight
                    and stiff.
And five-year-old Zehra smiles on the steppe,
so cut off from the world she doesn't know
                    that she has left the bed of a dead woman,
and so much part of it that she can carry
a jug bigger than herself
        and look after the train
            and smell the steppe
                and smile.

The train approached Etimesut.
Suddenly the antennas of a radio station rose up
(as if leaping up and shooting forth)
with their wires and T-beams.
They brought to this arrogant and sterile ground
the beauty of human labor, thought, and hope.

The train stopped at Etimesut.
Etimesut must be a model village.
For this reason, from its model schools

to its standard embroidery patterns, it was as false
and dead as all models and exemplary patterns.
Even as the prisoner-writer Halil thought this,
so the prisoner-fitter Fuat liked Etimesut.

The train started.
On the right, trees appeared on the steppe.
They were mostly acacias—
scared, wary, hesitant.
Yet acacias are brave,
and even if they're more abstemious than camels,
each of these had eaten up as much money as an Ankara contractor
to survive on this land.
Even as the prisoner-writer Halil thought this,
so the prisoner-fitter Fuat admired the acacias.

The train stopped at Gazi Station.
A taxi passed on the road to Ankara.
Three air force NCO's rode in the cab,
        together with a woman like a pomegranate blossom.
She sat between the pilot Yusuf and the radio operator Vedat;
the mechanic Rahmi sat next to the driver.
The mechanic, Sergeant Rahmi, was eighteen.
With his thin, pointed face he looked like a surprised young mouse.
And his tie didn't hang quite straight
                on his lead-blue uniform.
The mechanic, Sergeant Rahmi, was eighteen.
Eighteen.
At eighteen the heart shoots like a pebble from a slingshot
and the head doesn't sit on the shoulders—
                where is it? Where?
At eighteen you sleep without memories.
The bright spots lie ahead at eighteen:
on one side, the wide-open sea;
                on the other, the greenest forest.
On one side, the pit of hell;
                on the other, the world that begins with us.
On one side, bright sun;
                on the other, a dream.
On one side, lie back and watch the stars;

on the other, stretch out
                    and run as far as the eye can see.
On one side, all smoke and dust;
                    on the other, a blank.
Anthills are mountains and fleas are camels—
                    everything's larger than life.
At eighteen you don't think about memories,
                    you tell them.
But what could Rahmi the mechanic tell?
Before he entered the air force officers' school
                    he worked for a prison grocer.
Never filling up the ragged bags and sorry plates,
for a year and a half he carried tahini, dried beans, and coal
        between the stone shop and the iron door.
What could Rahmi the mechanic tell?
That he'd finished grade school on a hungry stomach and stolen pencils
or that after his father (a black-bearded pastry vendor) died,
he himself took men to his own mother?
What could Rahmi the mechanic tell?
About the prison grocer, Wrestler Huseyin?
Grumbling, Huseyin prowled his dark shop
        like an old bear on its hind legs.
His voice got as thin and high as a child's
                    when he was happy or swearing.
When his master beat him,
        Rahmi would squat right down,
                    cover his face with his hands,
and, for some reason, smile between his fingers
        at the grocer's wife, sly and innocent.
She was about fifty.
Tight black headscarf.
Stick-thin legs, flat chest.
False teeth and a wig.
But maybe her incredibly blue, untrustworthy, shameless eyes
                    prepared Rahmi for something.
Rahmi never thought
he'd get out of this shop
(would the grocer Huseyin want his help to become somebody?):
"I'll pass a hundred, a thousand, countless years
                    like this here.

And in the end
        they'll dig my grave
                in that dark corner, under the walnut sacks."

What could Rahmi the mechanic tell?
How he'd entered Officers School?
There was a teacher in the prison,
ill at ease because his heart was elsewhere.
His sentence inside was long, and his friends outside were many.
Jug-eared and very short,
he looked stupid.
But, unbelievably,
he'd write the prisoners' petitions for free.
He got the prison guard Mehmet a job outside
and saved a condemned man from the gallows.
He was tight friends with the prison warden,
even though a week never passed without more information on him
    coming in.

A circumciser had been in and out of prison.
A thief, a wit, and a heart patient, he was a giant of a man
                        blind in one eye.
Interested in acting,
        he directed plays at the Community Center.

The teacher sent Rahmi to the director
                        (unknown to the grocer Huseyin),
the director sent him to the county supervisor
                        (who was his uncle),
and Rahmi entered Officers School.
The whole business cost him 24 eggs and a kilo of olive oil,
                        plus a pure-bred
                        Denizli rooster
            (unknown to both the grocer Huseyin
                and his neighbor, the carpenter Ali).
What could Rahmi the mechanic tell?
Not a single jump or a single flight—
            his job was on the ground,
and how plane engines are cleaned in hangars
            wouldn't interest the woman like a pomegranate blossom.

Sergeant Rahmi,
   up next to the driver, had turned around,
    covered his face with his hands
   (who knows why),
and smiled between his fingers,
   sly and innocent, at the woman like a pomegranate blossom.
Her eyes were as shameless as those of the grocer's wife
    (but not treacherous or blue;
     soft and green,
    they didn't study Rahmi through the eyeliner,
   and maybe that's why he felt a slight pain
     in his heart, like a dull toothache,
       and a touch of sadness),
and they gazed longingly at Pilot Yusuf.
Pilot Yusuf was heavy-set, bold, and blond.
And the scar over his left eyebrow
   gave his pink-white face the air of a sulking spoiled child.
The woman like a pomegranate blossom
    —thirty-something,
    she resembled a pomegranate blossom
    because of her lipstick and silk print dress—
ran a plump finger over Yusuf's scar.
Her eyes still shameless,
   she asked, strangely pained,
    in the voice of a sister or even a mother:
"How did this happen?"
"That?
It's nothing—an old wound."
"Did you fall from a tree when you were small?"
Pilot Yusuf laughed scornfully
   (he wore a brown leather jacket over his uniform,
   with a thick wool scarf chosen for its weight):
"Not from a tree but from two thousand meters."
"From two thousand meters?
That's much higher than a minaret?
Oh, sweetheart!
So you fell from—an airplane?"
"Well, I didn't really fall,
   I jumped."
And Pilot Yusuf, smiling kindly at the woman, elaborated:

"I was on a training flight over Eskishehir
                    with Sergeant Rifat.
He keeps giving me orders,
                    but he doesn't know jack about this business.
I tried to ignore him
                    until I couldn't take it anymore
and I up and jumped out.
The parachute opened a little late.
I got wounded in the forehead."
He was quiet.
Then quickly added, pursing his child's lips:
"It couldn't matter less . . ."
The woman spoke as if hurt:
"Why did you go into this work?
I wouldn't have let you if"
                    —she almost said "if I were your mother"—
"I were your wife—I mean, your fiancée."
Yusuf answered in his ship-captain father's voice:
"Women have no say in these things.
And is there a higher calling than ours?
                    Higher or more honorable?
                    [Now he's in his own voice.]
Once we enter the war,
          you'll see what kind of man I am.
And then, yes,
          the country that loses air supremacy
                    [Now he spoke in a radio announcer's voice.]
                         is doomed to defeat . . ."
The woman dug her fire-red pointed nails
                    into Yusuf's knee:
"Sweetheart," she said, "I already know
          what kind of man you are.
But please, honey, let's not have war."
The radio operator, Sergeant Vedat,
          (nineteen, wheat-skinned, tall and thin)
                    agreed with her.
He didn't agree
out of fear
          (maybe he was still afraid of sleeping alone in the dark,
          and he was certainly still afraid of his father,

but it never occurred to him to fear war),
but because it would put his electrical business on hold.
Because as soon as the war ended,
    he planned to leave the military
      and set up shop in Izmir.
Sergeant Vedat's father was an official,
    he'd been a merchant, and they owned vineyards.
Vedat had been packed off to Officers School
   because he was a punk
    and needed shaping up.
"True.
Let's not go to war," he said.
"Sure," said Pilot Yusuf, as if sulking:
"His father has loads of rusty gold.
And we all know about the shop.
But what will us pilots do if we don't fight?
How will we prove ourselves?
Hauling passengers like bus drivers?"
"Don't go overboard. Civilian pilots make plenty."
"True,
but money's not everything for a man.
Forget civilian life.
It's the uniforms, my boy, the uniforms . . . "
"Yusuf, my sweet,
what if you die at this young age?"

All three sergeants stared at the woman, stunned.
Rahmi the mechanic shrugged his shoulders,
the radio operator Vedat laughed,
and Yusuf the pilot answered:
"So what?
[He spoke for all three]
   And do you die only in war?
Just last week, Lieutenant Ali and Sergeant-Major Hasan
   hit the ground from twenty meters and were toast.
Then, a month ago, Shahap and Selim broadsided a mountain in
  the fog
and then—who can count them all?
And if you die, you die—
   you can't fly without risking death."

(He said this just because that's how you bragged;
he didn't know just what he risked.
He was twenty,
and death meant nothing to him.)

Rahmi the mechanic joined the conversation
(proud and pleased with what he would be telling,
        but pleased especially to be joining in):
"Sergeant Rashit,
            a mechanic like me
                    —my age,
                        maybe a year older—
loved a girl in Gallipoli.
They gave the girl to someone else.
Rashit felt dissed.
He jumped in a trainer
        —supposedly it's forbidden for mechanics to fly—
        and the morning after the wedding,
                he crashed himself, motor and wings and all,
on the groom's roof.
The house, the girl, Rashit—
                    they all went up in flames together..."

Pilot Yusuf suddenly grabbed the woman's breasts
and mumbled the first words of a song:
"You're mad, wild heart..."
Then he yelled as if suddenly drunk:
"And if you die, you die..."

Their taxi had long passed the poultry farms.
The Etlik vineyards were up ahead on the left.
In the distance, Ankara Fortress.
On this spring morning on the asphalt road
the tires whispered of cool water.
The machine is in command of the driver
        (as no animal can be of a man)
and works like a pocket watch.
The driver sees the asphalt looming before them
        and disappearing under the wheels,
and in his heart bright circles widen out and out.

They approached the Hippodrome.

The driver sat as in a garden chair.
He was about forty.
Clean-shaven.
He was a close friend of the poet in prison
                    (who knows,
                        he may have been the source
                            of the poet's story of Ahmet in his epic).
He listened to the officers with interest.
"It was the cavalry in the armies of old," he thought,
                "now it's the air force.
Their uniforms were the fanciest,
                    and so are these.
They were chosen from among the youngest and wildest,
                    the same as these.
They were the closest to death back then,
                    as these are now."
And he looked at Yusuf's face in the mirror:
bold and blond,
        the full glory of life
                newly upon it.
He regarded Yusuf,
the radio operator Vedat,
and Rahmi the mechanic next to him.
All had unlined foreheads
            smooth as silk paper,
all hungry faces
                that didn't even know their hunger.
They'd only lived a drop
            and only had a drop of memories,
their burdens so light
            they could go so easily to their deaths . . .

They pass the Hippodrome.
And a brand-new city faces them:
                    proud and victorious,
                    disowning its suburbs,
            it rises in the middle of the steppe, no expense spared.

. . . .
. . . .

They pass the stadium:
this place stands in the city like a ready-to-wear suit
—strangely new, strangely pressed—displayed
                on a mannequin in a store window.

The woman called to the driver.
"Let me out here," she said.
The officers appreciated the woman's caution:
you never know,
and everyone lived in fear of the Commandant, "Iron Ali."

VIII

The 3:45 train out of Haydar Pasha
       quietly pulled into Ankara Station
at 8:15 a.m.
          (five minutes late).

Spring comes to Ankara Station
with heightened suppressed excitement in the station police,
      peasant construction workers in the third-class waiting room,
and, in the restaurant, a desire for Istanbul unfolding like a big head
   of lettuce.
Ankara Station is new, clean, and comfortable.
But despite all the light its marble
gives off, something in the air
so hard (or easy) to describe keeps people
from running or shouting or laughing out loud in Ankara Station.
So that
if you're caught off guard
when the loudspeakers announce a departure,
you'd think they called from another planet.

The prisoners got off the train

with their suitcases and guardsmen.
Handcuffed again,
they walked without attracting attention
(or else any aroused curiosity was well-hidden).
One woman just whispered to another:
"They're German spies."
                         (Suleyman was blond.)

The prisoners headed for the Guard station
                         (where they would wait for their connecting trains).
A peasant porter carried their bags.

The streets were deserted:
maybe it was too early
                         or too late
                              or a dead hour
or maybe life had withdrawn behind walls.
Stacks and stacks
                 masses upon masses
                              of marble
                                   concrete
                                        asphalt.
And statues
           statues
                 and more statues
but no people.
And then the steppe:
reaching deep into the city
                         despite everything
                              to pop up where least expected,
and then, suddenly, earth without end . . .

"Suleyman," the prisoner Halil said,
     "see the war between the city and the steppe?"
"Yes,
     the steppe still stands,
                         but it's losing ground."
The prisoner Fuat, a fitter,
stroked his fine mustache with the steel of his handcuffs
and surveyed the city as if it were a workbench:

"Brothers," he said, "I like Ankara.
        I don't know much about construction work,
                but you can tell our workers sweated over it,
                        and they've done a good job . . . "

The prisoner Melahat
gazed at the wide
                blue
                        peaceful sky.
"A rubber ball—
catch!"
She thought of her childhood and her daughter.
"Throw the ball up,
                high up in the sky!
My girl doesn't have a ball.
A letter to Istanbul:
'Mother, buy my girl a rubber ball,
big and red.
Sell my silver earrings.'
Throw the ball up,
                high up in the sky.
Where'll she play ball?
You can't see the sky from our street.
Pie in the sky—
forget it."
Melahat watched a lone cloud
the size of a child's shirt,
                        cute
                                and white,
float smiling across the infinite blue.

Still following the prisoners,
the university student stood across the street,
saw where Melahat was looking,
spotted the cloud in the sky,
and thought of Tolstoy's *War and Peace:*
"'All is vanity. Give up earthly struggle
and find the sky. There lies happiness
                        without fear or misery;
                                peaceful,

grand
and infinite,

it solves life's great mystery...'"
He smiled.
"Defeatism,"
he thought,
without losing his respect for the grand old man,
"giving up hope in humanity—
just after-dinner philosophizing."

And as he thought this,
the cloud the size of a child's shirt in the sky
got cut in two as if with a knife
by a trimotor plane.

The student saw the plane
and his thoughts ran one after another:
"Technique—
bringing freedom out of sweat and blood;
technique—
electricity, motors, fuel;
the pilot dives,
and I pace the length of Emirgan Woods—
plane tree,
rope swing,
the lover swinging back and forth;
if the pilot flips out
and drops a bomb
or opens machine-gun fire—
London, Belgrade, Rotterdam.
Tolstoy is a great man,
great despite everything!
How he has the enemy soldiers converse—
he drew on his memories of war in Sebastopol.
On the troop ships outside Sebastopol...
A note to the French translation of *War and Peace:*
'During cease-fires, enemy soldiers would gather together,
and even if they didn't know one another's language,
they'd laugh like brothers
and pat one another on the shoulder.

How much nobler their spirits
than those who made the war
and said, because they came from different countries,
they weren't men and brothers
                    but enemies . . . '
If I could be a great writer like Tolstoy!
'My love,
give me your hand—
not to kiss it
but to place it
            among hands weaving a new world.'
If I could finish this poem and publish it somewhere,
                    Selma would be so happy."

Turning the corner, they saw
        a two-story concrete building:
the Regional Headquarters of the National Guard.
The "cubic" style of Hungarian master builders
        in the hands of Ankara contractors
        had once more triumphed over wooden houses.

The prisoners and guardsmen went inside.
Melahat stayed outside
        in the hall leading to the privates' quarters.
Their handcuffs unlocked,
the others were detained
                    in the basement
                        with their suitcases.
The cement floor was bare and light.
They sat on their suitcases.
"I'm bushed,"
Suleyman said.
He leaned his head against the wall
and started humming his favorite song,
        a little mockery
                and a lot of longing in his thick voice:
"Come, let's sip life
                from a goblet of kisses."
Fuat was absorbed in the newspaper.
And involuntarily

Halil remembered
other detention rooms,
                    police stations,
                              and prisons.
Throbbing like separate hearts
                    in his smart grief,
they passed like milestones
                    on the road he'd taken.
The first detention room was near the border,
close to cornfields and a rebellious sea,
in the basement of a government building
        filled with the damp timbers of wrecked ships—
                    windowless
                              pitch-black
                                        and deep.
How hard it had been for Halil to search his pockets,
how long he had struggled to get a flame
                              from a match!
The air, naked and stinking like a corpse,
hung dead-still,
                    refusing to light.
Halil yelled and kicked the door
        until a sergeant brought candles.
Outside, it was nine o'clock on a sunny morning.
Then Halil smelled another person
and walked toward him with his candle.

The man
        was closed off
                    behind his eyes.
The man, a distant black mustache,
was like a dark
        empty window
                    in an abandoned house.
He stood on a broken keel;
they'd chained one leg to an anchor,
        as if a current might carry him away.
The man didn't return Halil's greeting:
he remained
        all alone behind his eyes.

Madness,
heartbreak,
melancholy.
They left Halil alone with the madman for three days and nights,
the madman in his chains
        and Halil with the candles he lit one after another.
Then they transferred them
        to the hold of a ship.
The journey lasted seven days and nights.
And as they crossed the Bridge in Istanbul
        (Halil chained to the madman
                and flanked by bayonets),
        kids started chasing them.
Halil was strangely embarrassed at first;
        then he felt great peace.
And he never lost this peace again.

Each time they raided his house,
        he opened the door with the same peace.
And each time he stood up from a beating at the station
                (his broken glasses down on his cheeks,
                        a humiliating pain in the soles of his feet),
        without having said anything
        or betrayed anyone,
                he felt in his heart
                        the same peace . . .
And his third time in Istanbul Prison,
he went on a hunger strike with the same peace:
he and his friends used their loaves of bread for pillows
and lay half-naked on the damp cement,
their legs in chains.

And in the eastern prison famous
for scorpions, dirt floors, and watermelons,
Kurdish lords set their henchmen on him,
and before he was knocked out by a truncheon
across the small of his back, he split open
                three heads with the same peace.

And in Ankara in solitary

—no books, pens, or people—
he played odds-and-evens with the same peace,
counting thrown handfuls of roast chickpeas by day
        and city lights out the window by night.

To understand
is the greatest peace.
The irresistible force of social necessity
and the struggle
—with head,
            heart,
                and fist,
with all-out hatred
                and malice,
with all-out compassion
                and love—
to end man's exploitation of man,
for a more just world
                and more beautiful country . . .

Fuat threw down the paper in a rage:
"Nuri Jemil is writing about patriotism," he said,
"about love of country—
                the man has no shame!"
Suleyman said with glee:
"Well, well—I've finally seen you angry.
What did you think?
Of course he writes about it.
They sell the country with one hand
            and write about patriotism with the other.
What do these bastards know about love of country?
Love of what country?
Love of positions, warehouses, factories,
                farms, and apartment buildings.
Take away their property and capital
and pull their chairs out from under them,
and the country would be enemy soil to these guys.
It's been the same through history.
During the French Revolution,
noblemen led enemy armies
        to defeat France

and save the monarchy...
And those who pulled the strings of the White Russian armies,
of Vrangel, Kolchak, Denikin,
                    were German, Japanese, and English capitalists.
And here
the Ottoman dynasty
and its supporters,
together with Venizelos and London bankers,
                    fought to take Anatolia from the Turkish people.
And just between us,
even
the Chinese Nationalist leader Chiang Kai-shek,
with American money and Japanese weapons..."

Fuat interrupted Suleyman:
"In Malraux's novel *Man's Fate,*
there's a scene where Chinese workers
                    are burned in the furnace of a locomotive..."

Suleyman continued:
"Franco, 'the greatest patriot' of the Iberian Peninsula,
set Moroccan Arabs and German planes
on his republican Spain.
And then there's Marshal Pétain, the hero of Verdun,
who handed France over to the enemy...
What do these bastards know about love of country?
Love of what country?"

Halil laughed:
"You're all worked up again."
"Of course
I'm worked up."

Fuat kidded:
"Now, with all that energy, how about a game of chess?"
"I'm up for that, too.
But you and Halil play first,
                    and I'll beat the winner."

Halil took the chess set from his suitcase.
They had painted the board

and carved the pieces themselves.

The match started quietly.
Halil had made a rule:
"No taking back a move."
On his sixth move, Fuat broke it.
Halil got mad.
The match went on.
Suleyman joined with Fuat.
Halil got really mad.
The match went on.
Suleyman kept butting in, telling Fuat what to do.
Now Fuat got mad:
"Shut up, you're confusing me."
The match went on.
Fuat's king was left alone on the board.
"Now you can mate me in ten moves, Halil,
                              or it's a stalemate."
"Not ten but fifteen."
Suleyman jumped in:
"No, twelve . . . "
Nobody knew how many moves it would take.
They all yelled
                and sounded off, proud and stubborn.
A knock came at the door:
"What's going on in there?
                You fighting?"
They fell quiet
and looked at one another, smiling.
Suleyman answered,
"We're not fighting, sergeant;
don't worry, we're talking."
"Good, don't fight.
But why can't you talk like people?"

The sergeant left,
and the match ended in a stalemate.

Halil took off his glasses,
his eyes like two naked children:

clean,
smiling a little sadly,
and cold.
Halil closed his eyes.
Red and green circles spun in the dark behind his eyelids,
then came pure-black stillness.
Halil immediately opened his eyes
and hurried to put his glasses back on.
His eyes were scared, like two fish in a bowl.
He looked:
warmer and clearer and clearer,
motion returned to objects and people, with light and color.
Suleyman asked:
"What's the matter, Halil?"
"Nothing.
Just a little matter of darkness."
"I don't understand."
"Darkness is bad, Suleyman,
to see only darkness—
nothing but darkness—is bad."
Suleyman laughed:
"Why don't you just say 'blindness'?
I agree it's the worst handicap."
Fuat joined in:
"Losing an arm or a leg beats going blind."
Halil, as if he'd just remembered something, asked Fuat:
"If your struggle demanded your eyes, would you give them?"
"I've never thought about it.
If it's absolutely necessary, I'll give them, too.
Why did you ask this now?"

Suleyman, worried, stared at Halil:
"Are your eyes tired again?"
"No.
[Halil turned to Fuat]
I was two years younger than you, Fuat, when I got into this business:
imagining the impossible,
ready for the highest sacrifice,
full of compassion,
utterly pitiless,

and an enemy of lyricism
and more than a bit of a romantic—
in short, a young intellectual
      with all his strengths and weaknesses.
You won't understand—
              thankfully, you're a worker—
                    but Suleyman will.
Young intellectuals are full of contradictions
              when they get their first whiff of the people,
              when they first join the masses:
on the one hand, they totally deny themselves as individuals;
on the other, they're self-absorbed.
I used to ask myself:
'Are you ready to give your all, Halil?'
'Yes.'
'Your eyes?'
'Yes.
After I'm blind, I can still speak and others can write it down;
      after I'm blind, I can still fight . . . '"

Fuat laughed:
"You're right," he said,
"but even the Devil couldn't think something like that out of the blue."
"An intellectual could."
Fuat asked:
"Did you wear glasses back then?"
"You mean, were my eyes sick back then?
I didn't wear glasses.
But maybe the disease had already set in.
I don't know, Fuat . . .
They still don't know what it is.
I still don't have a diagnosis.
But that's not important . . . "

The door was unbolted from the outside.
They all turned toward it.
Melahat appeared in the door with two guardsmen:
"I'm leaving, gang."
              (Melahat had been assigned to Ankara Prison,
              and the others would soon part ways:

Suleyman would go east, Fuat north,
and Halil to a prison on the steppe.)
"Just a minute, sister."
Fuat held out a red silk handkerchief:
"You can dry your tears with this as you think of your husband.
He gave it to me as a keepsake.
Better you should have it . . . "
Halil asked:
"You have fifteen liras, right?
Here's five to make it twenty.
Remember to write once a week.
Ankara Prison is fairly comfortable.
When you're settled, you can send for your daughter."

They all shook hands.
Melahat's eyes filled with tears.
She smiled
and disappeared.
The door slammed.
And was bolted again from the outside.

BOOK THREE

PART ONE

I

Earth
flat as far as the eye can see,
barren,
and bitter as red pepper.
In the west, a tall lone
                    poplar.

Though the smell of dried thyme still hangs in the air
                         of the steppe,
the skyflowers have all withered,
and the vetch is just thorns.

From Bashkoy to Bakirli
              takes eight hours.

Since the sunrise prayers, Nigar
      has been running away from her husband's village
                              with her lover.
Her breasts are sweaty.

It's almost noon.
The grass is warm,
the earth is humming.
Crickets and locusts sing
              the most hopeless of songs on the steppe.
Nigar holds her six-month-old in her arms.

Clouds pile up white and heavy over the steppe,
barely moving.
Nigar stops.
She calls to Mustafa
      walking ten steps ahead.

Mustafa, his cap pushed back on his head,

watches a hawk slip through the clouds.
The bird of prey
spreads its wings
and glides through the clouds,
silent
like a picture.

To be free as a bird in the clouds . . .

The poplar grows by a well.

Nigar sits on the wellstone,
her belly treacherous and soft
        under her long shawl.

The baby's fists stick out of the swaddling clothes.
The swaddling clothes have buttons—
              twenty-four,
              in two rows of twelve.

One of them is glass.
If a man bent over it,
he'd see himself inside it the size of an apple worm.

It's late afternoon.
The crickets and locusts
haven't yet finished
        their song on the steppe.

A fox passes below the road
and, before disappearing into the soapwort,
    turns to look at those on the wellstone.

The baby weighs on Nigar.
Her husband's seed.
Mustafa says:
"Kids die in the village
    all the time.
The death of a six-month-old
    isn't really a death."

The hawk is rapacious.
The fox sly.
The well deep.
The steppe endless
        and bitter as red pepper.

Inside the glass button
        a tiny poplar
                topples.

The baby drops
        from Nigar's arms into the well.
Better move on—
may the baby rest in peace . . .

But the baby wasn't the only one to rest in peace.
Mustafa and Nigar rested with the same peace
                                in prison.

The guards pace back and forth in the fortress,
blowing their whistles.
Stars appear behind the clouds.
"The lone fountain in the jail-yard
flows crooked, to one side.
Prison wouldn't be so hard
                if we weren't so far apart."

The sixth ward housed fourteen men.
Mustafa lay next to the door—
eyes softly closed,
                mouth open,
cheek in his palm, as if singing a song.
He rid himself of his fatigue in prison
                as if getting rid of grime in a bath.
His sleep was happy,
        and life was sweet.

On Mustafa's left, Hamza sat
cross-legged and tiny on his handful of a bed.
"Kill him," Nuri Bey, the landowner Hamza worked for,

told him, "kill Durzadé's shepherd."

If Durzadé didn't have the proper respect for Nuri Bey
—Nuri Bey, who could sit and chat
with the local National Guard sergeant—
and had his shepherd break the leg of the tawny cow,
that shepherd would have to be shot in the back
                              in an open field,
his white cloak reddening with blood . . .

Hamza had long forgotten the shepherd's face.
He wouldn't recognize him if he came back from the grave.
Nuri Bey didn't keep his promise.
"I won't let them convict you," he said.
                                        They did.
"I'll take care of you in prison," he said.
                                        He didn't.
This, especially, Hamza couldn't forgive.
And he'd write the prosecutor a letter
        if he didn't fear Nuri Bey.

It was getting light outside.
Hamza stood up for prayers.

In prison you find God,
all manner of flies, bedbugs, fleas, and lice,
accounts to be resettled,
enough hope to make a man cry with rage,
friendship and hatred,
loyalty and suspicion,
but one thing refuses to enter prison:
                              regret.
It's the dead man's fault
or the fault of those outside
or the judge's fault.

The ward doors opened.
The prison fountain no longer stood alone in the yard.
A ragged crowd
        gathered at the crooked-flowing fountain

like a herd of deer.

Hot plates were lit for coffee.
Kerim dug out his stashed knife and put it on.
Shakir Agha woke up on his four-mattress-high bed.
Musa had been beaten in the night and thrown in solitary.
The junkie Aptul flapped his arms and crowed like a rooster.
The gambling would be starting in the seventh ward.

Good morning, friends,
        have a pleasant trip.

. . . .

Halil had the head-guard's room
all to himself.
He had a bunk and a table,
and the walls were solid books.
Plus photographs of Aysha, Suleyman, and Fuat.
Two maps hung on the door:
North Africa and the Eastern Front.
Halil had it so good here he felt guilty and embarrassed.
It seemed he'd seen the last for now
        of hunger strikes and beatings
        by the Kurdish lords' henchmen in the east.

Halil tapped his pipe on his knee and emptied the ashes.
He looked toward the door.
Creaking on its hinges,
it opened shyly,
and Pater poked his round head in
        and entered like a timid bull.

The prison had long forgotten Pater's real name;
he'd probably forgotten it himself.
He had worked as a "father" in the juveniles ward,
        and the nickname "Pater" had stuck.

He walked up to Halil, pausing after each step.
Then he stood there,

pigeon-toed in his tattered combat boots,
                    his plump neck bowed.

"Hello, Papa," he said.
His voice matched his build, low and thick.
"Hello, Pater."
"You're not working, Papa—why aren't you working?"
"My eyes ache, Pater—I couldn't sleep last night."
"Why couldn't you sleep, Papa?
                    Were you thinking about your wife?"
Halil laughed:
"Yes."
"Did you just think of her?"
"No."
"Did you also think of me, Papa?"
"You didn't come to mind, Pater."
"So I didn't come to mind?"
"You didn't."

Pater squatted down before Halil
and pulled a cigarette out of his shirt.
He asked for a match.

He smoked as if practicing a savage rite.
His eyes shut tight with desire,
and his mouth pulled at the corners as if tearing.
          He sucked in the smoke with wheezing breaths.

He didn't say a word till he finished smoking.

"I've got something to tell you, Papa.
The judge who sentenced me in Afyon
          has been transferred here.
Now we'll write him a letter
and ask for pants and a jacket.
He provided them in Afyon.
He read the sentence:
                    'Son, I'm giving you 24 years.'
And what did I say?
'I'll do 24 years, judge.

But you send me a jacket and pants each year.'"
"Did he send them, Pater?"
"He did.
Then when I came here, he stopped.
Now I'll tell you, and you write, Papa:
'Your Honor,
first I greet you
and kiss your eyes.
I can't accept the sentence you gave me.
And why not?
You didn't keep your promise.
If you want to send me a suit of clothes,
                    send it.
If not, you can take your sentence back.'
Did you get that?"
"Yes. And the signature?"
"No need—it'll be hand-delivered."

For the first time, Halil was curious about Pater's crime:
"Pater, what are you in for?"
"Abducting a girl, Papa."
"But 24 years is a long time, Pater."
"There were also some people killed, Papa—
                    around two or three."
"How did all this happen?"

Pater thought a minute before answering:
"Papa," he said, "I'll tell you, and you write—
                    we'll publish it in the papers.
I worked two-and-a-half years for the girl's father.
But this guy decided in his old age
           to marry the girl to some rich family.
I told him: 'Father, this won't do,'
       but he still wouldn't let me have the girl.
And what did I do?
I went and got a gun, plus a dagger.
Where did I find the money?
I worked for the Ushak Company,
       two months in the sugar refinery.
If you work there, they pay you cash.

I got a gun, plus a dagger.
It was summer.
August.
Everyone was out in the fields, harvesting barley.
I went out, too.
I never thought anything would happen.
My plan
            was to intercept them on the way back
                            and grab the girl.
I hid in ambush and waited.
I watched:
they made a fire
                and had something to eat.
Afterwards they cut a little barley in the moonlight.
Then they went to sleep.
And what did I do?
I blackened my face with charcoal from the fire.
What was I thinking?
'So they won't recognize me.'
Then I quietly snuck up on them.
I grabbed the girl and wrapped her hair tight around my wrist.
It took all my strength to lift her off the ground.
When she screamed, 'Oy, mother, it hurts,'
                        I threw myself on her.
When she screamed, the one next to her
                —it must have been the mother—
                    couldn't bear the girl's pain
and went for my neck with her sickle.
When she went to hook me,
            what did I do?
                    Once with the knife.
                        She fell on her face.
Then someone else came.
I stuck him, too.
I slung the girl over my shoulder
and walked down the hill.
Then I put her down
and dragged and dragged her
                        till I couldn't move.
Time passed.

Two men crossed the field toward me:
                                                armed.
What did I think?
'They'll shoot me.' And I said to myself: 'I'm gonna leave this girl.'
I pulled off her pants
              and left her stark naked.
But why lie? I never touched her.
Then I stopped at the village
and got hold of a horse.
I roamed around Mount Murat for a month and a half.
Time passed.
I couldn't go on like that.
What did I think?
'Best turn myself in.'
And I learned the girl had died, too.
When she wouldn't move, I'd prodded her with the knife:
it killed the poor baby..."

"Is that all, Pater?"
"That's all,
but wait, there's something else.
I'll tell that, too, and you write.
I was ten when the Greeks entered our village.
Crowds and crowds,
          horses, what have you, all over the place.
I had a cousin, eighteen;
              they stuck him with a bayonet, and he went.
There was talk of rebels.
Gangs.
Then my uncle
          hit this Greek with his rifle butt,
                      and he swallowed his tongue and died.
Then the Greeks,
          maybe more than a hundred,
                      filled our house.
My poor mother couldn't leave me and run,
and since she couldn't run, she had to stay.
They wanted to take her into a room
                            and rape her,
and since she wouldn't go, they used the bayonet.

Time passed.
Two heathen boys shoot birds with a slingshot,
take them inside,
                 and pop their eyes out.
What can the poor bird do?
It flies up to the ceiling
                 and crashes to the floor.
And I think, 'Now why would they blind this bird?'
Of course, I'm ignorant,
and I tell them why not just cut off its head instead of taking its eyes out,
and they say, 'This is how we learned it from our fathers and forefathers.'
And then . . .
Time passed.
And then . . . Well, that's all, my esteemed Papa . . ."

Halil smiled:
"Pater, half of what you say is lies."

Pater scrunched up his face
          like a pudgy six-month-old baby
                       about to cry:
"It's not, Papa."
"Well, is it all true?"
Pater didn't answer.
Halil insisted:
"Come on, tell."
Pater spoke, openly evasive:
"There are some lies, too, Papa."
Then he laughed:
"You're a saint," he said.
"I better go down to the visiting area, Papa."
"Is this visiting day, Pater?"
"It's visiting day.
I don't have any visitors,
but I like to watch them."
He winked his swollen eyes:
"And there could be some food, Papa—
visitors love to do good deeds . . . "

Hamdi
came into the world in 1921
      in Squash Village near Cherkesh.
They rubbed him with salt.
He was soft.
They were glad he was a boy.
Before his fortieth day was out,
he looked up at the sun through the wheat.
He learned to sleep on the earth.
The house was dark,
      the earth beautiful.

He got smallpox in '22.
They bound his hands.
He walked in '23.
And until '24
      he roamed the world's 4 streets
                  and 36 houses.
He liked animals and rain.
Helva was made only on holidays.
Hamdi no longer cried
when his father beat his mother.

The winter of 1925
      (1340 by the old calendar)
        was stormy.
One of the oxen died.
His father got drafted.
It rained a lot.
They ate lots and lots of squash.
Guardsmen came,
they had Martini rifles.
A black bird preyed on the village chickens.

In '26 he was five.
They gave him a lame goat to look after.
He took the goat out to the fields.

Hamdi could never catch the clouds.
He never met with any wolves.
Hamdi came to know the grasses.
They ate lots and lots of bulgur.

There was a drought in '27.
The earth cracked.
The crops didn't bear.
The ground rumbled.
In the middle of that year
        his father returned from the army.
They ate very little squash.

Hamdi
wore long pants and a shirt.
He was circumcised (1928).

In '29 he went down to the Cherkesh market:
he sat on his father's lap on the donkey;
                        his mother walked behind.
In the market were fruits,
        mirrors, pocketknives, daggers.
It rained a lot that year.
They ate lots of *tarhana* soup.
There was a lot of squash.
And that same year
        he stuck his hand up a hen's behind
                        and took out the egg—
                        the hen didn't die.

They had a stormy winter
                in 1930.
The tax collector came:
he had a horse
        and a saddlebag
but no mustache.

The next year the boys and the girls together
        put the young lambs out to pasture.
Hamdi

wore socks and moccasins
          (1931, October 7).

In '32 the girls
      laid him on his back
         and grabbed his pants.
He screamed.
The girls had breasts.

The winter of 1933
        was stormy.
Fawn Creek froze.
That winter he went fishing for the first time.
He loaded wood on a donkey.
They met with a wild boar.
A barn burned in the village.
His father became a tenant farmer.
Girls had other things besides breasts.

In '34 they took the last name "Shenturk."
His father used it only for official business;
his mother never used it.
But Hamdi
       liked this name.
Hamdi Shenturk was thirteen.
They handed him the plow.
And Hamdi and the oxen
      went back and forth, drawing lines in the earth.
That night he smoked tobacco in secret
and got beaten by his father.
The next day
      he laid a girl in the hayloft.
He washed himself afterwards.

In '35 there was a drought.
The hills didn't green,
         the crops didn't bear.
A girl got abducted from the village.
The donkey died.
The fallow wasn't fertile.

His father beat his mother unconscious.
That year he went to the mosque for the first time.

In '36 his mother died.
The neighbors dug the grave.
He saw his father cry:
tears streamed down
              into his black beard.
He didn't sleep.
He almost smoked in front of his father.
It rained a lot that year.
They ate lots of squash.

The fallow was fertile in '37.
The earth swelled up.
In Cherkesh he ate watermelon for the first time.
He thought about being rich:
"If I had a hundred liras," he said.

He got married
(1938).
Fighting broke out with Tombs Village over rights to the mountain.
Shots rang out on both sides in the dark.
His taxes went unpaid.
He played quoits at the Youth Center.

The next winter was stormy.
In November of that year
       he went down to Zonguldak with two friends.
The sea
       stretched out forever.
He entered the mines.
One morning
       in December of that year
       they pulled Shenturk out from under the coal:
       his face bloody,
           his hands all black.
He said good-bye to life
       on a white bed
             (1939).

The late Hamdi Shenturk had a son
(1940).
They rubbed him with salt.
They named him Ahmet.
Hamdi's son, Ahmet Shenturk.
The end of that year
        brought more fighting with Tombs Village
                        over the mountain:
            shots rang out on both sides in the dark.
Three people were left dead
and three were sent to prison,
Ahmet's grandfather among them.

In 1941 Ahmet
        went to visit his grandfather in prison
                    in his mother's arms.
What can a baby know of the majesty of the law!
Ahmet took in the prison with a smile,
        his two front teeth showing in his pink mouth.
The visiting area had a wire fence with a wood railing
to separate the prisoners from the visitors,
but they all mingled together anyway.
Ahmet's grandfather held him in his arms
and shooed away Pater, who crowded too close.
People of the same earth and work,
        the peasant visitors all looked alike.
Only Shakir Agha's daughters-in-law stood out:
big-boned,
tall,
and beautiful,
the two women were like well-fed mares.
Their sashes were scarlet,
their skirts crimson.
With their gold-ringed fezzes
        and flaming-red shalvars,
they seemed to have descended from the sun
                    to brighten this poor festival.

The wire cage hummed like a bee hive,
fragments of sentences connecting in the air:

"What are you thinking?
It's too late for thinking.
You can think all you want—what's done is done."

"Spiders foretell sickness, death, and guests;
        they tell the time of the man without a watch."

"You go right for the bag—
        kiss your mother's hand first."
"So what? She was here just four days ago."
"Ah, son,
        mothers bleed, sons don't heed . . . "

"Money, did you bring any money?"

"Shakir Agha gave all the top officials ten kilos of flour each."

"My father lived during wartime:
        he went all the way to the land of swallows."

"Women are nine-tenths vanity,
                        one-tenth brains."

"We'll enter the war.
The Book says we will.
The hodjas divined it in the Koran
                by alphabetical numeration.
We'll go into Rumania and Bulgaria
                and come out at the mouth of the Danube.
Bulgaria's guns are aimed at us,
                ours at them."

"I brought your guard some bulgur."

"A man's lot—
you're born, grow up,
        roam all over,
        and end who-knows-where . . . "

"When the judge read my sentence,

I shouted, 'Long live the Republic!' "
"Was it a short sentence?"
"No, long.
But I liked
the judges lined up on the bench
                    in their gilt-embroidered robes—
                    I shouted with joy."

"A man is like a rose,
                    he can wither in a minute."

Only Twenty-Four Omer wasn't talking.
He'd squatted down,
pounding his fist on his knee.
The wood cigarette holder in his fist went up and down.
Eyes narrowed to slits,
Twenty-Four Omer stared into the face across from him
                    and thought:
"Summer is back,
        a man can find shade under the bushes . . . "

Halil looked out the window.
He could see the iron gate
and the visitors being searched
                    before getting in.
A peddler's horse neighed on the road opposite.
Halil sniffed the air.
On the steppe, winds rise suddenly
                    and fast turn to whirlwinds—
as they did now.
First came the smell of hot grass
as if a barn burned below.
The police-station flag flapped.
The poplars shivered, all spangles.
The air felt lukewarm, like blood.
A child's laugh
                    a cry
and in the next breath
                    clouds of dust.
Halil saw the sun

                 in the distance,
round,
      red,
               and smoky through the dust.
Halil shut the window.
He closed his eyes.
The sun stayed inside his head:
a fire the weight of three times a million times 2000 million tons.
Neither good
               nor bad
                    neither beautiful
                             nor ugly
                               neither right
                                       nor wrong—
just colossal
               boundless
                     life.
The force of 100,000 horsepower per square meter.
Neither evening
                    nor morning
                           neither hope
                                 nor alas
                                    neither more
                                            nor less.
Whirlwinds
               of white
                    gas
                       blowing 600,000 kilometers per hour.
Atoms ionized,
always dying
               always being born
                       always perfect,
and endlessly
splitting and fusing, independent of us,
               here before we were
                    and here long after us . . .

. . . .
. . . .

Halil opened the window.
The wind suddenly rising on the steppe
             had suddenly blown over.
Right across the road
stood the carpenter Shukru's wife, Zeynep,
holding her little daughter's hand.
Her other hand held a copper yogurt pot.
Her feet were bare,
her grave face inviolate.

They'd taken her husband away four years ago;
she'd followed him to town.
Shukru was in prison;
she hoed the fields.
And every day for four years,
                  rain or shine—
                        in mud, wind, heat,
                              or raging blizzards—
        she'd appeared at the iron gate at the same hour,
        and she would come every day for eleven more years.
And she'd still look at her man without raising her eyes,
still speak in whispers like a mother who asks for nothing,
             and quietly set the pot down and leave.

Halil looked up at the sun:
high
      in the distance,
                  red and clear,
no bigger than Zeynep's muddy bare feet,
                  it was small and heartless.

Happy to be human in spite of everything,
                  Halil smiled respectfully
and ran inside to get Shukru . . .

Twelve shops stood in the prison yard
                     at the foot of the stone wall,
           helpless and dwarfed
                     like lost trunks.

And like little shops all over the world,
          they all looked alike,
          lined up side by side;
          yet each was unhappy in its own way,
          alone at the foot of the stone wall.
They belonged to the government.
Leases were auctioned off to prisoners.
In the first sat the tailors, legs crossed
and heads on their chests as if cut at the neck.
Tailors,
the warden's shirts must be pressed.
Tailors,
your scissors fly like storks,
threads dangle from your lips.
Laughter is good, tailors, why not laugh?
                   Laughter lightens work.
Tailors.
The tailors' hands stumble and get up and run nonstop
      on nervous thin legs,
the stitching on the pants coming and going.
The tailors sit cross-legged.
Tailors.
The tailors' machine is a Singer,
                an 1897 model.

The second shop was the tinsmith Shaban's.
Sulfuric acid, hydrochloric acid, sand and copper,
                   and bright-red wet feet:
the boy apprentice writhes in the tinner's vat,
              narrow shoulders to the right, thin waist to the left,
             bare legs pressed together.
Below, the bellows like large animal lungs,

the fire looking up from a pit dug in the earth,
tin, cotton, and ammonia on a tray,
and on a sheepskin rug
                 the lord of the writhing and fire,
                          Master Shaban, sitting like a shah.

Empty for two years, the third shop is closed.
A cold
        dead heart,
                 the lock on its door doesn't tick.

Next door is the world of clunky shoes and rawhide soles:
the secondhand-shoe dealer Raif Agha,
                          toothless,
                                  cross-eyed,
                                         deaf,
but with 150 yellow gold coins in the warden's safe.

Modern Yusuf and his mirrors occupy the fifth shop.
The mirrors stare out from gilt stencils,
                          picture frames,
                 and borders of oil-paint red roses.
Naked women on the walls,
                 and a lithograph of a marshal.
Modern Yusuf has wavy blond hair parted on the side,
                 the light of filtered honey in his eyes,
                          a hawk-beak nose,
                          and a trim, bold mustache.
Modern Yusuf is the best-dressed man in the prison;
his yellow shoes are never seen unpolished.

Yusuf was born in Ilgaz, 1908.
Ilgaz.
Ever been there?
When?
4 quarters, 600 houses, 1,000 population,
city hall, police station and substation,
greasy spoon, bakery, ironsmith, saddler, coppersmith, dry-goods
    store,
orchards and fields—and fatigue unto death.

And 3 inns—rooms upstairs,
            coffeehouses below.

Ilgaz wakes up with the sun
            and goes to sleep two hours after sunset.
Boredom till morning.
Poker for the clerks,
            dice
                  for the young men,
                        and raki for both.
And far above, near the sky,
                  the highlands of deer and pines
            covered with the whitest snow.

Yusuf was born outside the town
            in the foothills of Ilgaz Mountain.
His father, Master Kadir,
            had been a tailor
                  but worked as a farmhand.
His mother: Shehriban.
Master Kadir died in the Balkan War.
Yusuf grew up with his grandfather
            (a retired guardsman
                  paid 3 liras a month
                        —paper money—
                  with a cow
                        a house
                              an ox
            and 4 acres of land).
At seven, Yusuf was apprenticed to a tailor
            and entered school.
He couldn't get the hang of tailoring
but studied right through middle school.
Then he joined a mule train:
Inebolu, Kastamonu, Chankiri, Ankara.
Military service in Istanbul.
He'd just been discharged and returned to Ilgaz when
"We braved ten years of war, with heads held high."
That night Yusuf got trashed.
And he lost his best friend over a snake-eyes:

he worked his piece.
They gave him 15 years.

He chose the last name "Modern."
For him, modernity
                was no
                        joke.
So that instead of using his last name last, as "Yusuf Modern,"
he chose to put it first
                        and became "Modern Yusuf."
Modern Yusuf liked his job.
Mirror-making counted as modern work:
                the fancy capitals of the new alphabet,
                        thin brushes,
                                oil paint, and chemistry.

The shop was crowded:
Pockmarked Ihsan Bey, in for embezzlement,
Grocer Sefer of Trabzon
                (forgery),
and Captain Ilyas
                (counterfeiting)
had joined Modern for tea.

Captain Ilyas
was no captain or counterfeiter—
                only a con man.
Captain Ilyas
        sipped his sweet tea
as he spoke
                with confidence
                        under his imposing hat:
"Today I declare myself a counterfeiter.
I was schooled in Sabranya,
                        blindfolded,
                                in a basement 80 steps down.
I don't know who taught me.
Everything's a mystery,
                top secret.
Bolsheviks, Mensheviks . . . "

Captain Ilyas had been in Batum
             when the Bolsheviks came,
                        that much was certain.
But how and why?
That wasn't clear—
maybe he smuggled.

"You must abolish money.
A G-note is God, a 500 the Prophet."

Modern Yusuf asked:
"And the angels?"
"50's and 25's."

Grocer Sefer's hairy face scowled.

Captain Ilyas continued,
             knowing and triumphant:
"Where there's money, there's God; no money, no God.
This is a big statement
             worth 4,800 words—
                        heavy stuff.
I'm into heavy stuff,
             Eastern stuff."

Sly, shy, and pleased,
             he smiled lightly.
He played with his jacket buttons.
He'd gone hungry in prison many times
             —he was an awful spendthrift and very generous—
and had pawned his hat and jacket
but never his yellow captain's buttons with anchors.

"There are as many winds as there are flowers.
A man is grass.
The spirit of grass is the wind.
All animals have special powers.
They speak silently with their bodies.
One will come up and look sideways like this
                        and twitch an ear.

The air the fish exhale
                    turns around to form letters
                                        and speak.
Even the grasses speak with one another
                    by way of the wind;
their voices hang in the air."

He crossed his legs and took off his hat:
a shaved
                    snow-white
                                        noble head
with wary
          sad jetblack eyes.

"Electricity was discovered in tin—
                    electricity-tin,
                    you see how they're alike.
That's how its patron saint discovered it.
The world is a science,
and work is everything
                    (but he himself was frighteningly,
                              unimaginably lazy).
We say that work is everything,
but people feed on one another's flesh."

Pater appeared at the shop door
and thrust his six-month-old baby's head in,
                    almost in tears.
"Captain Papa," he said,
          "you have a visitor, Papa."

The captain flushed red.
His sad black eyes beamed like two words of hope.
He put his hat on in a rush:
"That would be the village mayor."

He tossed Pater fifty kurush.
It was his last fifty kurush,
and if he couldn't get fifty liras out of the mayor
                    against the fifty thousand buried on the mountain,

the captain would go hungry tonight.
He leaned slightly forward,
rubbed his hands together,
and, as if warming up for a Zeybek dance,
        bent his knees, kicked up his heels to his coattails, ,
                                and left.

Pockmarked Ihsan Bey looked at Modern Yusuf
as if to say, "Let's get started—now's our chance."
Modern Yusuf understood
        and asked Grocer Sefer:
"This Captain Ilyas,
        I don't know,
                but you'd have dropped him
                        if you'd had him on March 31, no?"
"I'd have dropped him."
Pockmarked Ihsan asked:
"But, effendi agha,
there are a lot of contradictory reports about March 31.
You were in the navy back then,
                right?"
"I was stationed on the *Muini Victory*."
"Okay, how exactly did this March 31st thing happen?"
They knew the grocer Sefer's story by heart;
                they led him on today on purpose.

Grocer Sefer started talking
                through his suspicious gold teeth
                        and grizzled mustache:
"The officers put on civilian clothes in the morning
and, as they left, told the sergeant:
'The regular army is in rebellion.
If they come and ask you to go along,
go along but don't do any damage.'"

Pockmarked Ihsan Bey nudged Modern Yusuf and approved:
"Those were smart officers, effendi agha."
"They were both smart and mustached.
Anyway,
time went by,

and we heard a band march in from Parmakkapi.
Everyone fell in behind them.
They raided a police station in Beshiktash
                    and stole weapons.
But we didn't know where we were headed.
By the evening prayers we'd reached Yildiz Palace.
Three sergeants stood over us:
            one was Sergeant Mehmet Ali;
                        another, Sergeant Ibrahim.
We lined up outside the palace.
We shouted 'Long live the Sultan!' three times.
Sultan Hamid, the Heaven-Bound, appeared on the balcony.
'What is it, my children?' he asked.
Three men went before him:
            one was Sergeant Mehmet Ali;
                        another, Sergeant Ibrahim.
They passed around baskets of bread,
steaming hot.
He must have known we were coming.
Gunshots sounded in the distance:
'What's that?' 'Oh, nothing—
they saw an officer in civilian clothes
                    and shot him.'"
"Did you also open fire, effendi agha?"

Grocer Sefer regarded Ihsan Bey with deep-set suspicion:
"I didn't,
but if I did, I fired into the air.
Anyway,
Ethem Pasha arrived in a four-horse closed carriage.
The soldiers surrounded him.
Straight to Hagia Sophia Square.
Night fell, it got real dark.
They've mounted a high stand to speak from.
Ethem Pasha speaks.
Suddenly it's a celebration.
Gunfire.
They couldn't see it was a celebration—
'Are we surrounded and under attack?'
The navy withdrew.

257

Everyone ran away.
The band dispersed, the drums smashed.
Much later we returned to the docks."
"It sounds like there was some confusion, effendi agha."
"Yes, there was confusion for sure.
Anyway.
The next day we went to the armory.
An officer had been killed there.
We spread out through the city.
But there was no looting.
Shopkeepers freely gave stuff away.
Brothels, bars, shootings—
                    whatever your heart desired.
Two days later we hear the Movement Army is coming."

Grocer Sefer took a deep breath,
                    weary maybe
                        and maybe a little sad.
With his fingernails he scraped tartar off his gold teeth:
"Anyway," he said, "I thought to myself,
'Prayers five times a day,
        eat, drink, and pray for the Sultan,
                            and mind your own business.
Istanbul or Baghdad, what's the difference . . .
If it's like this here, what's it like out there . . .
Where's the government?
The military is finished.
I'll go back to the country.'"

Modern Yusuf mocked:
"Sure, when you heard about the Movement Army,
                    that was tough—you couldn't go spoiling for a fight."

Angry, Grocer Sefer started to answer,
but Ihsan Bey said, "Look, effendi agha,
                    look what I've got here . . ."
It was an old paper,
in the old alphabet
and torn in places.

"An ancient newspaper, effendi agha,

33 years old."
"Give it here."

Grocer Sefer snatched the paper.
Yusuf could barely keep from laughing.
As Grocer Sefer sniffed the newspaper,
his gold teeth sweetened in his mouth like apricots.
He put on his glasses:
"See, Ihsan Bey,
                no pictures,
        all Muslim writing.
Read it,
        so we can hear."

The grocer closed his eyes;
his mouth open,
his teeth gleamed like the hour for evening prayers.

"The paper is *Morning,* effendi agha,
dated '10 Rebiulahir 1327,
number 7038.'
The licensee, Mihran."
Modern Yusuf asked:
"So the owner was an Armenian?"
"Armenian, Schmarmenian—
        just read, Ihsan Bey . . . "
"I'm reading, effendi agha:
'Directeur-proprietaire.'"
        (He read the French as if reading Turkish.)
Grocer Sefer's eyes widened:
"What's that, Ihsan Bey?"
"That's French, effendi agha."
"True,
in the old days the heathen shops in Beyoghlu
wrote their signs in French.
It's good they've banned that now.
Those who eat Turkish bread should write Turkish.
Anyway,
read the columns."
"I'm reading, effendi agha:
'Communication of the State of Affairs to Abdul Hamid.'"

Modern Yusuf asked:
"What does that mean?"
"It means telling Abdul Hamid he's been deposed.
'Communication of the State of Affairs to Abdul Hamid.
The members of the committee:
Arif Hikmet Pasha, of the Senate,
Aram Effendi, of the Senate,
of the Assembly, Esat Pasha, Representative from Ishkodra,
and Emanuel Karasu Effendi—Salonika.
They arrived at Yildiz Palace
and informed the former press secretary of the Sultan, Jevat Bey,
that a committee had arrived to see Abdul Hamid.
Jevat Bey received Abdul Hamid's permission.'"

Modern couldn't stand it:
"Geeze, the bastards,
        they're still asking leave to enter the man's presence?"
Ihsan Bey continued:
"'The committee entered the room
                        where Abdul Hamid stood:
two tall mirrors,
            a grand chandelier,
                    many armchairs,
and another sofa with a blanket
and, beside Abdul Hamid, his son Abdurrahim Effendi.
Reportedly, it is here that Abdul Hamid pronounces
        the longest sentences and attends to the gravest matters.
And because this quarter is next to the harem,
        the committee could hear the women wailing.
Esat Pasha came within a meter of Abdul Hamid
                        and gave a military salute:
"We are here representing," he said, "the National Assembly.
The nation has given its sacred word as law.
Your safety, and that of your descendants, is guaranteed."
Abdul Hamid wore a black jacket
under an overcoat.
The overcoat was buttoned up.
His son Abdurrahim Effendi,
in an informal frockcoat, hands folded on his stomach,
            stood in a position of reverence.

When Esat Pasha finished his statement,
> Abdurrahim Effendi threw himself on the sofa
> and started bawling.

Abdul Hamid said: "I have a statement.
Do not leave me alone here.
Is my life safe?"
Esat Pasha said: "The Ottoman people are noble.
They know how to treat an injured sultan.
I repeat: your safety is guaranteed."
Abdul Hamid's chin trembled.
He looked ashen,
but his face was full of wrath:
"I knew that it would come to this," he said.
And when the former ruler said they hadn't been fed
for two days,
> he must have neglected to mention
the biscuits, candy, caviar, and butter.
We have been informed that the soldiers entering the palace
found baskets of food everywhere.'"
"Well!" shouted Grocer Sefer,
and laughed sharply.
His gold teeth flashed like lightning:
"Instead of getting mixed up in the March 31st affair,
> I should have joined the Movement Army.
> But no such luck."

Yusuf and Ihsan were taken aback.
This wasn't the reaction they'd expected from Grocer Sefer.

"Why don't you read, Ihsan Bey, why'd you stop?"
"I'm reading, effendi agha:
'Abdul Hamid's Deposing.'
That is, Abdul Hamid's leaving.
> You know, Yusuf, how they drove the man out."
Grocer Sefer confirmed:
"They drove him to Salonika.
But later, when Salonika went Greek, he came back.
He died in Istanbul during the Great War.
You should have seen
> the funeral they gave him.

Everyone died crying.
Leave this exile business, Ihsan Bey, read something else . . . "
"Okay.
'Abdul Hamid's Wealth.
Abdul Hamid had with him 700,000 shares
      of Orient Railways,
        worth 5 million, 150 thousand
                  liras.' "
Yusuf laughed:
"Clearly, he'd earned it with the sweat of his brow!"
Grocer Sefer peered at Yusuf over his glasses:
"Just like those today," he said;
             "whoever touches honey licks their fingers.
Isn't there any news, Ihsan Bey? Read the news."
"There is, but that part of the paper is really in pieces."
"Never mind, Ihsan Bey, read."
"'Tashkishla and its environs
were watered with
Ottoman, Albanian, Greek, Armenian, Jewish, and Bulgarian blood
      for the love of country
           and freedom . . . ' "
Stunned, Modern Yusuf asked:
"Weren't there any Turks?"
"It says 'Ottoman.' "
"Are they the same?"
"I don't know."
"Go on, read."

"'Armenian women assist soldiers
transporting artillery through Tatavla.' "

Ihsan Bey wanted to put down the paper;
he'd lost hope of making Grocer Sefer mad:
"I can't read it—
        it's in shreds."

This time Modern Yusuf insisted:
"Whatever is there, read it to the end."
"'Kamil Pasha's Escape.
  .   .   .   escaped on Sunday   .   .   .   .   .   .

from his mansion to Jaddebostan . . . . . .
. . . . . getting on a rowboat . . . .
reached safety on a steamboat . . . . . . ' "
Yusuf remembered he was in prison:
"God protect him—
            let's hope he doesn't get caught! . . . "

Ihsan Bey continued:
"'Incidents in Adana
   . . Satanic hands, disgraceful men . . . .
. . . the house of a married Armenian woman . .

.
   . . her husband comes and shoots three of these devils . .
taking this opportunity, attacks on Armenian homes . . . .
. . . official indifference. . . . . .
   . Muslims against Armenians, Armenians against Muslims. . .
. . houses burned . . . . . .
   . . fundamentalists loot the city . . . . .
. . . . Adana and the surrounding villages . .
. . . . . streets of Tarsus littered with bodies . '
Should I go on?"

"Read."

"'To the Honorable Chair of the National Assembly:
. . . . Your Honor. . .
. . . . Freedom Martyrs . . .
. . . . Funeral service . .
. . . . imperial edict in this matter . . . .
. . . . . . Mahmut Shevket Pasha . .
See how the Freedom Martyrs were buried:
. . . . . a cavalry unit in front . . .
. . . . . then police and city officials . . .
. . . . . . by the new sultan at the funeral .
first, prayers by one of the theologians . . . . .
. . . then a Senator . . . . . .
. . . then His Excellency Mahmut Shevket Pasha .
. . . no one else scheduled to speak . . . .
. . prayers for the souls of the Martyrs . . . . .
. Under protection of the new sultan's son (name illegible) . .

263

by the founders of the Ottoman Conservatory .

a monument will be erected . . donations from:

5000 . . . *Morning* owner Mihran .

20 . . . Tevfik, clerk at

108 . . . . merchant Halil

100 . . . . Attorney Samuel Anastasyadi

30 .

20 .

. . . reactions from Europe .

. . . . *La Turquie*

(must be a French paper)

. . . telegrams from European capitals .

The victory of the Young Turks

Paris, 28 April:

. . . . All newspapers . . Abdul Hamid's condition .

Budapest, 27 April:

. . . The press generally

Paris Bourse, 28 April:

. . . . . . trading is slow .

Ottoman holdings gained forty points

Orient Railways shares .

London Exchange also very quiet .

. . . . . . Ottoman shares .

. . . . Amsterdam .

Because the queen of the Netherlands gave birth last night

constitutional government in Iran .

. . . Freedom lovers growing stronger .

Advertisement:

Three-day trip to Alemdagh.

Famed for its charm, waters, and air

. . . A ten-piece band .

. . . . . . including two meals a day

. . . roundtrip .

. . . . . . tickets are two liras .

. . . . *World Philosophers* .

. . . . . and *The History of Education*

. . . this work by the former governor of Kozan

A miracle drug .

those afflicted with fainting spells and heart palpitations . . .'"

Ihsan threw the paper down.

They were silent for a while.
One of the mirrors caught Modern Yusuf's eye:
a blond young man in a tie stared at him.
For some reason he suddenly put on his hat
                           and smiled.

"Whew!"
Modern Yusuf said.
"We've come a long way . . . "
He took off his hat.
"What times those were!" he thought.
      "Thank God, I was born too late!"
He felt a gambler's joy:
not to have thrown a deuce
      when he might have.

Pockmarked Ihsan Bey and Grocer Sefer left.

Modern Yusuf had picked up the paper on the floor,
smoothing and folding it with care,
and was about to leave it on the table
            when right there
      he met with Prophet Ali's camel.
A hunchback camel
carrying a coffin.
An Arab
      in a headscarf
            led the camel.
Leading the camel
and lying in the coffin
      is Prophet Ali.

Stripes of green
      and red—
the shawl on the coffin
And, as long as the coffin
                  but bigger,
the Prophet's forked sword.

An angel in the sky,
on the left a deer,
a lion on the right,

Huseyin weeps,
            Hasan weeps.
And on the thin glass
        Prophet Ali's camel rides
                among the mirror-facets.

Those pictures sold well:
orders came from the most distant villages.
The model was an old design
with one addition—
        the angel in the sky.
He and Pockmarked Ihsan Bey
            had copied it from an Armenian prayer book.

Modern Yusuf left the paper on the camel
            and suddenly felt depressed.

He lit the brazier for casting mirrors:
glass clean, sparkling,
chemicals in perfume bottles
—silver nitrate, ammonia, Rochelle salt, distilled water—
and boredom growing in his heart.

He decided against casting mirrors
and stepped outside:
Tinsmith Shaban's apprentice leaned against the wall,
                taking a break,
as alone and forlorn as a village on the steppe.
Yusuf well knew how villages waste away
                in the badlands.
Halil emerged from the carpenter Shukru's shop.
Yusuf asked:
"Did you sketch another dresser for Shukru, Teacher?"
"No,
I told him his wife's here."
"I have some business with you, too."
"I know, Yusuf,
we're going to modernize Prophet Ali's camel."
"That's not it,
and anyway I'm not selling that junk any more.

My business—
        I've got something to ask you.
Well,
        I don't know,
                I wanted to ask if we've made progress
                        —have we become more modern?—
                                since Abdul Hamid's time."

Yusuf's question came as no surprise:
"Sure, we've made progress," Halil answered,
                                "and we'll continue to.
Think of it as climbing steps:
                the steps up, the last step,
                        the door;
                                the door will open
                —not by itself, of course,
                we'll open it—
                and we'll enter the house,
                                        comfortable
                                        and warm."

"Yes!
I don't know,
but talking to you makes me feel better.
Have some tea.
And I'll cast some mirrors before the fire goes."
Modern Yusuf cast his mirrors,
and Halil drew daisies to be painted on them.
Big
        yellow
                daisies
like his wife
        Aysha's
                eyes . . .

IV

The armory in the induction center yard
                            was empty.
        The trees:
        acacias, plums, and mulberries.

The yard was jammed.

The new draftees had come in groups
                        led by their mayors.
The crop of '21
        squatted on the ground.

A dreamland of white duffel bags.
And rawhide shoes.
And separation in downcast eyes.

Purple jackets and silk sashes
                        belong in songs
and festivals of leaping dances.
Who knows better than my peasants
        the hateful art of sewing patches?

The yard was jammed.
Brought in groups
in rawhide shoes,
with separation in downcast eyes
and their harsh, ragged desolation,
the crop of '21
        squatted on the ground.

The women stood
                at a distance,
                        dark and silent,
their farewells without end.

The yard was jammed.
Morning turned to afternoon.

Why did that slap come so fast?
Afternoon turned to evening.
Why did that curse come so easy?
Roll call was over.

In my beloved country, you know,
young men on their way to the barracks,
their grief still an open wound,
are shut up inside mosques and schools
under the endless emptiness of leaden domes.
And days
                go by outside like cranes
                                far, far away . . .

Clouds drifted through the sky;
a flock of cranes flew by.
The crop of '21
        filled the induction center armory.

The women
came like sick, hungry wolves.
They squatted on the ground
beyond the trees,
their hair tucked under scarves
and loaves of bread and yogurt pots in their laps
                                like helpless children.

The armory in the induction center yard
                                was dark.
And the trees were scarlet:
                acacias, plums, mulberries.
The eyes of the women in the yard,
even the ten-year-olds', were all mothers' eyes.
And the guards.

Weak pleas in the induction center yard:
"Son, guardsman—
guardsman, effendi agha.
Take him this pot of yogurt.
Why won't you take it, why?"

"Brother, guardsman—
guardsman, effendi agha.
Open the door so I can see him.
Why won't you open it, why?"

"Son, guardsman—
guardsman, effendi agha . . . "

The women
              started closing in:
"I'll see you dead, guardsman!"
"Guardsman, I'll see you laid out on the slab!"
"I'll see you in your coffin, guardsman!"

The guards knew
          (they were guardsmen and peasants both):
when womenfolk get mad, they really get bad.
A mad woman is the same as a Kurdish dog—
          the bravest horseman is no match for them.

They went at the women with rifle butts.
"It's forbidden . . . "

The women screamed and scattered.
They threw back stones.
They cursed the guardsmen's wives,
                          especially the wives.

The armory in the yard
                  was dark.
And the trees were jetblack—
              acacias, plums, mulberries.

A woman got hit with a rifle butt.
She dropped and sat up,
her mouth full of blood.
"I hope they cut you down like a poplar," she said.
"My son will be a guardsman, too, someday—
he'll go to your village
and do to your mother what you did to me!"

For some time
the heart of my heart,
the thirteen-year-old steelworker Kerim
(sapling-thin inside his blue overalls),
had been watching the women and the guards
from under his cocked cap.

"Hey, guardsman—
hey, you egg-suckers!" he yelled.
He checked to make sure no cops were around.
Like all poor city kids, Kerim
didn't pay guardsmen much mind,
but he feared and hated the police.

He'd sneaked into the commissioner's garden last night,
    and last night the commissioner's canary,
        sprung from his cage, went flying free.

He thought of it
and sniffled, his little nose black with coal
in his pale face.
And he went around to the back of the armory.

Kerim had worked three years in Jevat Bey's factory.
He could handle iron like dough
and temper steel with water.
But now he had only one thing in mind—
a yellow canary,
        in a wire cage, set free.

He took a huge key
        from the pocket of his overalls
and tried the lock on the back door of the armory.
Those inside
        flocked to the door.
Canaries set free—
but it was the wrong key.
He tried twice more.
        No luck.
He roundly cursed

the commissioner and the armory.
Then he bent down,
        put his mouth to the keyhole, and shouted:
"Don't lose hope, turkeys,
                        I'll be back tomorrow."

The black
        roofs
            below Severed Head Fortress
                        across,
                                with their
                                        incurable
                                                dread,
this smell in the air of bulgur cooked on wood fires,
this wall of sunbaked bricks,
the hole a lizard just slipped into,
these desolate
        acacias, plums, and mulberries,
the armory
            where men
                    are locked up,
the "It's forbidden,"
the women
            knocked down,
                    shawls and scarves torn—
he left this medieval world and the night
behind
        and walked on:
he walked, the heart of my heart,
the thirteen-year-old worker Kerim walked on,
        the most hopeful man of the twentieth century.

He turned down an inner-city street in my country.
The blacktop was far away,
            running between the train station and the city hall—
            about five hundred meters of desire.

Here the streets were unpaved:
holy ground forefathers
handed down,

and dried cowpies.

Beside doors with wrought-iron ring handles,
in the dark of branches drooping over wood fences,
　　　marble basins slept in their dumb emptiness.

Just the ground floors of the houses were built,
the second floors all awful, naked beams.

Behind the latticework shutters, gramophones,
　　　　　　　　　　thick voices,
　　　　　　　　　　　　　and babies crying.

Wheels leaned against the walls.
Never again to feel the joy of roads,
they'd stand and rot.

Kerim came to his house,
built of sundried bricks and wood.
The door was open,
his father home.

Kerim's father, Master Lutfullah,
　　　　　　　had been a blacksmith.
Now he was drunk and unemployed.
Kerim's day wages fed the household.
They had a weaver's loom.
His mother and sister wove lining cloth.
But Master Lutfullah took
　　　the women's work by force and sold it
　　　　to feed the woman he kept at the whorehouse.
And he didn't come home for weeks at a time.

When Kerim walked inside,
　　　　　　　his mother sat crouched in the corner,
　　　　　　her white scarf her shelter;
her frightened eyes looked twice as big.

His sister had collapsed over the frame of the loom,
　　　as if hit by a bullet in her neck.

The shuttle lay on the floor.
The spindle had fallen like a toppled poplar.
The warp had been cut with a knife:
                    the threads dangled,
                    trembling like long white hair
                    yanked in rage and let go.
And in the middle of the room,
his father—knife in hand,
barely able to stand.
Kerim understood.
And like the radical change of water into steam,
                    he walked up to his father.
He walked, the heart of my heart,
the thirteen-year-old worker Kerim walked:
"I don't want a drunk father," he said.
"And we don't need a man living off women.
From now on, I am the man of the house.
Enough is enough."

His father wanted to beat Kerim,
stomp him underfoot,
maybe knife him.
The women intervened.
The father swore,
then looked shocked,
and taking this shock as his cue to leave,
                    he dropped the knife,
                        then bent down and picked it back up,
                            and left.

The women sobbed.
Especially Kerim's mother,
squatting on the ground,
        her narrow shoulders shaking under her white scarf.
"Now he'll never leave that whore's bed,
never knock on our door again."

At first Kerim got mad:
"You crazy women, why you crying?"
Then suddenly he, too, began to cry

and snuggled up to his mother:
"Don't worry, Mom,
don't give up.
Father won't be mad at me.
And he won't drink again, you'll see.
And he'll quit the whore.
If you want,
        I'll leave right now
                and bring him back."

And talking and sobbing,
the heart of my heart—
            the thirteen-year-old worker Kerim,
                the most hopeful man of the twentieth century—
                fell asleep in his mother's arms . . .

                        V

Halil wrote a letter to his wife Aysha,
                gazing at the night
                        from his second-floor prison window:

"My love,
when a tidal wave breaking on the horizon
                rushes to engulf me,
when my head and heart spin
            in a whirlwind,
it's a disgrace
to sit back
in a wooden chair
        and rest . . .
But let's drop this subject . . .
My love,
I run my fingers through your hair,
its song playing in my hands.
You're six hundred kilometers away
                            and here beside me . . .
But that's a whole other subject.

In this year 1941,
              I won't discuss us two.
I'm not brave enough yet...

My love,
see how the electric light
          outside the white
                    house down the road burns blue
                              through the masking paper.
The road gleams under the moon.

In the induction center yard, the armory
              and the trees—
                    acacias, plums, mulberries.
There's also an arbor,
              which I can't see.

August first.
The nights are still short.
The guardsmen whistle.
The road is deserted.

Clouds drift through half the sky.

That's the Zonguldak train
              roaring by.

Despite the moon,
in the other half of the sky
              I can see stars
                    above the mountains.

The train just crossed the iron bridge
              behind the poplars.

The city has two parts:
Old Town, at the foot of the fortress,
                    is pitch-dark.

Kizli Coffeehouse didn't open this summer.

Its jetblack windows glimmer
                    in the moonlight.

New Town is near the station.
Its blue lights glow through the trees.
I hear a woman's voice,
kids crying.
I got a lump in my throat:
                    I miss my daughter so.

Two ghostly men,
        side by side,
                slowly
                        walk by.
Officials, I think,
                very somber and exhausted.
They mustn't have been talking.

Light leaks from the first floor of the white house:
                        they must be eating.

The train pulled out,
its whistles piercing
        like ears ringing.
I hope yours are, my wife.

Behind me I can hear the voice of the secondhand-shoe dealer,
                    Raif Agha, through the open door
                            of the fifth ward:
'They did my father wrong
            and me wrong.
Fights about land
        the shop
                property...'

Raif Agha is talking to himself,
                    deaf, cross-eyed, and toothless.
'I got an abandoned shop.
The dry-goods man, Ismail, did me wrong.
My sister, may she rest in peace, was his first wife.

"Ah," she told me,
         "you'll meet with disaster," she said.'

Raif Agha fell quiet.
The radio started,
         broadcast over loudspeakers from the Civic Center.
The armory
              is dark.
Yet it's packed with men.

Raif Agha starts again:
'They did me wrong, they did wrong,
                        my wife's brothers did me wrong.
Day and night, they cursed
                   my house.
They made me drink a potion in the fields.
My wife poisoned my food:
I couldn't get up
       I couldn't walk
              I couldn't talk
                     I couldn't go to the market.
They did me wrong, they did wrong, they did me wrong.'

Like a rope snapping, Raif Agha's voice suddenly stopped.

A man went down the road
                smoking a cigarette.

Raif Agha's voice again:
'My brother's wife did me this dirt.
Everyone was on their side:
         the police chief, everybody.
My brother's wife did me this dirt.
She cast a spell on me.
And it plagued me like this.
My wife's clan stoned my house, my village.
I took the money I'd hidden
                 in the foundation.
My brother's wife flashed me her evil amulet,
                        I saw it with my own eyes.

I went to the magistrate,
                        he wouldn't take my statement.
I saw they meant to drive me crazy—
I put my wife to death.
Blood on my hands, blood, blood on my hands.
Land disputes, shop disputes, property disputes.
The land split open, the shop trashed, the property torched.
They did me wrong, they did wrong, they did me wrong.'

Raif Agha now stopped for good,
I know:
        he suddenly dropped off.
I have a feeling
        he'll die tonight.

The governor's car drove past.
The governor has good-looking daughters.
The older one's wedding is tonight
                        at the Civic Center..."

As Halil continued his letter,
                        the wedding party went on at the Civic Center.
Behind the governor's happy, fatherly gaze
                        a crazy dream lingers:
scarlet fish, way down deep,
                sway tall, lazy rushes.
And his daughter, in a bridal swoon,
                lies bare-naked,
                        luminous in the watery green.

And now, as the city band plays a Zeybek tune
and the graceful bride visits tables around the room
and the mother-in-law gazes enrapt, loaded with diamonds and fat,
and as the groom
        —an engineer—
                follows the bride, erect,
                        with measured steps,
the governor-
        father
                recalls his dream—

remembering, he hides it from himself.
Maybe this crazy dream comes from seeing them sew,
                    five days ago,
                            his daughter's pink silk underclothes.

The governor took his eyes off his daughter
                    and checked the buffet:
it was jammed with flesh and clothing.
And Mr. Refik Basharan
                    gave the waiters orders.

Mr. Refik Basharan worked the hardest at the wedding,
and he was the happiest for working hardest.
Refik Basharan sat on the Party's State Administrative Committee.
The Air Force, the Society for the Protection of Children, the Red
    Crescent,
                    the Civic Center, and the Turkish-Ironspor Club—
the work of all their official balls, receptions, and important weddings
                    rested on his narrow shoulders.

He hadn't found time to get married yet.
If his uncle didn't look after the butcher shop his father left him,
and if his mother,
                    Fatma Hanum,
didn't traffic in drugs for hepatitis,
Refik Basharan would have starved to death
        unawares, running between the Party building and city hall.

His malaria-yellow forehead always in a sweat,
his thin legs always in a rush,
his bloodless lips smiling with a child's faith,
                    Refik Basharan spent himself as freely as water.

"Ox-like" in the governor's opinion,
"gung-ho as a Kurd," according to the Party chairman,
and "cracked" according to the court doctor,
he was merely
                    a Party man.

The Party chairman's head is shaved,

his scowling eyebrows are bushy,
his eyes big,
and his mustache is almond-shaped under his enormous nose—
in short,
"Praise to Prophet Ali!" is written all over his face, in the old alphabet.

The Party chair is a grain merchant.
As hard as a shroud is white.
Usury thick as a dull knife.
And a devout Muslim: prayers five times a day.

His wife avoids events where men are present.
           She takes sick the day before.
The Party chair is in love with his wife:
a woman who doesn't age,
      plump like good bread,
                     white
                        and soft,
     and whose flesh tastes like sea bass.
Sometimes the chair is so overwhelmed with joy
         he cries a river
                 on his wife's lap.
Not that he doesn't smell other roses.
But only once a year, when he goes
               to Istanbul.
The chair leaned over to the mayor and spoke
in the thin voice of a preteen
        reciting the Koran:
              it didn't go with his imposing nose.

The mayor: dark-skinned,
           graying,
              bald,
      short and thin.
He was all attention,
     listening to the chairman.
He listens closely to everybody.
He's good at flattery.
If all say something's bad, it's bad;
     if they say good, it's good.

The mayor is a retired major.
He commanded the division here during the Great War.
Assigning local people to nearby units,
            he won the city's good will.

His one dread
            —the beast of his nightmares,
a billy goat with a pointed red beard,
skipping from rooftop to rooftop—
            is to be thrown out of office.

The mayor's son is blessed.
He's engaged to all the girls in the city.
Long golden hair,
blue eyes wide with curiosity,
            a boy like the prophet Jesus.

The mayor took sick last year.
Burning up with fever,
skin and bones,
        he almost met
                his end.
And the blessed boy and his mother
divided the coppers and kilims,
yelling and haggling at the deathbed.

The mayor got well,
kicked out the son,
beat the wife with a whip,
and fed seven poor people
        for three days out of his own pocket.

The mayor is as proud of one thing in his life
as if he'd created two beautiful kids
—hazel eyes, skin in bloom—
            the city hall and the public restroom.

And the mayor has only one enemy—
the First Circuit Court judge, Rauf Bey.
And Judge Rauf Bey

is the city's archenemy,
not just here and now
but everywhere and always.
Anyone who comes up for a municipal fine
is let off;
if not, the case is postponed.
Rauf Bey rarely sentences anyone anyway.
His life is one big battle over points of law.
He gets mad at lawyers
and watches out for criminals' rights himself.
His personal convictions reign supreme.

Bear Ibrahim and Rauf Bey
and their wives
sat at the same table.
Ibrahim went on about the Sarikamish battle again.
And the judge dozed,
fatigued by his sixty years
and his young wife.

Rauf Bey's wife is a teacher.
They have two kids,
from the woman's first husband.
But Rauf Bey loves them so much
that nobody here knows they're adopted,
and even the kids have forgotten.

The band played the tango "Yesterday,"
an old native product.
Life . . .
Your wife is young, Rauf Bey,
loving her kids isn't enough;
your wife wants to dance, Rauf Bey,
you mustn't doze off.

Just when Bear Ibrahim had climbed Sarikamish's snowiest mountain,
Rauf Bey suddenly shook himself awake
and escorted his wife
onto the dance floor; his back straight,
he took her in his arms,

                    resigned to his fate.
And with her fresh, warm scent
and his thinning, well-groomed hair
                    and clean-shaven face,
without yielding to the drift of the accordion,
he moved around,
proud
        and shaky,
slightly dragging his half-paralyzed leg.
He was as brave as rebellion,
                        as sad as justice.

. . . .

Ibrahim, who couldn't finish his Sarikamish story,
                    served in the reserves during the Great War
and got wounded at Sarikamish.
He fought in the Independence War from start to finish.
It's not certain, but he must be fifty or so.
A Party member, he sits on the city council.
Barely fitting his huge frame into the smallest office,
                    he works writing petitions.

His wife is a skinny little woman.
Bear Ibrahim
admires her brains.
In the shop, the office, the coffeehouse, everywhere, always,
it's "My Hatché is like this
            and that,
my Hatché says,
            we'll ask Hatché.
Hatché, Hatché, Hatché . . . "

And he hates injustice.
Injustice, for Ibrahim, is hateful,
                    like a toothache.
When a citizen suffers some injustice,
                    Ibrahim's tooth aches.
He takes the citizen to his office,
and dispensing with formalities,

he writes killer petitions,
          the Persian compound adjectives raining fire.
And Ibrahim is pretty tight-fisted,
but when it comes to injustice,
money doesn't matter: he barrages
Ankara with telegrams out of his own pocket.

One morning two years ago
          he posted a sign in his office:
"Respected city residents,
the hand wielding a pen wields a lightning stroke of disaster
to damn injustice; so do not pass by this place but pay heed
and in your notebook take note, for one day it may be of need:
complaints against the City Collector
are exempt from petition and stamp fees."

The city and the Party, in the person of the Party chairman,
          acted immediately:
they tried to get Ibrahim declared insane.
But the garrison commander
          remembered Ibrahim had served as an officer
                    —even if a reserve—
          and pulled on his boots.

The next day, the City Collector resigned.
The sign came down.

Like all tangos from a certain era,
          the tango "Yesterday" ended with the requisite "te-dum."
And as Judge Rauf Bey returned to his table,
          he spotted the three brothers.

Three brothers, three brothers—
Hayrettin, Seyfi, and Sefer.
They, too, have come to the wedding
and sit lined up
          like corked medicine bottles.

The youngest of the three is a head all eyes,
and claws;

the master of the three brothers,
Hayrettin is the youngest of the three.

His office in Tuzpinar: empty cans and sacks,
the stink of rotting barley.
While the others, Seyfi and Sefer,
        hit the villages,
Hayrettin sits with his ledger
            and waits
                with the sad loneliness of a hunter spider.

Lady of roses, lady of roses.
Coy as a willow branch,
            the thin-waisted lady,
            the lady with the whitest hands.

Rosie Hanum, Hayrettin's wife, resigned
to your fate, you were doing fine—
why did you suddenly balk
one midnight
        and shoot your mother-in-law?
She who loved you the most,
who wouldn't hurt an ant,
the white lamb
        who'd borne
                three snakes,
collapsed on your red slippers.

Your husband started beating you again.
Always the same reason:
you were jealous of Hayrettin,
            without a word or a move—
                you were jealous of your husband.
The man with a face all eyes
                preferred
                Sarrach's son Ihsan to you.
Your husband started beating you again.
The gun lay in a drawer of the mirrored dresser
—among clothes smelling of hair and stream water—
and your hand reached in, white as marrow;

inside your coy head, the dark blazing,
what had built up
                    and built up
shot forth,
the seed husk splitting,
as the kicks landed on your naked thighs
                        and the gun fired.
And Hayrettin's mother,
who had come to your rescue once again,
collapsed on your red slippers.

The woman lived.
And Rosie Hanum was let off
                    by the criminal court judge, Rauf Bey.

End of story:
Rosie Hanum sold her gold
                    and bought off Sarrach's son;
maybe she slept with him, maybe not.
And six months ago she vanished.
She was last seen in Ankara, at Shehnaz's brothel . . .

The city band played "The Izmir March."
Refik Basharan ran to hush the band:
the governor would give a speech.
"My dear guests," the speech began,
and as it went on
under the light of the chandelier draped with colored crepe paper,
punctuated by clinking knives and forks and the attempts to stifle
    them, . . .

VI

. . . outside,
down on the street,
two men walked past the Civic Center.
One was tall and heavy,
                    the other short and slight.

Their shadows darkened the road in the moonlight.
The streets were deserted except for them.
They walked, slow and thoughtful,
                and spoke in hushed tones
                as if at a funeral . . .
The tall and heavy one, Shevki Bey, said:
"I'll try to console you—
consolation is good.
Sadly, I need consolation myself.
We're in such sorry circumstances—
                      personal, familial, national, international.
And the worst is old age
[Shevki Bey was close to sixty],
the worst is age—
the last stop of the journey.
And in the end,
before you can say, 'My country suffers, I suffer,'
                            you roll into the hole.
Don't misunderstand, son,
I'm not worried or desperate.
I see the facts
        like a Muslim—
            I mean, fully,
                like a man
                    seeing a waking dream—
        and with the patience only great hearts can muster,
        I see unknown adventures yet to come."

Shevki Bey's round black eyes glittered
under his long, thick, hairy eyebrows.
His cheeks were rosy.
Sixty years hadn't touched his body of a Mad Forest wrestler.

Shevki Bey went on:
"Am I talking gibberish?
No, son, I'm just
impatient:
        to see things before they happen,
            to have foreseen what's happening now years ago,
            to already see what will happen tomorrow,

and to be forced to stand by and watch
                              takes vast patience.
That's all.
For old age is accidental,
            and its end is youth.
Can anyone ever despair who sees and knows that life,
                    everything, moves onward, evolves, and perfects itself?
Except the slow, aimless pace of this evolution
                  gives me useless grief.
To know a mountain will erode in millions of years,
and all life,
              from even the tiniest animal to us,
will undergo millions of transformations
                                to achieve perfection,
to know all this
and then worry about material things and their accounting,
or try bending unchanging laws for our own comfort—
                              why,
                            I don't know..."

The little man Shevki Bey addressed
listened as if to voices far away.
Sparse, stunted, withering trees
lined the blacktop to the station;
they stood far apart, with nothing of green,
                  like men without hope.
Shevki Bey and the little man
              turned left off the blacktop
              into an empty lot.
Like all empty plots of land in the cities of my country
—maybe it's that way, too, in other countries—
this one under the moon evoked the same sick feeling,
                  the same spooky dread,
              as a corpse.
Shevki Bey stopped mid-field.
His giant body looming twice as big,
he breathed freer, as if this desolate place relieved his oppression,
                              and thrust out his right arm:
"Onward, son," he all but screamed,
                  "onward!

Read everything, learn everything.
Learn the minds of those who do not learn.
There's a line in the Koran:
'All creatures are manifest forms.'
Everyone acts according to his degree.
Make your mind your master
       and be delivered from all pain."

Years ago,
in the first National Assembly,
Shevki Bey would rise with his giant body,
       thrust out his right arm that way,
         and at the end of every speech
         would read, instead of a line from the Koran,
           this couplet:
    "In the name of conscience and faith, in the name of humanity,
     In the name of the blood shed for the right to liberty..."
He was in the opposition, unaffiliated.
His bravery surprised even Lame Osman.
They wouldn't let him stand for election again.
He fought.
He ended up in the Independence Court,
got out of prison,
and fled to Aleppo to continue his fight from exile,
but maybe his bravery no longer surprised Lame Osman;
maybe his flight smacked of blackmail a little.

The whole family starved in Aleppo.
And Shevki Bey—
       the corpse of a misunderstood hero in his heart,
        and the consolation that they'd still fear even this corpse,
        and a Protestant Koran under his arm—
           returned from Aleppo to his country.

Shevki Bey
rules his household like the caliph
of the Baghdad of fairy tales:
         with boundless compassion unique to him,
         cruel justice,
         incredible penury

                    and generosity...
And Shevki Bey has developed an interest in medicinal herbs;
            he gathers flowers and grasses from the fields.
From a handwritten Arabic book he learns their secrets
and names them with the aid of a French dictionary.
His family lives on his retirement pension
                    and the weekly pay of his tailor son.

Shevki Bey and the little man
            emerged from the empty lot onto a lit-up road.
A white house stood on the right,
                    the prison on the left.
And across, in the induction center yard, the armory.

Shevki Bey spoke,
        gloomy and enraged:
"As the sky rains rocks
and earthquakes reduce cities to rubble,
as floods roar through valleys,
                battering people on rocks and dragging their bodies out
    to sea,
and volcanoes rain lava of iron and copper,
when not the future but the present human condition is in question,
        how sad it is, son,
                that, in explaining the scientific causes of events,
                    the expert
                        bellows, *Je sais tout!'*
Don't be offended by the word 'bellows';
it's exactly right for this situation.
When it stops raining rocks, iron, and copper,
and the floods dry up,
            with the bodies they've drowned and dragged out to sea
                            and the mud they've amassed,
then, if anyone is left on earth,
            and if that sole survivor has the strength to listen,
then the expert
can confidently voice his explanations.
As for today,
my words, yours, or those of anyone who says 'I know'
            are far from finding anyone to listen—

                    very
                              far, son, very.
The wisdom, the sagacity the age demands
                    is to know how to watch calmly the march of events."

The little man
—Shevki Bey's son, the tailor Emin,
a swarthy young man with a long nose—
didn't seem to be listening anymore.
He'd fixed the blue eyes in his dark face on the prison walls.
He looked distracted,
                    enamoured,
                              expectant.
Two days ago he had written
          Halil, the man inside.
And he didn't hide it from Shevki Bey.
Shevki Bey, stunned to discover a side
to his son he didn't know about,
                              said nothing.
He didn't go to pick simples.
He thought for two days
and finally decided
on this night-time stroll.

Now, outside the prison,
                    he uttered his most terrible words:
"Don't stare at those walls, son.
I, too, did time inside.
I, too, sacrificed myself for the common good once,
but my family and children were the first to suffer.
Your mother passed away before her time,
your sister couldn't marry,
you were apprenticed to a tailor.
If you want to change the world,
          begin at home.
And know this, son:
except for the Divine Essence,
no system or belief,
          no sect or creed
                    or any of their followers,

can ever get close to us or befriend us.
If the power that rules the earth and the sky
           wanted humans to be happy,
                      He'd do it on the spot.
Which means He doesn't want it.
Well?
Backward thinking, right?
But son,
it's irrefutable.
It's the case, according to science, reason, and the facts.
Examine fairly yourself and your acts;
look around, left and right:
the same lies,
          the same savagery, the same hypocrisy
engulf humanity with iron persistence, adamant insistence.
The day you understand this
you will, like Montesquieu, form your principles
and say, 'Every nation gets what it deserves.'
It's not up to you to improve man's lot—
God would do it if He wanted to.
And if God doesn't want it, men can't.
Why fight obstinacy with obstinacy?
And 'All is God's will.'
Those words saved me from losing my mind.
To say 'God wants it this way' and then surrender to His will—
                          how good it is."

Suddenly Shevki Bey fell silent.
Whatever the reason, he seemed embarrassed for himself.
He knew he'd wasted his words,
          which made him furious.
He felt like beating his son unconscious,
        the way he'd done until five years ago.
Suddenly saddened,
       he spoke again, as if to apologize:
"Look at the countries who've lost their balance, son,
and the people who oppose those who profit from this imbalance,
                even people of the highest character
                [he included himself among them],
              have always been and will always be defeated.

Don't make anyone else's business yours,
don't even think about it to yourself.
Don't mind anything but your own business.
That's all."

He fell quiet again,
then added as if weeping:
"Let's hope that all ends well . . . "

They turned into their street,
leaving behind the white house,
                   the armory,
                          and the prison . . .

Writing his wife Aysha
by the window
on the second floor of the prison, Halil
     left his letter in the middle
and read—maybe for the fifth time—
            the letter he'd received from her that morning.
And he felt as free and happy as running water.
Aysha wrote in her letter:
"I'm stretched out on the cushion by the window,
with a blanket over my knees.
I'm warm and cozy.
I can see fields—
       lovely fields—
           and Chamlija Hill.
The air is so still
sounds make terrific echoes.
They're plowing a field right next to our yard:
two oxen,
a man in front pulling,
and another in back steering the plow.
The earth swells up,
big with life under the human hand.
I watch, amazed.
What an enormous,
        difficult task!
How can they do it so easily,

so simply?
They've brought alive a huge patch of earth since morning.
Let's see what they'll plant.
I'll write and tell you.
Night's coming on:
'The crows are flying home from school.'
We used to say that when I was a child.
Your daughter, Leyla, says it, too.
It's gotten dark.
I lit the lamp
and looked in the mirror.
A woman whose husband's in prison always looks
                                        in the mirror, always.

More than other women,
                    she fears getting old.
She wants the man she loves to like her still when he gets out,
no matter
              if it's thirty years later.
The woman in the mirror isn't old yet:
her hair is red,
              and her eyes
                        are now green,
                                  now honey-gold."

Halil folded Aysha's letter
and put it in his pocket.
And he went back to the letter he'd left in the middle:
"My only one,
of course your hair is red,
and yes, your eyes
                  are now green,
                            now honey-gold.
So you can see that?
Anyone could have seen it.
But I was the first
              to see their colors
                        because I was the first to put them in words.
And those words
are all I've written no one's said before
              in the world.

As you know,
I've given my life
   to what's most beautiful,
      most necessary,
        most certain.
But many others
   —more than you can count—
     have done the same before me,
       maybe with greater determination.

Yes, your hair is red,
and your eyes
   are now green,
       now honey-gold.
And something else you may not know:
your hands are amazing.

As you know,
people wear the stamp of their class
   on their hands.
The facts in this matter—
the role of the human hand, say, in social evolution—
       were discovered before me.
But I discovered
   the beauty of your hands,
     because I put it in writing first.

Yes, your hair is red,
and your eyes
   are now green,
       now honey-gold.
And your hands,
   you should know,
     are amazing.

My only one,
I thought we wouldn't talk about us two
     in this year 1941.
There's the world,
   our country,

                    hunger, death,
                                longing,
                                        hope and victory,
and here, along with and part
                    of the world and our country,
            are the two of us, with our separation and our love.

My only one,
first came the sounds
                    of ox carts
and then the carts, three in a row.
One was loaded with grapes.
They disappeared.
And for a long time
                    the road echoed after them.

The trainmen walked by:
they're the only ones who talk so loud.

The road is bright.
The radio played a song:
'No one comes, not a word.
            The days are long,
                    the roads far . . . '

Why?
But I
—but we—
know
        that word is sure to come now
                            very soon . . . "

PART TWO

I

On the recommendation of the forensic doctor
    Halil was sent to the hospital for his eyes.
The surgeon and chief of staff at the county hospital was Faik Bey
    (formerly a doctor for the police).
There were two other prisoners in the ward
    and two guardsmen.

The hospital stood in an open field outside the city.
Nothing grew much above the ground
    except a wild pear tree.
In the distance, some tall greens disappeared
    behind a mountain,
        a strange mountain
       they didn't climb
          but circled.

The building was single-story, concrete, square.
And like all concrete buildings of a certain vintage,
           the walls were cracked
             and wet in patches.
Wide stone steps led up to the door.
Faik Bey had told Halil:
"It's good these steps are so wide and comfortable.
For our peasants a hospital is the government, too,
    and at the government's door they have to squat against a wall;
    at least here they can sit on the stone steps."

It was Halil's fourth day at the hospital.
He and Dr. Faik Bey sat together
        on chairs
          on the landing.
Evening cast everything scarlet.
Against the plain stood Memet from Dumel,
        one side of his mouth

               toothless
                      from exactly the middle on,
          and his bleary blue eyes moist.
The autoclave hummed inside:
               Dumel's wife needs an operation.
The doctor and Dumel talked:
"Her intestine is blocked—
               we'll have to cut her belly."
"Will she die?"
"If we don't cut her belly, she'll die for sure;
if we cut her belly, she might make it."
"She's got two babies."
"We'll cut her belly."
"Will she make it?"
"She might, if we cut her belly."
"She's got two babies.
We left them with the neighbors and came.
If she dies . . . "
"If we don't cut her belly, she's sure to die."
"At night in the threshing field, you know,
and we didn't have any covers or anything.
And the babies were there, too.
In the threshing field, you know—
'Oy, mother!' she screams,
          grabs her belly,
          and starts writhing around.
Will she die?
Maybe if you wrote a medicine."
"Medicine won't help.
We'll cut her belly."
"You know best.
At night in the threshing field we were naked, you know.
Maybe if you gave her a yellow pill."
"There's no other way than to cut her belly."
"Will she make it?"
"If we don't cut her belly, she's sure to die."
"We left the babies with the neighbors and came.
The harvest is like we left it."
"Father, brother,
her intestine is blocked in her belly!"

"Won't it unblock?"
"Not by itself.
I'm going to open her belly
and free the intestine."
"With your hands?"
"With my hands.
Hear that sound?
They're boiling the instruments
all sparkling clean."
"Will she make it?"
"If we don't cut her belly, she'll die for sure."
"Maybe a yellow pill?"
"Can't be.
If you want, take your patient back.
Without your permission
        we can't open her belly.
You give your permission,
I'll use the knife.
That's the law.
You sign a paper."
"What paper?"
"Saying you give consent.
Walk around.
Think it over."
"Will she die?"
"We have to open her belly.
But she's your property.
That's what the law says."
"Will she make it?"
"If we cut her belly, she might make it;
if we don't cut her belly, she'll die for sure.
Sit under this pear tree.
Think it over.
Then come and put your seal on the paper."
"I don't have a seal."
"Use your thumb-print."

Dumel walked away.
Dr. Faik Bey asked Halil:
"Did you notice Dumel's mouth?

Typical case of pyorrhea.
On the right the teeth are fine, white.
The left side has all fallen out.
It's like half his mouth wasn't there."
"He has blue eyes."
"Yes, and a red beard.
Look, Halil Bey, look
          how he squats there.
An old, cornered jackal.
And it's like he's afraid
          to lean back on the tree.
He must come
          from the hinterlands, from the steppe.
The steppe leaves its mark on a man.
He doesn't like me at all.
I'm the enemy.
And he's desperate.
I'm the effendi in this big building,
the man who gives him grief out of sheer spite
          instead of giving him a yellow pill.
The county clerk and me—
          we're both the same.
He'll put his thumb on the paper,
not because he believes in it
          but because I ordered him to.
And now he isn't thinking about anything,
          except maybe the harvest.
He's done all he could,
          and if his wife dies, it's my fault.
Me,
the effendi of this big building.
He doesn't like me,
          I'm the enemy.
Did you see his wife?
She's like a piece of earth,
                              a handful.
Not from sickness—
          from *years*.
And she's pregnant,
          with two babies already.

Which means she's still cooking,
          she can still be gone to bed with.
I saw her birth certificate:
                              1903.
She could be a year old,
          she could be a thousand—
                    she hasn't *lived*.
For instance:
oh, I don't know,
she has no idea of the sea.
For instance:
she hasn't heard of stuffed eggplant.
And each time she's stared
with amazement
          as her husband wound his watch—
                              if he has one.
And for instance:
          she hasn't even dreamed
                    anyone could sleep
                              past dawn.
Don't look at me so warmly.
I'm not about to rot in prison.
I know
          we only live once.
And death doesn't unite—
                    it separates.
I die, she goes on living;
          she dies,
                    I go on living.
Nice and easy
          equality of life?
Could be.
But today life is a lottery:
          I win,
                    she loses.
What can you do?
But I know
outside of me,
independent of me,
          life with its masses of people

is changing, moving on.
I know.
But for now
      I'm satisfied with my ticket.
I've just fallen in your eyes.
You can't possibly forgive me.
And I don't want you to.
You don't like me,
      and neither does he squatting under the pear tree . . . "
Halil started to answer
      when the head nurse came up in a coy flutter.
She wore her cap with the red crescent like a bridal crown.
"We're ready, doctor," she said.

Halil was left alone.
But not for long.
One or two at a time, people filled the stone steps.
On the plain, dusk was a rainbow of colors.
The hospital clerk (a man about forty, interested
in books and pictures) sat down on the chair the doctor had left,
and pointed to the mountain in the distance:
"Mornings," he said,
      "and then again at this time
              in the evening,
the mountain takes on the color of lilacs.
It's a strange mountain.
The area is volcanic,
maybe certain minerals create this effect.
A mysterious light:
      something's there all right.
In the surrounding villages
      the trees are thick,
          and the animals tall,
             and the kids beautiful.
Later, the kids go bad.
If we could just spread that mountain around this country
              of cracked earth
                and gravel!

It's still fairly green in the town itself.
Here we're at the edge of the steppe.

Behind us,
  entering the hinterlands,
    Huseyinli, Chukuroren,
      Black Market, the county seat—
sixteen hours without seeing a single tree,
in dense light.
I've been in the desert.
The desert is something else.
This will seem strange to you,
  but its desolation is like a dark forest.
Jules Verne's novels
  have South American forests.
Do you remember?
Darkness
   forever slowly rises
      up from the ground
  to the tops of trees with fearsome names.
And for weeks the shipwrecked wander in that vegetating darkness.
It's exactly the same—
  the treeless steppe is just like that."

The nurse Ismet Hanum appeared.
She was from Istanbul.
Halil asked her:
"Has the operation started?"
"It's started."
"Was she easy to put under?"
"Very easy."

The Aksaray quarter was written all over
  Ismet Hanum's upturned sable eyebrows.
She tapped Huseyin on the shoulder as if knocking on a door:
"You're smoking again, dear."
Huseyin came from deep in the back country.
He'd been in the hospital two months.
Medically, he should have died long ago.
But he played death for a fool
  with his long, skinny chest and sly, peasant stubbornness.
"I lit one," he said.
"If you do that, Huseyin, you'll bleed again."

"Ismet Hanum, is tobacco to blame?
        The doctor smokes, too."
"But you're sick, dear."
"Okay,
        I'll just finish this and won't smoke again."
"You'll smoke again.
And didn't I tell you not to sit on stone?"
"I'm sitting on a step."
"The steps are stone."
"Okay.
        I won't sit again."
"You'll sit—it's useless."

Huseyin stayed seated on the steps
as Ismet Hanum pointed into the distance:
"Oh, look at that cloud over the fortress—
                    it's a sailboat.

How slowly
            it floats by!
Ah, Istanbul!
Don't you miss it, Halil Bey?"
"Sure, now and then."
Emin Effendi butted in:
"Gypsy Ismail brought a bee basket from Istanbul.
It's one of those modern baskets,
        but the bees wouldn't stick around—they took off."

Emin Effendi was a minor clerk,
but he probably had a mysterious
                    major illness.
Huseyin asked Halil:
"Airplanes drop men from the sky—
                    is it true, bey?"
"It's true."
Ismet Hanum sighed:
"God,
        let's hope we don't go to war!"
Huseyin mumbled to himself:
"That beats all—
        from the sky, huh?"

Emin Effendi broke in:
"Like my bees.
Bees will travel an hour for a flower,
mothers and sons separate.
If they're caught in the rain on the way,
  they duck into the branches of an oak."
The hospital clerk—curious at first,
    then mocking—asked:
"And if there isn't an oak, Emin Effendi?"
"There'll be a poplar."
"Suppose there's no poplar, Emin Effendi?"
"Well, any tree, then."
"And no trees at all?"
Emin Effendi stared at the clerk, round-eyed like a child:
"How can that be?"
Huseyin sided with the clerk:
"The clerk effendi is right.
    Why not?
Where I come from, there are no trees.
When it rains, the bees
  dive into the weeds."
Halil asked Emin Effendi:
"Didn't you ever go outside the town?"
"I did—
  I went as far as the groves.
I'm single,
my mother died a year back.
My bees get around for me."
"Army?"
"Exempt."
"And how about traveling,
  seeing the world some?"
Emin Effendi stuck his thick lips out
    under his bushy mustache
     as if spitting:
"Travel for what,
what's there to see?
A man needs water and bread,
  plus a bed.
   And if he's got some bees . . . "

Huseyin interrupted Emin Effendi in a hoarse voice.
"I wish I'd traveled, bey," he said to Halil.
"Where I come from is nothing but gravel.
No trees, no mountains.
Of twenty households, eighteen are only people.
In anything, what counts is brains.
If I had some brains in me!
I've been a sharecropper eight years
       and I still can't buy a goat.
If I had any brains . . . "
"What would you do?"
"What do you mean, what would I do, bey?
I'd give up on the land and move to a city.
You know the best—
cities
       a man could wander for a month
       and never reach the end.
I planned to go to Istanbul
and check out life there.
Isn't Istanbul the best in Turkey, bey?
It wasn't in the cards.
Had this trouble inside me . . .
It just keeps eating at me."
"Don't worry, you'll get well."
"God willing."

"I'm here, aghas."
Those on the stone steps took in the newcomer.
He swayed back and forth.
His beard had swallowed up his face to just below his eyes,
except for a point of white skin right in the middle.
He was like a hairy bug, and a mess.
"You're late, Vasfi," Ismet Hanum said.
       "The wound-dresser is in the operating room."
Emin Effendi said proudly:
"How many times have I told you?
A man should be on time, like bees."
Vasfi sat down on the bottom step.
"I'll wait," he said.
Ismet Hanum twitched her sable eyebrows:

"It's up to you,
        but the wound-dresser will be tired after the operation.
        If he says he can't do it, don't blame me, dear."
Emin Effendi seconded her:
"Sure, he may not do it.
        He works for a living—
                he's only human."
Vasfi grumbled:
"And me?
Aren't I a human being?
Just because I'm a drunk, a gambler . . .
My wound can't take the heat, it gets maggots . . . "
Emin Effendi laughed, suddenly rich and happy:
"You need my bees, too.
If you mash tobacco in honey
        and put it on a wound . . . "
Ismet Hanum scolded him:
"What kind of talk is that, Emin Effendi?
You just wait for the wound-dresser, Vasfi."
"I'll wait.
I've lived with this pain a year.
It's them wound-dressers.
Shouldn't a hernia close up in two days?
        Mine didn't.
I became a drunk, a gambler.
They took out my hernia in Ankara.
There was this wound-dresser
                        like a water buffalo,
                                        jetblack.
The doctor turned me over to him after the operation.
The s.o.b. had a thing for fresh wounds,
        the guy lived on fresh wounds.
He undid the bandages after only two hours.
Such blood gushed out, brothers—
        the bed, the sheets, a red river.
The stitches popped.
I holler and swear
        and the s.o.b. just laughs.
'I'll tell the doctor in the morning,' I say.
'Fat chance you'll see the doctor again,' he says,

                              'you're in my hands now.'
'The patients are witnesses,' I say.
Not a peep out of the patients.
'Patients!' I say.
The patients keep silent.
All the patients are asleep.
And the building is so big,
        if you fired a cannon at one end
                        they wouldn't hear it at the other.
I was scared, friends.
I shook like a mutt in the dead of winter.
The s.o.b. wrapped up the wound and left:
        out in the hall he couldn't stop laughing.
I waited till he was gone.
It got halfway light out,
and I slipped out of the hospital in my underwear.
My clothes are still there.
I reached the inn.
And they took me to the village.
They said I'd be in trouble with the law
        but thankfully no one came after me.
But once the wound changed its mind,
        it wouldn't close, it got maggots.
A man can't just laze around in the village.
So I went back to the city:
        this wound made me a drunk, a gambler.
I became a drunk, a gambler."

For some time it was quiet.
The hospital clerk asked Halil:
"So you're writing a new book?"
"I'm working on it."
"May I ask what it's called?"
"'Social Stratification in Anatolia
Between 1908 and 1939.'"

Ismet Hanum suddenly cried out:
"Ooh! . . .
        Look at the moon!
'The moon I see,

Allah I believe.'"
The clerk teased her:
"You're a real Muslim, nurse."
"I just remembered when I was a kid, dear.
                It's good luck to spot the moon
                                before dark.
I've tested it lots of times.
[She turned to Halil.]
I like twilight
                far from the city like this
                                out in the open fields.
Oh, look at the fireflies!
Where are they going, sparkling like that?
You're quiet, Halil Bey."
Halil asked as if waking from sleep:
"Think she'll make it?"
"Who?"
"The woman they're operating on."
"The doctor has a light touch.
My God,
        how lovely the world is!
Out there it reminds me of Istanbul
                                when the houses disappear
                                        and the lights come on."

One of Halil's guards, Corporal Refik, came up.
He reported like a child bearing good news:
"I watched inside through the glass door.
They laid the woman on white sheets.
At first it's scary,
        then curiosity takes over.
[He grabbed Halil's arm.]
Come and look if you want, bey."
"I don't want to, corporal."
"But it's worth seeing."
"It's been half an hour."
"And more."

Huseyin called out:
"Someone's there in the dark—

who's out there?"
"It's me, effendi agha."

Ismet Hanum recognized him:
"Oh, dear, it's the husband of the woman in surgery.
What do you want?"
"Nothing."
"You were going to say something?"
Halil called to Memet from Dumel:
"Come on over.
The operation isn't finished yet."
"It will be, effendi agha, God willing."

Corporal Refik explained as if drilling soldiers:
"I watched, brothers.
         It's no human hand in there—
                  the doctor's hands are bird wings,
                           they flutter this way and that.
The man couldn't work harder for his own mother."

Halil showed a place to Memet from Dumel:
"Why don't you sit down?"
"I'll just stand.
Will it be over soon?"
"It'll be a little longer."
"So it won't be over soon?"
"Can't tell.
         But it's more than half over."
"I'll go into town and get some apples."
Ismet Hanum laughed, shaking her round shoulders:
"Bless you!
         Is this any time to think of apples, dear?"
"I'll be right back.
She likes apples."
"She may like them, but she can't eat them *now*."
"She can eat them later.
I'll be right back.
Apples are good.
Will it last another quarter hour?"
"Yes."

"I'll be right back.
She likes apples."

And Memet from Dumel hunched up his shoulders
                          and disappeared into the dark.

Huseyin spoke as if giving good news:
"I'm hungry."
The hospital clerk leaned over to Halil:
"Hunger," he said,
          "hunger is not eating nothing.
It's eating grits
                  till your intestine blocks.
Imagine:
the village under knee-deep snow,
we went into this house.
No one around.
We went out to the barn:
          there they all were, buried in manure.
The ones in your prisons are still the healthiest—
                                        rations,
                                            sleep."

Halil thought:
"Freedom doesn't give rations or sleep."

They called from inside:
"Dinner!"

Emin Effendi and Huseyin scrambled to their feet.
Vasfi, who'd come for the wound-dresser, begged Ismet Hanum:
"Be good and save me some food."
"Do you have bread?"
"Not hardly."
"I'll see if anything is left.
And I know you come late
          so you can beg food.
Come at noon,
          and I'll gladly give you something for lunch."
Vasfi smiled shyly:

312

"At noon you're too crowded—
                    everybody's rushed."

Ismet Hanum asked Halil:
"Aren't you going to dinner, dear?"
"I'll eat later."

Ismet Hanum and the clerk left.
Vasfi and Halil remained on the stone steps.

After the sun sets,
         just like open seas, high mountains, and deep forests,
                              the steppe cools off fast.
And at this hour in such places, the idle person—
                    if he's not feeling well
                         and especially if he's one of the enlightened—
withdraws into himself, like an animal in its shell.
A variety of this experience came over Halil:
he buttoned his jacket,
hunched up his shoulders, and fixed his eyes
on the distant city lights, lost in thought.
"I should send word to the prison tomorrow,"
                              he thought,
               "there's probably a letter from Aysha.
It's strange
how the light out there flickers on and off.
Why?
They must be carrying a lamp from room to room.
Where did I read it—
a black-haired woman in a white dress
     sends signals this way.
Will the woman make it?
To touch living, human intestines
               even with gloves on.
Hunger
is not eating nothing . . .
The village under knee-deep snow,
there they all were, buried in manure.
India, the Congo, China.
     Natives in colonies.

The light went out again
                    and came back on.
Why?
They must be carrying a lamp . . .
I should send word to the prison tomorrow.
There's probably a letter from Aysha.
I love Aysha so much.
Lately she doesn't write 'my sweet' in her letters—
                              why not?
How plump and white her neck is!
Will my daughter look like her mother?
If I go blind, my daughter will grow up in the dark—
                         darkness for me.
I won't see how she changes."
"Effendi!"
"You calling me, Vasfi?"
"If you've got a cigarette . . . "
"Just tobacco.
Have any paper?"
"No, but I'll take the tobacco anyway."

Halil gave Vasfi the tobacco
              and suddenly felt angry:
"Why won't his wound heal?" he thought.
          "Has he got diabetes?
How come they don't all die wholesale?
What diehards my people are!
The ones in prisons are the healthiest.
The right to life,
            to life."

"They took out my hernia in half an hour—
                    isn't this over yet?"
"Almost."
"God willing."
"The light there came on again," Halil thought.
"Should send word to the prison tomorrow.
Still, our prisoners are better off than they are in Europe,
          and if you have a visitor once a month . . .
I wish I could see Aysha.

It's more than half over.
I haven't told them yet—
                    it'll be a happy surprise."

Ismet Hanum took Vasfi food.
"The operation is over, Halil Bey," she said,
                    "we put the woman in her bed.
The doctor asked about you—he's on his way.
He likes you a lot, dear.
Of course, we all do . . .
You take your food and go in the back, Vasfi.
Don't expect anything from the wound-dresser tonight . . ."

Halil greeted the doctor:
"Nice going, Faik Bey.
Is she in the clear?"
"Too early to tell.
The surgery went fine.
But in a case like this, the danger is afterwards."
"What are her chances?"
"Thirty percent.
Where's her husband?"
"He went into town for apples."
"He was too hasty."
"We told him, but he wouldn't listen.
You're tired."
"Not too."
"So it's thirty percent?"
"About that.
          Less even."

They fell silent.
Everything looked bright as day under the moon.
The city across, with lights burning here and there,
the crackle of insects filling the air,
and the earth saying, "I'm right here":
the steppe was at peace.

The doctor flicked his cigarette away:
it glowed on the ground like a phosphorescent bug.

Halil tapped his pipe against his knee and emptied the ashes.
Suddenly the doctor asked:
"Have you ever seriously thought about dying?
     I mean, have you thought about it long and hard
as if thinking through a math problem?
That's all I think about these last few years.
At night I get into bed,
close my eyes,
     and whistle a tune through my teeth
        —always something I've made up,
       something very sad—
       and I think about death.
I'm overcome with the sorrow and loneliness
     of someone thinking about his death
         without love or hate.
My ties to people break,
     and I find myself alone with death.
Then I calculate:
     I'm forty-eight,
     I could live to seventy-five at most,
       which leaves me twenty-seven more.
I measure the remaining twenty-seven against the past forty-eight:
         it's a crime.
Strange, isn't it?
     Twenty-seven at most,
       and then, once upon a time there was Dr. Faik Bey."

He was quiet.
Then, as if begging for help, he asked Halil:
"How old are you?"
"Thirty-nine, I think."
"What do you mean, 'I think'?"
"My birth certificate says thirty-nine.
But my mother always said they had me written up a year older."
For some reason, Faik Bey all but snapped at Halil:
"Forget your mother—
     call it thirty-nine."
Halil laughed:
"You could even say forty."
"No,

no need to be generous:
                    a year is a year.
Well, have you calculated?"
"What?"
"What's left?"
"No."
"You've got to calculate.
You have thirty-six left.
Nine more than me.
You're old enough to make this calculation:
        more than half your life has slipped through your fingers.
You can compare what's gone with what remains.
Before thirty, years and even death are just abstractions.
                    Then they become facts.
And you're taken aback
                how soon so little time remains.
Haven't you ever been amazed by this?"
"No.
But I understand you."
"What do you understand?"
"You have the time and chance to think a lot."
"Don't you?"
"Sure, I have that privilege, too."
"What do you mean 'privilege'?"
"'Privilege' means this, Faik Bey:
        the woman you just operated on,
        who you yourself said
hasn't even dreamed of sleeping past dawn,
who's condemned to a half-animal, half-vegetable existence,
                    this Dumel's wife
                    and Dumel himself
and most of the people in our country and on earth
don't have the satisfaction of thinking a lot.
They don't have the time or chance.
They work so hard and get so tired
        that when they fall into bed at night—even at sixty—
                sleep descends on them like lead.
You might dream in sleep, but you can't think."
He was quiet.
Then Halil added with a smile:

"And when they think,
they think of life,
                not death . . . "
"Okay, say they had the time and chance
                                to think of death."
"Even then, they wouldn't think about it like you do."
"Why?"
"This is why, Faik Bey:
because you are alone in life,
        you are alone in death.
If you'd stayed a doctor for the police
        and kept your ties,
if you hadn't cut the strings between you and your class,
or if you'd gone over to the other side
        after this operation
                and become attached to other people with other ties,
then this chronic disease that now grows unchecked
                would flare up but rarely . . . "

Faik Bey laughed out loud:
"You sound like a doctor," he said,
"but look, rarely or not, it would still flare up."
"Yes, it would flare up, Faik Bey.
        A tree bends only when it's green,
                and it's not that easy to change headquarters:
                we carry inside us something from the cradle.
And then . . . "

Memet from Dumel appeared under the pear tree.
Halil saw him
and jumped up, happy.
"He's back," he said, "here he is . . . "
They greeted Dumel.
And in the yellow light of the door and window,
        they stood without speaking,
                on their feet like three trees.
Dumel held a big paper bag in his arms.
He seemed scared he'd drop it.
He clearly wasn't used to paper bags.
He looked at the doctor

318

as if to say, "No good can come from you,
                 but go ahead and tell me anyway,"
      with tears in his eyes.
"Good news, brother," Halil said, "it's over."
Dumel dropped the paper bag.
The apples scattered on the ground with childlike joy.
With Halil's help, Dumel collected the apples,
                 put them back in the paper bag,
                 and set them down on the stone steps.
Then he took two apples,
         rubbed them on his shirtsleeve,
                 and offered them to Halil and the doctor.
His half-toothless mouth was smiling,
                 his bleary blue eyes still crying.
After some pushing and pulling back on both sides,
                         he kissed the doctor's hand.
He went for Halil's hands,
but Halil was faster—they hugged.
Still holding Halil,
         Dumel quickened with a new joy and listened:
the sound of ox carts
         starting from the left end of town.
Cutting like a stone axe
         and rising with slow sparks under the moon,
                 it was the savage song
                 of the unyielding steppe.

Halil heard it, too.
And the darkness of men defeated by the earth
                 and the sadness of his beloved country
passed over him with a shiver.

"Our people," said Memet from Dumel,
I'll go meet them:
they left when I did just a while back.
We'll put her on a cart, she won't get tired.
[He turned to the doctor.]
Effendi agha, you tell her to get ready."
And he started to run toward the sound of the ox carts.
The doctor grabbed his arm.

"Wait," he said, "she isn't even awake."
"She'll be awake when I get back."
"She may wake up, but she can't travel."
"She'll ride on a cart—
at most she'll walk from here to there . . . "
"Can't be."
"Don't do it, effendi agha,
    she's got two babies.
We left them with the neighbors and came.
The harvest is like we left it."
"Can't be, father."
"Okay, so she won't walk—
    we'll bring the cart right up here."
"She can't get out of bed.
She has to lie on her back at least fifteen days."
"She'll lie at home."
"Can't be."
"She's got two babies."
"Don't drive me insane—I said no."
"I'll put my thumb on the paper."
"What for?"
"Didn't you say she's my property?
I'll put my thumb on it that I took my property back in one piece."
"Can't be."
"A seal?"
"I thought you didn't have a seal."
"Don't play with me:
    I'll do whatever you want.
        Give the kids' mother so we can go—
            the harvest is like we left it.
[And Dumel turned to Halil.]
Effendi, you tell him . . . "

Halil fought back tears.
"Let's go inside," he said, "and check your patient.
See if she's in any shape to move."

Internal medicine, surgery, contagious diseases, maternity,
                        women, men, children:
        the county hospital had fifty-nine beds,

but the patients numbered seventy-two.
The overflow lay on the floor,
                and some beds held two patients . . .
Dumel saw his wife.
She wasn't awake.
Shaved head,
swollen face like a potato.
She could have been a sickly little boy.
And her hands lay on the white cambric sheet
        like two roots shot out of the ground.

Dumel put the apples at the foot of the bed.
He stared long and hard,
        squinting his bleary blue eyes.
"Nothing left in her now," he said, "she's gone bad.
My piebald ox got this way a year back:
        he laid down and never got up.
Give her these, she can eat them.
She likes apples.
God bless you, effendi agha . . . "

And Dumel walked out, crying.
That was that—
                they never saw him again.
And three days later the woman died . . .

II

Early in the morning,
        day just breaking above the hospital,
Dr. Faik Bey suddenly woke up.
(Single, he slept at the hospital.)
The room was still half dark.
But outside the wide, bare window,
                light like cold water
                took pity.
"What time is it?" thought Faik Bey.
He reached toward the table to see

but couldn't make it out.
He switched on the lamp,
his room as sad as train stations at dawn—
                    all fading lights
                        and absence.
Faik Bey lay on his back, naked.
(Summer and winter he slept without clothes.)
He forgot to check the clock.
He stared at the ceiling
and counted the beams.
He studied the wall opposite:
a bedbug
made its tiny way across the vast, chalky whiteness
                    like someone lost in the endless
                        snows of the pole, alone
                            as a star in space . . .

"Alone as a star in space,"
        Faik Bey repeated out loud.
And he lowered his head, chin on his chest:
before his eyes he saw
        his headless, naked body stretched out
            to the ends of his toenails.
He saw it as if for the first time.
And he did see it in this light for the first time,
                    surprised
                        curious
                            and sad:
belly dark and sunken,
        long, thin, flabby legs,
aged skin.
He felt his belly:
jelly-soft disgust.
He flexed his right leg:
the calf sagged.
On the heel, wrinkles creasing the anklebone.
And the loneliness of that headless old body.

Faced with his body,
        Faik Bey thought of its death.

What came to mind first
                    wasn't being washed or wound in a shroud
                            but an image of it in the morgue.
Laid out naked this way on the stone slab.
Then descending into a hole,
then the smell of moist earth,
the worms starting to bore through the wood coffin
(he couldn't bear to think of them crawling over his body),
then the worst:
            unhearing
                    unseeing
                            unmoving loneliness . . .
Faik Bey pressed the bell
                    again
                            and again.
Then he quickly gathered himself up against the pillow,
                    shrank into a ball,
                            pulled the sheet over his knees,
                                    and waited.

The door opened.
Ismet Hanum, the Istanbul nurse, rushed in, all in a flutter.
Maybe Faik Bey was expecting her,
        maybe he wasn't expecting anyone.
He grabbed the young woman's wrists:
"Don't be afraid, don't scream, shh—
        for God's sake, save me!" he said.
Startled at first, Ismet Hanum struggled,
but before long,
with "Oh, doctor, they'll see, they'll hear, the door's open,"
                            and so on,
                    she switched off the lamp
                    and didn't make another sound.

Outside the wide window,
                light like cold water
                took pity . . .

Early in the morning,
        day just breaking above the hospital,

Halil suddenly woke up
        and got out of bed.
He called to the dozing guardsman on duty:
"I'll be outside
        by the stone steps."

He went into the hall:
the smell of sleep and medicine,
moans that sounded fake,
a far-off metallic tinkle,
and fading lights,
        the sadness of train stations at dawn,
                        absence . . .

The door of the women's ward was open.
A patient sat
                in bed, combing her hair,
her face pale,
hair jetblack.

Halil descended the stone steps
and stood on the earth.
He stretched his arms, breathing deep:
the air muggy,
the sun rising,
the sky squeaky-clean as if wiped with a damp cloth.
A faint haze at the base of the mountain
                        dissolving like gossamer.
Ahead, the trees brightening,
        sun hitting their left side.
And off in the distance the city,
as if back in port after a long voyage.
The landscape is pure light, all pastels,
and at this hour
        nature is healthy, young,
                and kind.

"Is the doctor awake, effendi agha?"
Halil turned to the boy.
The thirteen-year-old worker Kerim

—the heart of my heart!—
        stood there in his coal-blackened overalls
    like an imp sprung up from the ground.
Halil was happy, as if he'd met an old friend when least expected:
"How about saying hello first, young man?"
Kerim smiled:
"Hello, mister."
"Hello—what's your name?"
"Kerim."
"What's your business with the doctor, Master Kerim?"
Kerim's little red-nosed face frowned:
"I'm far from a master worker," he said.
"Why?"
Kerim took his right hand out of his pocket:
his thumb was wrapped in a thick bandage.
Halil gasped:
"What happened?"
"The press crushed it last night."
And suddenly, as if feeling the pain all over again,
        he groaned, tears filling his eyes:
"Oy, mother,
    it hurts."
"Well, what have you done for it since last night?"
"Nothing.
Master Ahmet wrapped it in a rag,
and we changed it at home.
Mother said to go to the hospital and show it to the doctor.
I came early so I wouldn't miss work today."

Halil and Kerim went inside
and found the head nurse.
They had the wound dressed.
Halil offered Kerim tea:
they got better acquainted.
They agreed to be friends,
        and Kerim left.

Although it was time,
    the morning rounds hadn't begun.
Halil met the nurse Ismet Hanum in the hall.

The young woman's dark eyebrows were all mussed up
                    (usually they looked brushed),
and she carried a tray of empty soup bowls.
Halil asked:
"Have you seen the doctor?"
Ismet Hanum stopped.
Her face flushed beet-red.
"The chief of staff, Faik Bey?
No, I haven't seen him.
But—well . . .
Toward morning
                he rang.
I was on duty.
He wanted water.
I took him some.
I haven't seen him since . . .
Why do you ask?
He must be in the wards.
But the head nurse just said we're running late.
What time is it?"
Over the empty soup bowls Ismet Hanum
        regarded Halil with increasing suspicion.
And like all liars, she jumped around,
                        saying too much
                        too fast.

Halil didn't notice she was flustered.
"Thank you," he said,
        and went back to his ward
            and sat on the bed.
He leaned forward.
As his face grew thoughtful, his nose looked thinner and longer.
His glasses flashed—
two helpless pieces of glass.
His arms hung at his sides.
And his hands, palms up, rested on his knees.
Halil now knew the nature of his disease:
atrophying blood vessels of the eyes.
For years building up slowly, little by little,
        and one day, one instant, in a single leap: blindness.

Here, too, the dialectic,
               Halil,
                    always the dialectic.
But maybe . . . ?
A new discovery in treatment?
A leap toward recovery?
And not lose the light before death . . .

Halil forgot his eye disease from time to time,
               and from time to time he remembered:
then it would be as if a tiny blood vessel had burst
               under his skin somewhere,
                    and his heart would race,
leaving him breathless.
Then, peace.
Then, absence.
Halil would drift off, and it would be like walking through a door
                    into the courtyard of an old Istanbul house
with its snow-white muslin, well, and bright tin cup:
                         quiet
                              cool
with a little something of sad old stories in the dappled light . . .

The patients in the ward had all gathered around two beds.
In the first bed, Arab Ali
               knelt as if praying.
Orange bandanna draped over his left knee,
eyes and mustache gleaming jetblack,
and the wrinkled scar of an Antep boil on his cheek,
Ali told his dream,
               and the others listened respectfully.
Their respect is not for the dreamer
                         but for his dream:
"May it augur well."
"If you deem it's good, it will be."
"I saw a stretch of land
               watered just so.
I was plowing with bay horses.
They no longer plowed with oxen in the village.
A gun went off behind me."

Someone broke in to ask:
"Did you hear it go off?"
"No."
"Good—it's good you didn't, very good."
"But wait,
          maybe I did."
"No harm done—
          it's okay if you heard it, too,
                    as long as the field was watered
                    and big besides . . . "

At the second bed they passed around a photo magazine
Halil had given them last night.
There were war pictures: people, machines, fires.
"Hey, look—look at the Mehmets!"
"Those aren't Mehmets, they're English soldiers."
"Whatever—they're all Mehmets."
"And are these Italian?"
"You can tell by their hats—Italian."
"The Italians
          aren't fighters,
                    they're refined people."
Rejep butted in out of the blue:
"When you go to war, if you kill a heathen
                    and drink one mouthful of his blood,
                              you won't fear anything ever again."
They all stared at Rejep.
He was fifteen or sixteen.
A butterball.
He would mock everyone,
          and when he was cornered he'd drop his eyes
                              and smile coyly.
He liked to read.
He knew by heart
all the townships and counties in all the provinces.
"Now where'd you hear that, punk?"
"I heard it from my father who died in the war:
he was killed in action
                    when I was six months."
Sergeant Talip from Aydin whacked Rejep on the head

with the magazine:
"Go to the Devil, Rejep."

Sergeant Talip had thin blond hair and green eyes.
His face looked cast in wax.
He would speak very softly,
suddenly get mad
and sulk at you for days.
He was friends with Rejep.
Rejep called the sergeant "Mother."

Corporal Refik broke in:
"'You'll be finished in six months,'
                    the Germans told the Russians—
                        we read it in the magazine."
The tinsmith Muslim from Cherkesh answered
(his face as if hewn with an axe):
"Father Russia won't fall so easy..."
"I hear it's rotten to the core..."
"Don't listen to that.
Have you been to Kayseri?
Those guys built us a textile factory there—
                    nothing like it in the world.
The governor's mansion
        was nothing next to their workers' lodgings."

Sergeant Talip said softly:
"Now the English are with the Russians."
Corporal Refik objected:
"They say the English are buying time."

The magazine had reached Rejep.
On the last page
he stared at the bare white legs
        of girls entertaining English soldiers in the desert,
        and his squinting eyes in his round face
                had no mockery in them.

Excited voices filled the hall.
The patients dispersed, ready for the morning rounds.

Halil came to himself.
The door flew open:
Ismet Hanum from Istanbul stood on the threshold.
"Halil Bey," she said,
            "the doctor is dead."
Nothing had changed about Ismet Hanum's face
                                    or her voice.
And even her eyebrows were no longer mussed up:
            they looked like brushed sable again.
"Dr. Faik Bey is dead,"
                    she repeated.
She pulled the door shut and was gone.
The patients were stunned.
A doctor's death
        —especially a chief of staff's—
                    was unthinkable to them.
And with one blow it dashed their hopes of health.
Arab Ali murmured:
"God have mercy on him—
may God give his family strength."
Sergeant Talip said softly:
"They say he had no one at all.
He was alone in the world . . . "

And as suddenly as the ward had been shocked stock-still,
it just as suddenly snapped into motion:
                the patients burst into the hall.

Halil met the hospital clerk,
who grabbed his hands:
"Suicide," he said, "suicide . . .
He poisoned himself.
We found him in his bed, stark-naked.
When he was so late, we wondered.
His door was locked.
I have a duplicate key.
The assistant and I opened it together.
Oh, don't ask . . . "

Halil pulled his hands free.

His voice cracking,
and without knowing why himself,
                              he asked:
"He was forty-eight, wasn't he?"
And making like wiping his glasses
                              to cover his eyes,
he walked away
and down the stone steps into the sun.
The plain was bright and lukewarm . . .

Suddenly Faik Bey's death seemed like a lie to Halil,
especially his suicide—
                    and by poison!
(Yet a minute ago Halil had explained it all in his head.)
He went back inside
and, for reasons unknown even to himself,
hurried down the hall toward Faik Bey's room.
The door opened.
They carried the body out on a stretcher.
It was covered with a white sheet.
Halil squeezed against the wall to make room.
They passed:
Dr. Faik Bey's body first,
then the clerk
        followed by the public prosecutor, hands in his pockets.
The patients had flocked to the doors,
and they regarded the doctor's stretcher
                              with curiosity,
                    not the usual anxiety and dread.
Faik Bey's body was taken to the morgue.
The ward doors closed.
And for some time Halil stood before
                    the empty
                         silent
                              length of the hall.

He heard a woman scream right in his ear.
Startled, Halil turned to look.
The door of the operating room stood ajar,
and the frosted glass was lit up from inside

with a light like a blind, all-white eye
        or pure, disembodied mind.
Halil went up to the door.
And thinking he was somehow doing wrong,
ashamed to be looking where he shouldn't,
                                he peered inside.
There, in the same bloodless, cold, unfeeling light
        he'd just seen on the frosted glass,
a woman lay capsized on her back on the delivery table,
        surrounded by sparkling instruments.
Her legs were spread wide,
and between the white cloths covering her groin
the place of copulation looked like a huge, naked, awesome flower.
The woman shuddered, groaning.
Ismet Hanum held her wrists;
the head nurse assisted the internist.
"Instead of Faik Bey," Halil thought.
        "But what does an internist know about this?
                Just so he doesn't mess up . . . "
The woman shook and screamed again.
Her head rolled to the left.
Halil recognized her
as the woman combing her black hair in bed this morning.
Her belly tightened and swelled with the pains,
her genitals protruded,
        and some half-bloody stuff oozed out.
"Like all mammals," Halil thought,
                "like cows, cats, dogs.
Like the universe," Halil thought,
                "like life-bearing trees, stars, societies."

The center of the naked, awesome flower
                opened in the shape of an egg.
Something dark appeared in its depths—
the soft wet hair of the child on the way.
And with each push the mouth of the passageway opened wider.
Then, at last, darkness the size of a baby's head.
With a gauze tampon the doctor's rubber-gloved hand
pressed the woman's anus.
And suddenly Halil felt very embarrassed:

"So Aysha gave birth like this, too?"

he thought.

The baby's head emerged.
The doctor turned the baby's face
            toward the inside of the mother's right thigh.
Then he eased out the left shoulder, then the right,
and then the arms, body, legs:
the doctor held the baby in his hands.
And it was tied to its mother from its navel.
The doctor grasped the cord with the forceps
                        and cut it with the scissors.
And at that instant Halil heard
            the most beautiful sound in the world—
                the first victory cry of the newborn.
And with his heart full of joy,
        he softly closed the door.

BOOK FOUR

and all manner of chimneys . . .
But soon the city was left behind
           like a fallen nestling.
Heavy wings barely moving,
beaks pointed straight ahead, necks taut,
needle-thin legs sticking out behind,
               the storks headed south,
more floating in the air than flying.
That evening they entered the province of Ankara
and spent the night in the fields outside Chandir,
        standing balanced on one leg,
               beaks thrust under wings . . .
And at dawn they took off.
The journey south lasted days.
They got out of Ankara fast,
but the province of Konya was endless:
flat sky above,
        flat earth below.
Mountains appeared at last,
not hills but real mountains
with snow and forests.
They crossed a lake and a river.

Then they reached the province of X,
the air warming up by the hour.
Then one Wednesday afternoon
        —way off in the distance,
               fused with the sky,
clear, and serene,
        like a long-drawn-out flash—
               the Mediterranean.
The storks clacked their beaks in glee
and stopped overnight in the harvested rice paddies.
The next day they spread out
               in flocks and pairs.
Only the leader flew alone
               toward the provincial capital.
Fields passed below
        and turned into groves:
        oranges, lemons, and tangerines

                    (still green).
The sea sped closer, widening and vast.
And now the stork flew over the city:
tree-lined boulevards, roofs, and chimneys.
The city stood on a bluff above the water.
Far out in the harbor, a single ship lay anchored.
The hot salt air
                smelled of bananas.
The stork circled the city,
then veered left,
flexed its wings,
let go,
        and glided down.
Up on a chimney,
its old nest swayed closer.
The stork swerved to the right
        to miss the wires on the adjacent roof
                (radio antennas,
                        over twenty),
but couldn't clear its left wing:
it spun around, thrashing, and collapsed on the roof,
        tangled in broken wires
        just twenty meters from its nest . . .

Suddenly a strange static
        silenced the voice of America.
Jevdet Bey didn't panic.
He put on his glasses
to check it out:
no sound on any station.
He went over to a second set,
        a 1940 RCA:
nothing there, either.
He tried the third set,
a six-tube Telefunken:
silence.
The fourth set: the same thing.
Strange.
Jevdet Bey chewed on his long white mustache.
He stepped back

and sat down in the only chair, at the exact center of the room.
Eyes narrowed, he studied the sets:
going back to when radios first came on the world market
(from those with earphones to those with gramophones),
the most famous models of every make
stood lined up by year and number of tubes.
Jevdet Bey slapped his bald head,
and his white mustache popped out of his mouth:
"Eureka!" he cried.

He rushed from the room—
hallway, steps, attic, roof, antennas.
He repaired the antennas.
And rushing back—
roof, attic, steps, hallway—
Jevdet Bey returned to the radio room with a huge stork.
The bird had a broken leg.
He bandaged it.
Then he clipped the wings
     so the bird wouldn't try to fly
       (it wasn't easy—bird and man both struggled).
Then he took some meat from the refrigerator
     and offered it to the bird.
The bird ate
     and limped off to a corner.
And it stared at Jevdet Bey in amazement.
"I hope you enjoyed the meal, Haji Baba," said Jevdet Bey.
"We'll be bosom buddies from this day forward.
I'll reserve the adjoining room for you.
      Just make yourself at home there.
Of course, my whole house is yours to enjoy.
But you're not allowed in here without me
        because, God forbid, you might break my toys.
Feel free to use the yard during the day.
After all, you're a stork:
      you might get bored listening to radios all day.
They're all I had in the world,
      but now I have you, too.
And now I'm all you have—
      plus my radios.

Just as there are
        heroin junkies,
                cocaine junkies,
                        nicotine junkies,
                                power junkies, and so on,
I'm a fifty-five-year-old radio junkie.
I mean,
        I suffer from radiomania.
I listen to the voices of people
calling me from the four corners of the world.
We have a distant relationship:
I could care less what they do,
I'm just curious how they tell about it.
And I must admit I like their songs, too—
all the world's songs,
                in any language or style.
But have you noticed?
These days they sing
        even as they're at one another's throat again.
And when they tell how they fight,
you'd think they were singing love songs.
Now, with your permission,
                we'll turn to Berlin.
You don't know German, do you?
I'll translate.
It won't do you much good,
but I can practice translating out loud."
Jevdet Bey had always known French and Arabic,
but he'd taught himself German, English, Russian, and Italian
after he caught radiomania.

Jevdet Bey tuned in Berlin
                and translated:
"The Ukraine capital of Kiev has been taken.
665,000 prisoners . . .
Tanks, artillery . . .
Okay.
Cut.
I already heard that last night.
So nothing new has come in from Berlin.

Let's try London.
The number killed in last month's air raids.
I've heard that, too.
While in London, let's find you a jazz band
                    just a few frequencies away.
Here you go . . . "

The noise of the jazz band filled the room, scaring the stork.
The bird flapped its clipped wings
and tried to run away
but couldn't with its bad leg.
Jevdet Bey laughed:
"So jazz doesn't do it for you, Haji Baba?
Then let's go to Spain, to Barcelona.
Barcelona, Spain . . .
How and why
        did Dolores Ibarruri La Pasionaria fall silent?
The woman had a voice like sunlight.
I still search the Spanish stations for a voice like hers—
                            deep
                                luminous
                                    warm . . .
I don't know Spanish,
        but she could ream you out and you'd love listening . . . "

And Jevdet Bey turned hopelessly to Barcelona.

II

The Mediterranean coast of my Anatolia
                    has such lovely cities:
small,
sunny as oranges,
shimmering like fish,
and colorful like bitter oleanders.

The city of X has a population of 45,000:
Cretans, Arabs, and native Turks.

The houses are mostly wood
             (the finest those left by the Greeks),
       the new ones are concrete, modern,
and all are set in gardens glittering with running brooks.
And it has two parks, two outdoor cafés,
a "City Club" and an "Army Lodge"
             (an infantry regiment is based in the city).
One moviehouse, two hospitals
             (county and military).
A Village Institute, a high school,
and a Home Arts Center for Girls.
Electricity.
Mills: 4 rice, 3 flour, 2 sesame.
Locker plants: 2.
Markets: 2
             (one farmers', one for meat and fish).
A Chamber of Commerce and banks:
             Ottoman, Agriculture, Labor.
And the Grain Exchange.
The province produces 100 million kilos of barley, wheat, and oats;
corn—10 million,
rice—15,
millet and white beans—10,
       sesame seeds—100 million.
Then tangerines, oranges, bananas,
             Seville oranges, and lemons.
Tomatoes, peppers, artichokes especially,
             cauliflowers, and eggplants...
Fish:
       red sea-bream, red mullets, sea bass...

. . . .
. . . .
. . . .

Fifteen minutes outside the city,
             the Nomads pulled down their camels.
The camels were tall and long-haired,
and their bristly black sacks bulged with wheat.
The camels grumbled, and the copper bells

on their long necks chimed high and low and fell still.
The donkey set to grazing.
The Nomads unloaded the sacks
as if unloading sunken ships.
The men loomed twice as big and tall
                    among the kneeling camels in the dusk.

At sunup, peasants in horse carts passed the Nomads,
also on their way to town with wheat
                              or maybe sesame seeds.
They greeted one another coldly.
"Dirty, hairy Nomad," the peasants muttered
                    and cracked their whips.
"Fuck off, greasy Turk," a brown-bearded Nomad mumbled.
And the one on his left seconded him:
"Better a Nomad in the mountains
            than a Turk in a village."

. . . .
. . . .
. . . .
. . . .

The Grain Exchange is a two-story, squat, concrete building.
Climb the steps: a glass partition;
                    go through the door: the hall,
                    divided by a wood railing;
                    at the far end, the Exchange Commission;
        ahead, individual tables with chairs on one side of the railing
        and, on the other, wood benches.
The adjacent rooms house the Agriculture Office.

The Exchange Commissioner and his staff were seated.
Koyunzadé Sherif Bey entered the hall,
        flanked by his middle son and two accountants
        and followed by his broker and twenty-odd peasants and Nomads
        with grain samples in handkerchiefs and paper bags . . .
The peasants and Nomads
remained standing by the wood benches
                    as if at funeral prayers:

rough dark hands folded over their sashes,
worried heads drooping on their chests,
lips moving under their mustaches,
                    foreheads creased with grief . . .

Koyunzadé Sherif Bey complimented the Exchange Commissioner
and sat down with his son
              at his table,
                    the one on the far right . . .
Samples were laid on the table, and the grain
was recorded under Sherif Bey's name.
Koyunzadé Sherif Bey had gray hair.
He was fifty or fifty-five.
His handsome, manly head on his broad shoulders
                    looked down at others as if giving orders.
The Koyunzadés came from noble stock,
      descendants of Nomad chiefs who'd settled in town long ago.
They owned fifteen thousand acres of land
and one of the rice mills.

Sherif Bey has three sons and three daughters:
the girls, one uglier than the other,
                    and the boys, one handsomer than the other.
The property belongs to the father.
When Sherif Bey dies, his eldest son will replace him,
and the property will pass down undivided.
One of his son-in-laws is an agronomist, the other a judge.
The oldest daughter is unmarried.
She replaced her dead mother.
Tall, bony, dark.
Her thin lips have never smiled.
She beats the servants with logs
              (the way her father beats the hired hands).
And at night she shuts herself in her room
and reads Alfred de Musset and weeps.
Even Sherif Bey respects his daughter as if she were his elder.
The whole family dresses in high style:
                    the mansion follows English fashions.
But their politics are racist and pro-German.
They've done business with Germany since the Constitution.

Huseyin Yavuz entered the Exchange hall
           with his peasants, Nomads, samples, and brokers.
Peasants stood with peasants, Nomads with Nomads.
Huseyin Yavuz greeted the Commissioner
                     and hailed Sherif Bey: "Hello, Beyzadé."
And he sat down at the third table,
                                which was his.
The grain was duly recorded.

Ayatollah Effendi of the ulema of Erzurum,
with his snow-white turban, carpetbag, and jetblack beard,
                     takes the trouble to fare far from his homeland
           and comes down to this Mediterranean city (1899).
And with his strong breath he exorcises the evil spirits molesting
                                a local widowed woman.
He marries her,
along with her orange groves and 5 thousand acres of land.
Huseyin Yavuz is the issue of this marriage.
His father and mother have long since gone to their eternal rest,
but the land and the orange groves
                     have increased and multiplied year by year.

Huseyin Yavuz is very tall and skinny,
slightly hunchbacked,
pop-eyed,
        and jug-eared,
                his hair thinning.
His daughter studies at the College in Istanbul:
                     the girl is a beauty, a living doll.
Each year he himself delivers her to school
                and takes her home on holidays himself.
Sometimes he thinks
        if his daughter died, he'd kill himself—he couldn't live.
And when this thought occurs to him,
                he locks himself in his room and drinks day and night;
                                he's a drunk anyway.

His wife—about 45, short and plump,
                cloaked and scarfed—
                is the banker Fevzi Bey's mistress.

Huseyin Yavuz sends students to Europe out of his own pocket
                    but hides the fact
              and denies it if asked:
                         "Good deeds and bad should be kept secret."

He likes politics.
And because the English took him prisoner in the Great War,
                              he's friendly with the Germans.
And he admires America:
"Just think what it means to be a billionaire,
                    a bil-lion-aire!
Oil barons, steel magnates, coal moguls—
                         Americans all.
If the guys took us up, we'd be home free."
Yavuz exported sesame seeds to America before the war . . .

Mustafa Shen arrived and settled himself at the second table,
              between Koyunzadé Sherif Bey and Huseyin Yavuz.
Mustafa Shen was a redheaded little man
              with an incredibly long nose.
His freckled white hands were in constant motion,
and his colorless eyelashes fluttered constantly.
He'd worked years as a clerk
and saved up his first capital by facilitating bribes.
His father came from Syria, his mother from Burdur,
and it's rumored he's a bastard.

Mustafa Shen has a big office in Istanbul:
he's partners with Greek and Armenian exporters
(he dropped the Jews
              after the 21 June pact with Germany).
He plays the *saz* like a pro
              and has a voice as sweet and syrupy as filtered honey.
And he gambles.
Mustafa Shen advises all the "aghas,"
              even Koyunzadé Sherif Bey.
Since the "Office monopoly" was established,
Mustafa has smuggled wheat to Rhodes, to the Italians,
              and brought back cement and tin.
The governor

knows about the matter
but looks the other way so the city gets its cement and tin . . .

Ali Chavish entered the hall
and spoke with Mustafa Shen before taking a seat.
"Mustafa Bey, have you thought about that Office man?"
"I have, agha."
"What did you decide?"
"Here's what I thought:
you'll take the Office man to D,
          stay there a week,
                    then bring him back.
Leave the rest to me.
Understand?"
"Got it."
Ali Chavish grinned—
a greasy, wrinkled darkness split with pure white teeth.
Ali Chavish was a gigantic black.
He came from Tripoli.
He was about sixty-five.
Illiterate.
Till the end of the Great War,
          he was a pirate, a smuggler, a bandit.
With the Republic, he opened his first office.
Now, at tax time,
        his accountants carry the deeds to all his properties in carpetbags.
He likes white women,
                especially buxom blondes,
but he hates blue eyes;
he thinks they're bad luck.
His first wife was a Greek girl from Chios
with plump, fleshy arms and hands:
put hazelnuts in her finger joints, and they'd stick.
She disappeared during the Balkan War:
they said she ran away,
          but she could have been killed
          —maybe by her husband, maybe the local Greeks.
Ali Chavish abducted his second wife from a village of Elmali.
A peach of a Turkish girl.
She bore a son

white as paper
and then the poor woman died.
The boy studied law in Germany;
now he's in business,
            partners with his father—
and not only in business
                but in his stepmother's bed
                (yet he just wed
                one of the governor's daughters).
Ali Chavish found his third wife in a whorehouse:
broad, white, rock-solid hips,
dreamy hazel eyes shaded by jetblack lashes,
and solid gold bracelets
            from her thick wrists to her elbows.

Once, they hinted about his son to Ali Chavish.
But unlike Othello, Chavish was not at all jealous.
He licked his thick purple lips with his pointed pink tongue:
"Yes," he said, "y-e-e-e-s,
my son is my partner;
he has to help his old father in all ways.
His mother won't need to depend on strangers,
and the cost is cut in half—
a young woman doesn't come cheap."

Ali Chavish went bareheaded
        —he never wore a hat—
        and his pants were patched.

Jemil Bey from Crete entered the Exchange floor.
He had long, curly hair and a pointed beard
that hid the scar on his chin.
His eyes were like a bird's—
                        round
                    with almost no whites.
With his sweet, Cretan accent, Jemil Bey gossiped
                something fierce and set everyone at loggerheads.
From the governor to the tax collector,
from the Koyunzadés to the corner grocer,
he kept confidential files on everyone he knew,

organized files updated monthly.

Jemil Bey owned rice and flour mills
and was the CEO of Cretan Enterprises.

The floor of the Grain Exchange was packed:
on one side of the railing, the "aghas" at their tables
                —the five big effendis of the province—
            with their brokers and accountants,
joking with one another across the tables
but enemies underneath.
On the other side, Nomads and peasants,
most still standing . . .
They muttered among themselves,
but with so many people muttering,
              the din was deafening.
Koyunzadé Sherif Bey yelled:
"Enough! Shut up—
          we can't hear ourselves think!"

They stopped,
and the hall was quiet except for Chavish's childlike black laughter
          and the clacking keys of the Commission's typewriter.
Everything was ready.
They waited for the head of the Agriculture Office to arrive.

Next door, in the rooms of the Office, the head, Kemal Bey,
                talked to the peasant Ahmet.
The peasant's face looked like a dried-up walnut
and seemed to be smiling through tears.
Kemal was a young man
     at his first government job.

As required by the regulations of the governing board,
thirty to seventy-five percent of the grain
               (30–50–75%,
                  depending on the total produced)
     had to be sold to the Agriculture Office.
The rest didn't need to be sold,
         but if it was, it also had to be sold to the Office.

The peasants and the Nomads, after they sold their percentages to the
    Office,
                took the remainder to "their aghas,"
who turned it over to the Office through the Exchange,
and this made Kemal Bey furious.

Kemal discussed this business with the peasant again:
"You gave the Office thirty percent,
                        it's required."
"I did, bey, it's required."
"So seventy percent is left."
"It's left."
"But you won't sell it to the Office."
"I won't."
"Who'll you take it to?"
"The Koyunzadés."
"But Koyunzadé will sell it to us:
                        it's required,
                        he can't sell it anywhere else."
"He'll sell it to you, bey, it's required."
"Not to me—to the Office."
"To the Office."
"Then why take it to Koyunzadé?
        You'll give the guy two-percent commission off your back,
                plus one percent to the broker,
                then the weighing fee,
                apart from the whole other problem of rigged scales."
The peasant laughed;
at first diffident,
then bolder, he said:
"That's the problem, the scales.
Yours show less."
Kemal Bey glared at the peasant:
"So the problem is that our scales show less,
                        not theirs?
When we weigh the thirty percent, do we still show less?"
"No, then you show more.
Bey, you're the government—
                would the government cheat itself?"
Kemal laughed:

"So our scales . . . "
The peasant lowered his eyes and slyly whispered:
"Are rigged."
"Who says?"
"Everyone,
          even the hairy Nomads."
"Do you know about scales and numbers?"
"No."
"Do the Nomads?"
"Of course not,
               the guys are just shepherds."
"So who knows about scales and numbers?"
"The aghas:
          Mustafa Bey, Ali Chavish, Koyunzadé Sherif Bey,
                                        all the aghas.
               They know about scales and numbers . . . "
Kemal turned beet-red:
"So they spread this propaganda.
Those assholes.
I'll write the head office."
The peasant got scared
          and looked confused.
He'd never heard a government man curse the aghas.
Kemal asked:
"Do you owe Koyunzadé money?"
The peasant hesitated to answer.
"Come on—do you owe him?"
"Yes, about two hundred bills."
"Why didn't you get the money from the Bank of Agriculture?"
"The agha gets it from the bank and passes it along to us."
"How much interest will you pay?"
"Ten notes on the hundred, so twenty for two hundred.
And I worked a little in the agha's rice paddies."
"Did you get paid?"
"What's a little field work?
And if I have government business, he takes care of it for free."
"Why go to that pimp?
Why not take care of it yourself?"

The peasant got more and more confused:

on the one hand, he thought, "Is this hairless kid totally dumb
                                                or plain crazy?"
And, on the other, he felt strangely sad:
"They won't let him stay here, they'll drive him out," he thought.
"Even if the governor backs him, the aghas will pull strings and get rid
    of him."

"If our business is small, we take care of it ourselves,
but if it gets big, we put ourselves in the aghas' hands."
"That's just great."
Kemal Bey stood up in a rage:
"So you won't sell the seventy percent to the Office?"
The peasant kept silent.
"Or did you already take it to Koyunzadé?"
"I did."
"Then come watch how he sells it to me,
                                it's required . . . "
"It's required."
"But he'll pocket your two percent."
"He will."
Kemal laughed:
"That's also required?"
The peasant laughed:
"It's required . . . "

III

The province of D borders the province of X.
The city of D is the provincial capital . . .

Although ringed by bare hills,
D is crisscrossed by streams,
and the whole area is groves and vineyards.
The vineyards yield a faint-smelling wine heavy as molasses;
one sip,
        and it sticks to your lips,
and its fire burns for days, not in your belly
                but in your heart.

One bottle
    and, if you're not used to it, it hits you like lightning
                and knocks you out.
And once you get hooked on it
    you crave it night and day;
your head swims like a gold sun in a blue haze,
laziness seizes all your joints,
your belly swells,
and your wife kicks you out of bed:
           bye-bye, manhood . . .

D depends on weaving for its livelihood
    (the wine isn't for export; the men consume it on the spot).
Every house has a loom.
Only the women weave and run the business;
they own the looms.
The big,
    chubby-faced, apple-cheeked women of the city
    have set up something like a matriarchy:
they're complete sluts.
And the city doesn't even have a whorehouse.

The Office head, Kemal Bey, couldn't believe it:
"How can it be?"
"Why not?
My third wife comes from there."
"So you knock on any door you want . . . "
"But there's a 'but': the woman has to like you, too."
"Don't put me on, Ali Agha—it can't be . . . "
The man stuck out his long-fingered black hand:
"Wanna bet, Kemal Bey?
         Let's shake . . . "
Kemal didn't extend his hand:
"What do you mean? What kind of bet?"
"We'll go to D,
and if what I say is true, you buy dinner;
           if it's a lie, I buy."
"And how much do these women get?"
"You think they're whores?
We just have to cover the food and drink . . . "

And Ali Chavish, following Mustafa Shen's directive,
                took the Office man to the city of D.
It was late afternoon when they stepped off the bus,
and that very night, Kemal Bey
        —surprised by the two hand looms still at work on the first floor,
up in a room with rugs on the floors, walls, and divans
and a grand walnut bed—
lost the bet with a dark beauty, a mother of two.
The woman could play the lute beautifully,
and Kemal noticed:
the kids, around five or six, didn't look anything alike.
He met the woman's husband as well:
a red-cheeked, outgoing man with a pot belly,
who drank a glass of wine at dinner and left.

Kemal lost the bet,
but Ali Chavish bought dinner anyway.
They stayed at separate houses for a week.
And when they got back, Ali Chavish left Kemal Bey at the Office
                        and ran to Mustafa Shen.
Mustafa Shen rubbed his freckled hands together:
"This job is done," he said, "it, too, is done.
He won't make any more trouble at the Office . . . "

But Mustafa Shen was wrong—
            the "job" wasn't done.
A week later, Cretan Enterprises offered the Office rice
                            at 40 kurush
            (rice sales weren't regulated yet); Kemal Bey gave 35.
Ali Chavish intervened,
            to no effect.
Koyunzadé wanted to sell the Office his rotten rice
                    at 35.
Kemal Bey didn't buy.
The bank director tried to mediate—
            it didn't work.
The police chief intervened,
            to no effect.
Still, resorting one morning
to a fait accompli,

Koyunzadé dumped his rice sacks outside the Office granary.
Kemal Bey ignored them.
Toward noon, the statehouse called Kemal Bey:
     "The Party Inspector wants to see you ASAP."
"I can't make it, I'm busy right now. I'll stop by this afternoon," he
 said.
In less than half an hour
   the regiment's mess officer showed up at the Office
   —he came from Kemal Bey's hometown—
   and, in a barrage of words, dragged Kemal Bey to the Party.

The Party Inspector's face was white and hollow—as if cast in plaster—
              above his double chin.

He liked folklore
and collected folk songs like stamps.

When Kemal Bey entered the room,
the Inspector's back faced the door,
his thick fingers playing the trumpet on the window pane.
He didn't turn around to look
but kept playing.
Kemal stood waiting for a while,
then sat down in one of the armchairs,
      taking care to make noise.
The Inspector spun around:
"Why don't you come when you're called?"
Kemal stood up:
"I had urgent business, sir."
"You look like a headstrong young man.
Did the government establish the Office so you can make it hard for
 the people?"
"I don't make anything hard for the people, sir."
The Inspector opened his pale blue eyes as wide as he could:
"If you don't make it hard for the people,
do you show any respect for the town fathers?
Do you know what a member of the General Assembly means?"
"I do, sir."
"That's a lie—
you know nothing.
Why didn't you buy Koyunzadé Sherif Bey's rice?
Because he wouldn't bribe you?"

356

"I don't take bribes, sir.
Koyunzadé's rice had rotted.
If I bought it, I'd be responsible, and the Treasury would lose."
"And it's your business to worry about the Treasury?
So what am I doing here?
I'm not thinking about the Treasury?
Now go
        buy that rice, pronto,
                        at 35.
He's delivered it to your door anyway—
the poor man shows such good will.
Son, don't make life hard for the producers.
It's our duty to protect the national wealth.
We must make it easy for the Republic's economy.
Do you understand, son?
Don't distinguish yourself as a petty bureaucrat
                but by helping the people.
One of our six principles is populism.
Now, son,
        don't embarrass me—
I promised Sherif Bey."
Pained, Kemal spoke,
more pleading than defiant:
"I can't, sir, I'd be responsible . . . "
The Inspector regarded Kemal's hazel eyes with disgust:
"When you wanted to buy the Cretans' rice,
            where was your responsibility?"
"Their stuff wasn't rotten, sir,
                it was a little cracked—
                    so I gave 35."
The Inspector shot his short arms into the air:
"So you offer 35 for the Cretans' filthy cracked rice,
but a real Turk's grain isn't good enough.
And in these critical years we knock ourselves out
            —the Party, the government, Parliament—
to establish Turkish hegemony on Turkish soil!"
The Inspector lowered his arms
and fell quiet.
He paced up and down,
then stopped in front of the window
            to play the trumpet again.

He turned back around and stood before Kemal,
                leaned down to the young man,
                and asked as if slapping him:
"Where're you from?"
"Akshehir."
"That's a lie.
The people of Akshehir are Turks, and brave.
You're an enemy of the Turkish race.
Look at me, young man.
[He stuck two fingers in Kemal's face.]
I can pluck a man's eyes out.
Do you know who I am?"
Kemal's thin face reddened as if dipped in blood,
his shoulders and arms shook,
and he broke down, sobbing like a rebellious, helpless child.
He tried to stop,
but the sobs kept coming,
and tears rained down his dark cheeks.
Finally, he blurted in one breath:
"I won't buy it—
                I will not buy Koyunzadé's rice,
                                        I won't..."
And he covered his face with his hands,
                backed away,
                turned around,
                and, hanging his head, walked out the door.

. . . .
. . . .
. . . .

Kemal lay awake all night,
rebelling against injustice and fearing getting fired.
In the early hours, rebellion took the lead,
but near morning fear pulled ahead.
And when he sat down at his desk at eight,
Kemal Bey felt totally defeated:
"You're an idiot,
        a complete ass," he told himself.
He waited for a telegram from Ankara:

"Please resign immediately."
And he waited for the phone to ring:
"Koyunzadé came down five kurush—
don't drag it out, just buy at thirty."
Neither the telegram nor the call came,
but toward nine, loud noises and shouts
                    came from outside,
            along with the sound of shattering glass.
The accountant rushed into the room:
he was short and fat,
and his hands were lost in the overlong sleeves of his jacket.
"Kemal Bey," he said, puffing his cheeks,
                    "they've attacked the Exchange!
                They're headed our way…"
"Who's attacking? What's happening?"
"The people.
All the barefooted of the city are on our steps.
They want wheat."
"Call the cops right away—
                I'll go see."
As the accountant called the police from Kemal's desk, Kemal
                                    rushed out the door.

Outside, crowds of people
        mobbed the Exchange floor and the steps.
They numbered about a hundred and fifty
but looked like millions to Kemal.
Men, women, and children—
bare feet, wood clogs, caps, scarves, bare heads,
            unshaven faces, feverish eyes,
                millions of people like millions of ants.
The glass partition was smashed.
Kemal felt dizzy,
and his hazy eyes saw only a girl
sitting on the floor below a black skirt,
                        crying,
her muddy little bare foot cut by shards of glass,
                            bleeding.
The shouting mounted when Kemal appeared:
"We want bread!"

"Bring out the wheat—who you saving it for?"
"They eat the best bread themselves, the pigs!"
"Sure they do, they've got the wheat."
"I'm not budging without wheat . . . "

They'd come from the city's outskirts,
from bamboo-thatched mud huts.
They worked in the rice paddies.

Four cops appeared below.
They tried to climb the steps.
The people wouldn't let them.
Two kept trying
and got beaten.

Kemal ran back to his room
and phoned the governor:
"Sir, it's the Office—
                    there's a mob of people outside!"
"I know,
we've got about five hundred here.
Some are looting Koyunzadé's rice sacks
                            outside your granary.
I'll be right there."

The governor arrived,
along with hundreds of people chasing his car.
The acacia-lined street was wall-to-wall people.

Yelling and screaming, they let the governor through;
someone threw a corn-cob after him.
The governor went upstairs,
but the cops couldn't follow.
The governor entered Kemal's room.
He pleaded like a beggar asking for change:
"Give them some wheat—for God's sake, quick!"
Kemal stared at the governor's pale, sweating face:
"I can't, sir, unless I have orders from the head office; I'd be responsible."
The governor's scream fell like a fist on Kemal's ears;
his two front teeth, platinum, flashed:

"You'd be responsible, and what would I be?
There'll be a revolt,
                    blood will flow..."
And he eased into Kemal's chair,
                    exhausted, and whispered:
"If this gets any bigger, they'll dismiss me.
I have a family, son.
You're young and single."
"We'll wire Ankara, Governor, the head office."
"It'll take too long to get an answer.
We can't wait."
"Then you give me written orders, Governor."
"I can't—
I'd be responsible,
I can't overstep my authority."

The roar outside swelled.
A rock flew through the window,
and they kicked in the locked door of the room.
Police whistles blew nonstop.
The governor jumped up:
"I'm calling in the regiment. They need to send soldiers.
The cops can't handle it."
He picked up the phone
and looked at Kemal as if to say, "Help!"
Kemal said nothing.
The governor put down the phone.
"No, that won't do—
calling in the regiment won't do, will it?
They'll say I couldn't handle this little thing,
                    won't they?
Answer me.
Why don't you say something?
Tell me what to do!"

Kemal's long thin face suddenly flushed with enormous pride:
he felt in one irresistible rush
the secret egotism of self-sacrifice.
With deep compassion for himself
he said, his voice cracking:

"I'll release the wheat
and assume full responsibility.
If they want, they can take me to court.
How many tons of wheat do you want, sir?"
"Fifty,
        I don't know—
                make it sixty."
"I'll give you four hundred."

He released the wheat
and immediately wired Ankara.
Two days later, the answer came:
"Continue to handle the situation."
And so the problem disappeared.
And Kemal felt so good about himself, so powerful, and so hugely happy,
he said, "Why hurt the Party Inspector's feelings?
                                I may as well buy Koyunzadé's rice, too."
And he bought what was left after the looting at 40 kurush.
And he tucked a blue envelope
        into the outside pocket of his jacket—his first bribe.
And the next day he went to the city of D:
he had missed the dark young mother of two, her lute,
                                        and her bed.

PART TWO

I

"I'm lying on the bottom of the Atlantic, effendi,
                leaning on my elbow
                        at the bottom of the Atlantic.

I look up:
I see a submarine
high overhead
cruising fifty meters deep
like a fish, effendi,
sealed off and secretive like a fish

inside its armor and the water.
Up there the light is bottle-green.
There, effendi, it's all sparkles,
star-spangles,
a million candles
blazing bright green.
And there, my steel-propelled soul,
are couplings without thrashing, births without screams,
the first moving flesh of our world—
there, effendi, the voluptuous intimacy
                    of a steaming bath
and the red hair of the first woman I had.
There, rainbow-colored grasses, rootless trees,
            wiggly creatures of the world below the brine,
life, salt, and iodine:
there, Haji Baba, there
            is our origin,
and there, stealthy, treacherous, and steely,
                    is a submarine.

Light seeps down about four hundred meters.
Then, the deep dark,
        the deepest darkness.
Sometimes strange fish
        crack the darkness,
                scattering light.
Then they're gone, too.
Now just ply on ply of thick water
        all the way down, final and absolute,
            and at the very bottom—me.
I'm lying, Haji Baba, at the very bottom of the Atlantic,
                        leaning on my elbow
                        and looking up.
America and Europe are separate just on the surface,
                    not at the bottom of the Atlantic.
Tankers pass overhead, one after another:
I see their spines,
            their keels.
Their propellers spin happily,
and the rudders look so odd underwater

I want to reach up to turn them myself.
Sharks glided by below—
I saw their mouths
        on their bellies.
Suddenly the ships panic.
It's not the sharks for sure.
No, effendi, it's a torpedo:
        the submarine has fired a torpedo.
Rudders frantic,
            in a fright,
keels scanning the water for help,
the tankers try to protect their soft underbellies
            like men fending off knives.
Now there are three, then six, seven, eight submarines.
And the tankers go down,
firing at the enemy
            and spilling their cargo and men into the sea.
Diesel oil, kerosene, gasoline—
the sea surface bursts into flame.
Now a river of fire flows up there,
effendi, a fiery river
        slick with oil.
Blood-red, sky-blue, pitch-black—
a scene from the chaos of the earth's creation.
The water boils at the surface,
the foam choked with wreckage.
See that tanker, effendi, sinking
like a sleepwalker,
                a lunatic?
It's passed through the tumult
and entered the sea's paradisal calm.
But it keeps falling,
lost in the liquid dark.
Soon, now, it will explode from the pressure.
And a mast, effendi, or a smokestack
                may land next to me.
The sea up there teems with men.
They drift down like sediment,
        Haji Baba, settling to the bottom like sediment.
Feet first or headfirst,

arms and legs reaching out and pulling back,
searching for something.
Not finding anything anywhere to grab onto,
        they sink to the bottom, too.

Suddenly a submarine lands next to me.
The hatch on the bridge snaps open like a busted coffin lid,
and out steps Hans Mueller from Munich.

Before becoming a submariner in the spring of '39,
        Hans Mueller from Munich
was the third soldier from the right in the Fourth Squadron
        of the First Company of the Sixth Battalion
                of Hitler's Storm Troopers.
Hans Mueller
        had three loves:
1) A foaming golden brew.
2) Anna, fleshy and white like an East Prussian potato.
3) Sauerkraut.
Hans Mueller
        had three duties:
1) To salute his superiors
        like lightning.
2) To take an oath on a gun.
3) To round up a minimum of three Jews a day
        and damn the sly ones who got away.
Hans Mueller had three fears
in his head and heart and on his tongue:
1) Der Fuehrer.
2) Der Fuehrer.
3) Der Fuehrer.
Hans Mueller
with his loves, duties, and fears
                        lived
                happily
                        until the spring of '39.
And he was surprised
        to hear Anna
—magnificent as a C major in a Wagnerian opera,
fleshy and white as an East Prussian potato—

complain so
                about the shortages of eggs and butter.
He'd say to her:
'Just think, Anna,
I'll have a brand-new gun belt
and wear bright shiny boots.
You'll put on a long white dress and wear
                        wax flowers in your hair.
We'll walk under crossed swords.
And we'll have a dozen kids—
all boys, of course.
Look, Anna, if today
we don't make cannons and guns
just so we can have our eggs and butter,
how will our twelve sons
fight the battles of tomorrow?'

Mueller's twelve sons never got to fight,
because they never got born—
because, effendi, before the nuptials could be consummated
        Hans Mueller himself went to war.
And now in late
        autumn of 1941,
                he stands before me on the ocean floor.
His fine blond hair is wet,
his pointed red nose shows regret,
        and his thin lips are drawn with sorrow.
Though he's right beside me
he gazes at me from far away,
the way the dead do.
I know he'll never see Anna again
or drink a brew
                or eat sauerkraut.
All this, effendi, I know,
but he does not.
His eyes fill with tears,
never to be wiped dry.
His pocket is full of money,
never to increase or decrease.
But the strangest thing is,

he can't kill anyone
or die anymore.
Soon he'll swell up
and rise to the top,
rocking on the waves,
his pointed nose nibbled by fish.

I stared at Hans Mueller, Haji Baba, thinking all this
when suddenly there appeared next to us
                              Harry Thompson of Liverpool.
He was a quartermaster on one of the tankers.
His eyebrows and lashes were burnt,
his eyes shut tight.
He was clean-shaven and overweight.
Thompson had a wife,
effendi, a broomstick of a woman:
tall and skinny, neat and fastidious,
and, like a broomstick, slightly ridiculous.
And Thompson had a son,
Haji Baba, a six-year-old
all peaches-and-cream, cuddly, plump, and blond.
I took Thompson's hand.
He didn't open his eyes.
I said: 'You died.'
'Yes,' he said, 'for freedom and the British Empire—
for the freedom to curse Churchill if I want, even in wartime,
and the freedom to go hungry, even if I don't want.
But this last freedom will change:
we won't go hungry or jobless after the war.
One of our lords is working on the solution:
justice without revolution.
Churchill said: "I'm not here to break up the British Empire."
And I'm not here to make a revolution:
the Archbishop of Canterbury,
                the president of our union,
                              and my wife
stand in opposition.
I beg your pardon.
That's all—
                period. The end.'

Thompson fell silent.
And he didn't open his mouth again.
The English don't like to talk a lot,
        especially dead English with a dry sense of humor.

I laid Thompson and Mueller side by side.
Together they swelled up,
and together they rose to the top.
The fish thoroughly enjoyed Thompson,
but they wouldn't touch the other—
scared, I guess, that Hans's flesh was poison.
Don't say they're just animals, Haji Baba;
you're an animal, too,
                    but smart . . . "

And Jevdet Bey gazed fondly at the stork.

The night air hung heavy with the fragrance
                            of Seville oranges.
Jevdet Bey sat in the garden with his stork
and listened to the radio he'd taken outside:
news of the Atlantic war on the London report.
Slowly getting high, he had a good time
        imagining himself at the bottom of the Atlantic.
Wings clipped,
the stork rested its straight red beak
                            on its white chest
and napped up on one leg.
In the harbor below,
the Mediterranean lay like a young mother
                with generous bare breasts
                            and smiling eyes.
And up above, the sweet williams craned their long, thin necks,
                            listening to the air.
The orange trees burst with stars.
And now Jevdet Bey's garden, glass, and heart
        filled with the memory of a woman he couldn't forget.
Now, no bottom of the Atlantic
                or those at the bottom of the Atlantic.
Those who've died at our side

drive off the distant dead.
And five years ago Jevdet Bey's wife, Leyla Hanum,
      had died in his arms
          (not for Hitler
or the British Empire and the freedom to curse Churchill
or even from something like pneumonia or cancer),
      just because her appointed time
        to go had come.

"Have they reached Moscow yet, Jevdet Bey?"
"Jevdet Bey, won't you tell us the good news?"
"Jevdet Bey, what's the word from London?"
"Have they reached Moscow yet, Jevdet Bey?"

Jevdet Bey awoke from his revery
and shivered as if suddenly chilly.
He turned to the voices:
Koyunzadé, Mustafa Shen, and Jemil Bey from Crete
     —three of the five biggest effendis of the province—
stood at the garden gate.
They were returning from the club,
half-lit,
and life was sweet
     under the acacias
        on this warm, happy Mediterranean night.

"Jevdet Bey, what's the word from London?"
"Have they they reached Moscow yet, Jevdet Bey?"

And without waiting for Jevdet Bey's answer,
they burst into laughter
and sauntered off, swaying slightly.

Jevdet Bey lay back on his chaise longue
and gazed up at the oranges and the stars.
The oranges were close by, the stars far away.
And Jevdet Bey wanted to touch the distant stars
             beyond the oranges.
He put on his glasses
and, still lying down

and without looking,
                felt around for Moscow on the radio.
World and country,
house and tree,
man, jackal, and wolf,
all rivers
(Ganges, Amazon, Volga, Nile, Meander),
all actions and all words:
closer and louder, a grand
                music filled the Mediterranean garden.
Jevdet Bey closed his eyes
and, as if surrendering himself to the sea,
abandoned his old heart to the symphony.

The radio under the orange trees was an eight-tube, '39 model.
The dial glittered with the station names
like the faery king's magic kingdom.

The radio at the prison was a four-tube, '29 model.
It was sent over from the Civic Center fifteen days ago
and installed in the corridor.

In the chill glassy night outside,
the steppe was frozen stiff, hairs all on end.
Inside, the prison slept.
Only four men were still awake:
the guard at his post
                (keeping warm by the fire he'd lit on the landing)
and Halil, Painter Ali, and Beethoven Hasan around the radio.
The volume turned low,
they listened to the symphony that filled the orange grove
                                        five hundred kilometers south of them
from Moscow, thousands of kilometers to the northeast.
Beethoven Hasan holds his head in his hands,
his fingers in his long black curly hair.
Painter Ali's face could be carved in ivory;
he keeps licking his thick red lips.
Halil stands.
He doesn't know whether to feel rage, anger, or grief.
At this moment he wants to split his chest open

                   and be free
to give his whole heart
                   to his beloved people.

And the symphony plays on.
Soprano, alto, tenor,
the violins are human,
               human and proud,
                         and they ask:
"White, yellow, red, black,
didn't they all reject
enslavement of race by race, nation by nation,
the exploitation
          of men by men?
Didn't they declare human labor sacred
and make the greatest freedom possible?"

And the flutes speak with my sister's voice:
"Respecting children, stars, and songs,
loving the earth, machines, and books,
their windows flashing in the sun with joy,
unresting in their ceaseless passion to create—
                    they are the men of life and love."

Seizing on the flutes' last phrase,
          the alto viola is a knife to the heart:
"The men of life and love
               are bathed in blood from head to toe;
vengeance in their eyes, bewildered,
the men of life and love
retreat inland, fighting,
and leave behind
a path of fire,
a vast stretch of scorched earth."

Now the cornets and bass viols have the floor:
their gravity outweighs all other sounds.
And their indictment is certain of its justice:
"The enemy is deceitful, unjust, ruthless;
the armored men approaching worship death.

They believe men are born in sin,
and they destroy the mind in men.
And they burn books . . .
Their foreheads stone,
their breath rancid
        like weedy water
                rotten grass
                        and putrid flesh,
their hands clutch their machines like bird claws,
and, determined not to spare a single sapling
        that doesn't surrender to them
        or a single human hopeful as life,
        they come, crouching behind their tanks.
They die like swarms of locusts,
gaps open in their ranks,
they fill the gaps and once again attack.
They've taken Kiev
and push on to Leningrad and Moscow
        to beat the snow."

All the strings fell quiet,
and now the lush tenor
of a single violoncello speaks:
"Countrymen,
                brothers and sisters,
soldiers of our army and navy—
friends, I call on you:
death to the men of death . . . "

In response,
                the conductor calls all the instruments into action.
A north wind storms through a hornbeam forest,
then the clarinets slowly advance
to tell the story of one who answered the call:
"He was born in a village,
grew up on a kolkhoz,
and worked at a power plant.
He liked books and children.
And before he joined the army,
                hook-nosed Ivan

ran the children's park library.
His unit was stationed on the Belorussian-Polish border.
His watch ended toward morning.
The air outside was like fresh-drawn milk,
the earth soft and moist,
the trees in mist,
the birds about to start.
Then rosy dawn:
how sweet to be young and healthy at the break of day!
Ivan's slanted blue eyes surveyed
the valley stretched out flat
                    in surrender.
The kolkhozes back east
                    would be just waking up.
And girls with thick, white calves
                    would soon mount the tractors.
He lit a cigarette of strong black tobacco.
And, hooked nose receding into his face,
            he smiled, happy with his country.
He walked away.
Turning at the door for a last look behind,
            he entered the barracks.
Everyone in deep sleep.
Ahmet from Turkestan lay on his left,
Yurchenko from Ukraine on his right,
Sagamanian from Armenia in the upper bunk.
The smell of male sweat and fatigues.
He took off his jacket and hung it up.
Sleep soft as velvet settled on his eyes.
Ivan sat on his bunk
and, yawning, untied his boots.
He took off the left.
Then sat up and listened:
a din came from outside.
Suddenly the door burst open,
and the watchman whistled and yelled: "Man your guns!"
They all shot outside.
Ivan was the first to leave,
one foot booted,
            the other not.

The huge forest to the northwest was burning,
the air like blood flowing unchecked.
Sounds of cannons and more cannons.
A formation of planes flew high overhead.
And the first enemy tanks appeared to the south:
                    one after another,
                              six coal-black iron beasts.

The year: 1941.
The day: 22 June.

Ivan had never fought with anyone in his life
(not even with the good-hearted but very prickly
                    Armenian Sagamanian),
          not because he was afraid
                    but because he loved peace.
And he harbored no ill will toward any nation.
Ivan had one weakness:
he was easily amazed, like a child.
And he was strangely pained and amazed
by Hitler's rise in Germany.
"Despite the Social Democrats' betrayal,
the nation of Marx and Engels, Beethoven and Schiller,
the proletariat, our Communist comrades, and Telman
          will bring him down for sure,"
                              Ivan thought.

Hitler was not brought down.
Ivan was more amazed, more pained.
And now
on 22 June, at dawn,
"The Fascists are coming," he thought,
"but we from up here and the German people from within,
                    we'll clean up on them."

Ivan fought from up there.
Germans, Rumanians, Finns, Italians, and Hungarians
attacked under one flag of death.
Czech, Belgian, Dutch, and French factories
          worked for the swastika.

Hitler's tanks and planes were many.
Ivan's knowledge of the martial arts wasn't much,
and despite everything,
        he was still a child amazed by it all.
He fought as he retreated inland,
leaving behind
a vast stretch of scorched earth.
Ivan fought,
but the German people
        continued to be Hitler's hunting dogs
                and amaze Ivan.
And this amazement lasted till he saw his first German POW.
The Red Army soldiers had flocked around the prisoner.
They looked at him as at a strange tool they'd never seen before.
Ivan, too, looked on,
and never to be shocked by anything again,
he dropped his amazement then and there
like an old toothbrush.
For Ivan understood:
the half-beast half-man
standing before him
was straight out of H. G. Wells's *Island of Dr. Moreau.*

The sopranos had long since receded
with their pastel blues, pinks, and greens.
The altos and tenors faded into the background,
orange, chestnut, coral,
and the crimson baritones and basses came to the fore:
"The ants carry off their flooded nest.
A country is rolled up
                like a carpet, from end to end.
A woman uproots barley with her bare hands,
                to keep it from the enemy,
                        and her palms ooze blood.
A country is loaded
                on human ships, their hearts the sails.
And like mothers snatching children from cradles to flee fire,
                they dismantle workshops and move inland,
                crushed by the weight
                but relaying them from hand to hand

without dropping a single screw.
If they could, they'd shoulder cities, forests, rivers, the very earth
and, leaving nothing but partisans behind,
        migrate wholesale to the east
       and the turning point of the battle.
A woman uproots barley with her bare hands,
            and her palms ooze blood.
Ivan sees the woman uprooting barley.
Their eyes meet.
The female eyes ask the male:
"Where are you going?
I'm not finished with the barley."

One afternoon on the steppe, Ivan's retreating battalion comes upon
   a road.
The road is wide
and long.
Hearts in combat boots,
the boots in stones and dirt.
Feet don't ache in retreats so much as the shoulder with the gun . . .
The road stretches from the Occident to the Orient.
The road is wide
and long.
And littered:
        samovars
          beds
            blankets.
And potato sacks, bellies burst.
Enemy planes have clearly
      strafed the area.
They've attacked the migrating kolkhoz
maybe caught walking in the noonday heat.
Carts are overturned, wheels in the air.
Wheels in the air—
     they'll spin at a touch.
Bodies line both sides of the road.
Bodies lie in the wheat field.
Nailed by a bullet in the back as they ran.
Fell on their faces as they ran.
Their tense backs frozen

in an instant, in motion.
Who's there in the oat field?
What's there in the oat field?
A stray cow grazes in the oat field,
          pausing to lick the wound on its left shoulder.
And, suspended on an invisible thread,
          a winged insect bobs above a dead mule.
The air is hot.
Glittering specks rise, spiraling into the air.
A tree.
An apple tree.
The apples are green
the apples are sour.
Ivan sees the tree.
The tree asks:
"Ivan, where are you going,
          leaving me here?"

A body.
The body of a little girl.
Her dress is red with white polka-dots.
Her bare legs are thin as twigs, long as branches.
Ivan bends down.
He strokes the dead girl's hair.
The hair asks:
"Ivan, where are you going,
          leaving me here?"

And Ivan asks himself:
"Where, where, where?
Where will we stop?
          Where, how, and when?"

Ivan learned malice
as if learning a savage but enchanting song.
And as he burned the tanks with white swastikas on their backs
and brought down the carcass of each dog,
his country became twice as precious in his eyes.
He grew silent and furious.
And he now knew hatred

                without mercy.
The medieval hordes kept coming,
medieval hordes
        descending on parachutes
                and riding motorcycles.
Their commanding officer:
a fanatic,
        a true believer:
to question
        is forbidden,
to think a sin.
And his insolence is like a monocle under a raised eyebrow.
And like a fish inside his armor, he's arrogant—
                                a superman.
And a rapist and a glutton.

Ivan wasted five of such officers before they reached Kiev.
Just before Kiev, he found the Armenian Sagamanian next to him.
They hugged silently.
And the dark man's unsmiling face
                smiled for the first time:
"Give me a cigarette," he said.
He had never yet asked anyone for a cigarette.
Ivan fought twice as hard.
And he and Ahmet from Turkestan became sergeant-majors on the
    same day.
"We're retreating, yes,
but when we liberate Europe,
                I want to make general," said Ahmet.
Now they pulled back.
Europe receded before them,
                Moscow closed in behind.
But they were certain:
the world would not regress to the Middle Ages
                        or stand still and mark time.
These are birth pangs;
                the earth is pregnant.
Friends, I call on you—
hear me, friends!"

And with spring colors against a clear red,

calm and full of light, the symphony ended.
Beethoven Hasan
stopped playing with his hair,
sat up, and asked:
"That's beautiful!
                Is it Beethoven?"
Halil respectfully turned off the radio:
"No."
The peasant Painter Ali asked:
"You want the Soviets to win, don't you?"
"Yes,
and you?"
"I want the Soviets, too."
"Why?"
"Because you want it."
"How can that be?"
"Why not?
You're a good man—
would a good man want something bad?"
Halil laughed,
then said as if scolding:
"Good man, bad man,
forget that.
You love your country, don't you, Ali?
Not just your village
but besides your village,
Anatolia and Rumelia?"
"Sure,
we all love our country . . . "
"Then listen:
anyone who loves his country,
not just here but everywhere
in Asia, Europe, America, Africa,
anyone who really loves his country
—not for personal property, houses or land or profit,
                but from the heart,
the way the people love their country—
and anyone who hasn't done anything to make him fear the people,
                        who hasn't sold out his country,
whether Turk or Bulgarian, French or, I don't know, Sumatran
                                or even German,

would want the Soviets to win."
Halil was quiet.
He waited, then said:
"Well, why don't you ask why?"
"Why ask?
I know:
if they win, the poor peasants will live better.
Their generals are all peasants and workers and stuff.
The newspaper
sang the praises of the German commanders,
all aristocrats from lines of generals going back generations.
And they have their own country:
                    East Prussia.
It wrote about the Soviets, too,
as if to mock them:
they're all peasants and stuff.
It means to say they'll lose.
But they won't.
As long as the generals are peasants.
You know us peasants,
we're shrewd, cunning people.
And if a whole country were ours,
mountains couldn't stop us, let alone Germans . . . "
Beethoven Hasan laughed:
"Forget the Germans—it's models should fear you."

The peasant Painter Ali was 25.
He'd shot an agha's son over a girl.
His face paper-white,
he had the gold eyes of a fawn
and full, red lips.
Ali held a diploma from his three-grade village school
and had started oil painting three months ago.
He'd seen Halil painting one day.
At first hesitant, then bolder,
                his long fingers caressed the canvas.
Then for two days his breath warmed Halil's neck.
Then he asked him for oils
and painted his self-portrait, from a mirror, on wood.
It was incredible.

They immediately sent for painting books from Istanbul.
Ali read them in one night but didn't understand a word.
And the next day he asked Halil:
"What's an 'academy figure study'?"
"'Academy figure'
means to draw nudes.
It's an absolute must for you."
Ali understood,
and three days later Beethoven Hasan landed in the infirmary with
    pneumonia.
Ali had sat him before the open window
of the ward, completely naked
                    (except for his privates),
and done an "academy study."
They barely saved Beethoven's life.

Beethoven Hasan, a typesetter, came from Istanbul.
Before he went to prison seven years ago at sixteen,
                    he had three consuming passions:
movies, sports, and Western music.
His first two passions landed him in prison:
he wanted to see the Olympics, wherever they were, in person.
He had no money.
He said, "I'll do like the gangster in that movie."
He couldn't and got caught.
And he got seven-and-a-half years at exactly sixteen:
they didn't think sports could build up a body,
they didn't believe his birth certificate.
He owes the nickname "Beethoven" to his third passion.
He couldn't read notes or play an instrument,
but he composed symphonies.
With a typesetter's care, he'd line up his ideas on paper,
then give them voice.
"My heart is a paradise of symphonies,"
                    he'd say,
                        "and my mouth is my orchestra."
Many times he gave concerts for the peasant prisoners.
And they didn't mock him,
because he never messed with anyone
                    and packed a mean punch.

"I'll write a symphony
of what you said, Halil,
            Ali's answer,
                    and my thoughts.
It's called: 'The Unvanquished.'
It goes like this."
And Beethoven Hasan began humming.
Then he suddenly stopped.
His black eyes looked as sad and unforgiving
                    as a child unjustly beaten.
Halil asked:
"Why did you stop, Hasan?"
"I don't have any right to make such a symphony:
                            I'm a thief,
                            a gangster."
Halil pulled Hasan's black hair:
"No, Hasan,
        you're a typesetter
        and an honest composer.
Get on with your great big beautiful work.
Well, guys, it's one o'clock—
time to sleep."

Outside, the air of the steppe
        was frozen like a block of ice.
Don't touch—your fingers will stick to your chopper.
It's so cold the foxes are shitting copper.

Inside, a chestnut fire flickered.
Rags on its back,
            hunched over a brazier,
                    the prison shivered.

Halil laid the map of the Eastern Front
        on the concrete floor of his room.
It was pieced together from newspaper clippings,
each segment on a different scale.
The Baltic sat right next to the Black Sea,
Warsaw rubbed shoulders with Kiev.
Orel was as far from Briansk as could be.

And on Halil's map, Moscow lay
     here a stone's throw, there half the world away.

Halil has drawn eyes in the margins of his map.
Some frontal views, some profiles.
From a gashed eyebrow, blood
               trickles down the lid
                         of a bold, glaring eyeball.
Some eyes are in pairs, some single.
There are single eyes as sneaky as a submarine periscope.
Some eyes are jumbled together,
               all over one another.
Some open wide,
               their fate frightfully legible.
And some are closed tight, like locked walnut boxes:
what are they hiding?
There are eyes
               of mothers.
There are eyes:
               just two pupils gleaming
                         with hate and rancor.
There are eyes
               of love.
There are eyes
               like a wheat harvest in the sun.
And over and over,
that same eye:
               the gashed eyebrow, the blood
                    trickling down the lid,
                    the bold, glaring eyeball.

Halil squats before the map on the concrete,
and behind his glasses are his own eyes,
doomed sooner or later to lose the light.
And Halil can't decide
          what causes the pain in his eyes:
atrophying blood vessels or sitting with his hands tied
          while the whole world fights.
To be on the frozen lakes of Finland now
or in the Libyan desert

or the Yugoslav mountains
or Istanbul or Izmir; at the front;
or in Paris, alongside Gabriel Peri now.

Radio Ankara said:
"Within ten days
        the Fuehrer's tanks may be rolling through Moscow."
Halil knew it was impossible.
But not to be there in the flesh
        among those fighting to make it impossible,
to squat on the concrete instead
with needles pricking his sick eyes,
with Luminal to let him sleep
if only for a couple hours,
to be down on the concrete
marking the latest changes on the Moscow front,
drawing in pencil
                what they drew in blood . . .

And with a chewed-on pencil
between his dark bony fingers,
Halil marked the latest changes on the Moscow front.
The line began at Kalinin
        and, curving slightly east,
                ended above Efremov.
The front is less than seventy kilometers from Moscow:
twelve hours by foot,
ten minutes by plane,
and one-and-a-half centimeters on the map.
There's no snow on the map,
                no wind,
no day or night, no life or death,
                no people.
The map is a piece of paper,
a picture.
The front is one-and-a-half centimeters from Moscow on the map
and less than seventy kilometers on the snow-covered earth.
But on the snow-covered earth
bright life fought death.
And the enemy

was incredibly far away:
as far from Moscow as the height of a new man.

It was the sixteenth of November in '41.
50 divisions, thirteen armored,
3,000 artillery pieces,
and 700 planes
would attack Moscow once more.
The plan:
to seal off the Soviet capital on two sides,
penetrate deep in the north and south,
isolate the units defending the city,
                    and wipe them out.
Hitler is in a better position with respect to the number of tanks.
Tanks
        matter, without a doubt.
But with us, men drive the tanks;
        with them, tanks drove the men.

The men tanks drove
        had marched off one summer morning.
Their hair was combed, their uniforms looked sharp.
And they marched, bleeding, the length of two seasons,
and, one winter night, paradise lay all before them.
But now they weren't quite so well groomed,
                    their uniforms didn't look so sharp.
Waist-deep in snow they marched,
heads buried in their shoulders,
unshaven for weeks,
the skin on their foreheads cracked in patches.
The army that had come to conquer Moscow
                was wounded, hungry, cold.
They'd grabbed anything warm:
women's skirts covered their shoulders,
        children's socks served as gloves.
And paradise lay all before them.
But first they had to get past
        that endless pack
        of red devils all in white.
The white plain went on forever.

And paradise lay all before them:
before them lay Moscow,
the end of bleeding, hunger, cold—
Moscow
        was so close.
Moscow was a stove,
a larder,
a feather pillow.
Hot running water
and stores full of furs.
Just break the lock with your bayonet
and throw the warmest, softest skin on your back!
Everywhere you look, caviar;
sausages everywhere you look,
and mountains of butter.
Then pillows, beds,
and sleep
        on a full stomach.
No more raids, fronts, or partisans.
Sleep
wake up
warm up
eat.
Sleep
wake up
warm up.
Till not a lump of coal remains to burn
or a shot of vodka to drink.
Then the war can end,
and they can go back,
heroes.

The army that had come to conquer Moscow
was wounded, hungry, cold.
But with the instinct of an animal
        left out in the snow
        wounded, hungry, and cold,
                with the instinct of an animal
                —raging, head down, tail taut—
                it fought

for food and warmth.
Hairs all on end, it fought,
and Moscow was still in danger...

It was the sixteenth of November in '41.
The shadows of German tanks
darken the Volokolamsk asphalt.
Twenty of them.
Coal-black.
Huge.
Each advances like a blind rhinoceros,
                    pathetic and scary.
And ugly, like a dumb wrestler.
And they look like scorpions, though they're nothing like them.

In the Petelino trenches 28 men saw them come.
Exhausted, they all stared at one another.
They'd fought for hours
            and had just dispatched an enemy company.
Bodies were stacked on top of one another, side by side, outside the
    trench.
The tanks rumbled closer.
In the trench, Mustafa Sungurbay narrowed his grape-black eyes:
"Oy, mother," he said, "oy,
                20 of 'em."
And he laughed like a hunter sighting twenty wolves.
Klochkoff jumped into the trench from behind.
He was the company's political officer,
                    a Communist;
"Hey, guys," he said
and paused, as if about to give good news.
The company called him "Worker."
Bondarenko from Ukraine had given him the nickname
for working nonstop.
He was prolific as an olive tree,
industrious as an ant;
how did he find time to fall in love or eat or sleep
when life was the dough
        his huge hands couldn't knead enough?
Those in the trench were glad to see him.

"Worker" Klochkoff gave his good news
                    in a level voice:
"The way I figure it,
they're 20, we're 29:
that's one tank
        for every one point forty-five men.
We're forty-five percent ahead of them."

But "Worker" proved five-percent off in his calculations:
one of their 29 was a coward.
When a German in the first tank to approach the trench
shouted "Surrender!"
        he put up his hands and rose.
Spontaneous gunfire brought the coward down
        as fast as he'd stood up.
Twenty-eight were left in the trench.
The fight lasted four hours.
Fourteen tanks
        and seven men were rendered inactive.
The fight seemed almost won.
But "Worker" Klochkoff
                    spotted 30 more tanks.
They moved in, cutting through the dark night.
They outweighed those before.
Ballistics, radios, engines, steel:
equipped with all the technical know-how of the twentieth century.
Yet they looked like medieval contraptions,
devices suggesting
witches and alchemy and such.
"Worker" Klochkoff asked the men in the trench:
"Did you count the new ones?"
"No."
"I did: 30,
        plus the six left over from before make 36.
We're twenty-one.
Without splitting hairs,
                    that comes to two tanks per man.
And we can't retreat:
behind us is Moscow.
I mean, what I'm saying is . . . "

Kujebergunoff spoke:
"Let's all hug."
They stared at him, taken aback:
serious and sedate to the point of boring,
the man never sang or told jokes
or spoke unless spoken to,
and lived buried in himself
                like fish that keep to their own waters.
Kujebergunoff repeated:
"Let's all hug while there's time."
They all hugged . . .
The new tanks bore down on the trench.
The battle lasted half an hour.
It took away seven or eight more tanks
and sixteen more men.
The men ran out of ammunition.
One last grenade was left in Klochkoff's hand.
The men ran out of ammunition,
but they knew an honest man's heart,
              that giant, can never die.

        We live together with others,
        we fight together with others,
        but we die our own deaths.

When they ran out of ammunition, Kujebergunoff shot from the trench
              like water springing from the ground.
Crossing his arms on his chest, erect,
          he strode toward the tanks . . .
"To be or not to be"
      was outside Kujebergunoff's concern
          because he lived completely inside life.
Bullets raked his belly.
He smiled proudly.
His arms stayed crossed as he collapsed.
That's how Kujebergunoff died.

Three men struggled to escape
         a tank on fire.
Mustafa Sungurbay saw them.

"Oy, mother," he said, "oy . . . "
He drew his knife and clenched it between his teeth.
His two front teeth gleamed on the steel with joy.
And Mustafa calmly left the trench
                    like water flowing on the ground.
Crawling like a master hunter, he glided by.
Those in the tank got knifed.
And they burned, along with Mustafa Sungurbay.
That's how Mustafa Sungurbay died.

Nikolai Maslenko
threw a snowball at the tanks when he ran out of ammunition.
He swore, he yelled, and overcome with rage,
he grabbed with his bare hands the treads of the nearest tank
and was crushed under the heavy steel plates.
But his torn fingers stayed stuck in the treads;
the treads buried them,
not them the treads.
That's how Nikolai Maslenko died.

"Worker" Klochkoff tossed the last grenade,
the tank stopped, and as it caved in, it opened fire.
Klochkoff fell, shot through with holes.
His eyes softly closed.
He breathed his last: at ease, content,
he died as if on a white bed
                    at a hundred.

Nataroff was the last man alive in the trench.
Wounded, he left the trench at nightfall
and entered the forest, dragging himself on his elbows.
He wandered, bleeding, for days.
He didn't shout or moan but saved his voice—
                    he saved it like a trust.
Finally, he met with friends.
In one breath, he turned his voice over to them:
he told the story of the twenty-eight
                    and died.
                    That's how Nataroff died.

Behind them, Moscow was still standing,

blood on its white bandages,
200 million people acting as one.
Behind them, Moscow was still standing,
calm and confident.
It fired its anti-aircraft guns
          and carried in its pocket
                    a dogeared poetry book.
It attended the theater, movies, concerts,
          listening to Strauss and Tchaikovsky
                    between bursts of artillery,
and played chess behind windows hung with black drapery.
It sent its young workers ahead to the front
and shipped its new machinery back to the interior.
The old workers retooled old machine shops
                    and made them run like clocks.
Moscow dug tank traps and built barricades.
And Pushkin, his cast-bronze shoulders covered with snow,
stood in a daze,
maybe writing a new *Eugene Onegin*.
And the steel man in the Kremlin,
the Bolshevik in the Kremlin,
with his cool, imperturbable, unflinching eyes
and bushy mustache covering
          one of the wisest mouths of the century.
And in his granite tomb, Lenin.
And his winning smile over the snow.

The enemy reached Yakroma to the north of Moscow
                    and Tula to the south.
And in late November
and early December
they brought up their reserves
                    all along the front.
In the first days of December
the situation was critical.

And in the first days of December,
near Vereja in Petrishchevo,
the Germans hanged an eighteen-year-old girl
against a snow-blue sky.
Eighteen-year-old girls might get engaged,

but she got hanged.

She came from Moscow.
She was young and a partisan.
She loved, understood, believed,
                    and took action.
The girl dangling from a rope by her slender neck
                    had all the grandeur of a human being.

As if turning the pages of *War and Peace,*
a young girl's fingers had worked in the snowy dark.
In Petrishchevo, phone lines were cut.
Then a barn burned, with 17 German army horses.
And the next day the partisan got caught.

The partisan got caught at the site of her new target
                    suddenly, from behind, and red-handed.
Stars filling the sky,
her heart racing,
her heartbeat in her pulse,
the gasoline in the bottle,
the match ready to strike.
But it wasn't struck.
She reached for her gun.
They fell on her.
They took her away.
They brought her in.
In the middle of the room, the partisan stood up straight,
her bag on her shoulder,
fur hat on her head, sheepskin coat on her back,
and cotton pants and felt boots on her legs.
The officers looked closer at the partisan:
like a fresh almond inside its green shell,
inside all that cotton, felt, and fur was a tender slip of a girl.

A samovar simmered on the table:
five gun belts and a gun on the checked cloth,
and a green bottle of cognac.
Pork sausage and bread crumbs on a plate.

The homeowners had been shut in the kitchen.

The lamp had burned out;
the room glowed red in the firelight.
And it smelled like crushed beetles.
The owners—a woman, a child, and an old man—
huddled close together,
far from the world,
alone on a deserted mountain, fair game for wolves.

Voices from the next room.
They ask:
"I don't know," she says.
They ask:
"No," she says.
They ask:
"I won't tell you," she says.
They ask:
"I don't know," she says. "No," she says. "I won't tell you," she says.
And the voice that's forgotten everything but these words
is clear as the skin of a healthy child
and straight as the shortest distance between two points.

A leather belt cracks in the next room:
                    the partisan is quiet.
                    Bare human flesh answers.
One after another, belts crack.
The snakes hiss as they leap toward the sun and fall back.
A young German officer enters the kitchen
and sinks down in a chair.
He covers his ears with his hands,
shuts his eyes tight,
and stays that way, motionless, throughout the interrogation.
Belts crack in the next room.
The homeowners count:
                    200.
The questioning resumes:
They ask: "I don't know," she says.
They ask: "No," she says.
They ask: "I won't tell you," she says.
The voice is proud
but no longer clear:
                    it's choked like a bloody fist.

The partisan is hauled outside.
No fur hat on her head,
sheepskin coat on her back,
or cotton pants and felt boots on her legs,
she's stripped to her underwear.
Her lips are swollen from biting,
her forehead, neck, and legs all blood.
Barefoot in the snow,
arms tied behind her back with rope,
flanked by bayonets,
the partisan walks.

They put her in Vasili Klulik's hovel.
She sat down on a wooden bench,
frowning and distracted.
She asked for water.
The guard refused her.
The German soldiers came in,
attacking like insects.
They pushed and shoved her.
One kept lighting matches under her chin,
another ran a saw across her back
till the toothed metal dripped blood.
Then they went off to sleep.
The guard marched her outside at bayonet point.

A child with wide blue eyes
looks out the window:
the world in ice,
the street alone in snow
              under the stars.

A child with wide blue eyes
looks out the window.
He'll forget what he sees,
he'll grow up and marry,
but one summer night
or one afternoon, asleep,
suddenly he'll dream
of a young girl

walking barefoot on stars in the snow.

The length of the street in the snow,
the street alone in the snow.
The partisan in the snow
—feet bare,
arms tied behind her back,
in her underwear—
walks ahead of the bayonet
        up and down the length of the street.

The guard got cold, they returned to the hovel.
He warmed up, they left.
That went on from 10 until 2 a.m.
At two the watch changed,
and the partisan on the wood bench couldn't move.
The partisan
is 18.
The partisan
knows she'll be killed.
In the red glare of her rage
she sees little difference
between dying and being killed.
She's too young and healthy to fear death
                        or feel regret.
She looks at her feet:
swollen,
cracked, frostbitten, scarlet.
But pain
        can't touch the partisan:
her rage and faith
        protect her like a second skin . . .
Her mind wanders to her mother.
And her schoolbooks.
She remembers a glazed earthenware pot,
                    the one before Ilyich's picture,
                    filled with the bluest flowers.
She thinks of her childhood,
so close
        she can almost feel

the colors of her short dresses.
She remembers the first air raid.
The battalions of workers on their way to the front,
              marching and singing through the streets,
              the kids chasing after.
She keeps remembering the trolley stop
                    where she said good-bye to her mother.
She remembers a Young Communists meeting.
It's so close
        she can almost feel
              the glass of water on the red tablecloth
                    and even her own shaking voice.
And now she thinks only of her own voice:
her voice sure and strong,
saying no,
saying I won't tell you,
hiding even her name
        so as not to tell the enemy anything true.

        Her name was ZOE;
        she told them it was TANYA.

        (Tanya,
        your picture's here in front of me in Bursa Prison.
        Bursa Prison.
        You probably never heard of Bursa.
        My Bursa is soft and green.
        Your picture's here in front of me in Bursa Prison.
        It's no longer 1941—
                the year is 1945.
        Your side no longer fights at the gates of Moscow
                but at the gates of Berlin—
                    your side, our side,
                        the side of all the decent people in the world.

        Tanya,
        I love my country
                as much as you loved yours.
        You were a Young Communist;
        I'm 42, an old Communist,

you a Russian, me a Turk,
but both Communists.
They hanged you for loving your country,
I'm in prison for loving mine.
But I'm alive,
and you are dead.
You left the world long ago,
and your time here was brief—
just eighteen years.
You never got your share of the sun's warmth.

You're the hanged partisan,
Tanya,
and I'm the poet in prison.
My daughter, my comrade,
I bend over your picture:
your eyebrows are thin,
your eyes almond-shaped.
I can't tell their color from the picture.
But it says here
they were dark chestnut.
That color is seen a lot in my country, too.
Tanya,
your hair is cut so short,
almost like my son Memet's.
Your forehead is so high,
like moonlight
bringing peace and dreams.
Your face is long and thin,
your ears a little big.
Your neck is still a girl's—
I can tell it hasn't felt a man's touch.
And something with a tassel dangles from your collar,
a decoration for the little lady.

I called in my friends to look at your picture:
"Tanya,
I've got a daughter your age."
"Tanya,
my sister's your age."

"Tanya,
she's your age, the girl I love.
We live in a warm country:
        girls become women overnight."
"Tanya,
I have friends your age in schools, factories, and fields."
"Tanya,
you died—
so many good people have been and are being killed.
But I
—I'm ashamed to say it—
I've never once
put my life on the line
in seven years of war and live perfectly fine,
                        even in prison.")

In the morning they put Tanya's clothes back on,
except her boots, hat, and coat:
                those they kept.
They brought out her bag:
bottles of gasoline, matches, bullets, sugar, salt.
They strung the bottles around her neck,
threw the bag on her back,
and wrote across her chest:
                "PARTISAN."

In the village square they set up the gallows.
The cavalry had drawn swords,
and the infantry formed a circle.
They forced the villagers to come and watch.

Two wood crates were stacked up,
two spaghetti crates.
Above the crates
        dangled the greased rope,
                the end knotted in a noose.

The partisan ascended her throne.
The partisan,
arms tied behind her back,

stood up straight under the rope.

They slipped the noose around her long, slender neck.

One of the officers liked photography.
The officer has taken out a Kodak.
He wants a snapshot.
The noose around her neck, Tanya calls out to the farmers:
"Brothers, don't lose heart!
Now's the time for courage.
Don't let the Fascists breathe—
smash, slash, burn, kill . . . "

A German slapped the partisan across the mouth,
and blood ran down the girl's swollen white chin.
But the partisan turned to the soldiers and went on:
"We're two hundred million strong.
Can you hang two hundred million?
I may go now,
but more of us will come.
Surrender while there's time . . . "

The farmers cried.
The hangman yanked the rope.
The slender-necked swan started to choke.
But the partisan stood on tiptoes,
and the HUMAN called out to life:
"Comrades,
            so long!
Comrades,
            the fight is to the end!
I hear hoofbeats—our people are on their way!"

The hangman kicked the crates.
The crates rolled away.
And Tanya swung from the end of the rope.

On the sixth of December the Red Army launched a counterattack
                              along the Moscow front.
On the eleventh the situation is as follows.

In the north: Rogachev is taken, Klin is surrounded,
the enemy has been driven from Yakroma,
and Istra has been liberated.
Three divisions have been defeated in the north:
seven tank battalions, two motorized cavalry, three infantry, and one SS.
Plus the four infantry battalions decimated at the center.
In the south: with two tank battalions crushed
and the "Great Germany" SS battalion retreating before them,
they're advancing to the northeast of Tula.
And the horsemen who routed the 17th Tank Battalion
cut through two infantry battalions—one motorized—
and, in pursuit of stragglers,
      swept into Venev like the wind,
felt saddlecloths flapping like eagles' wings in the snowy sky.
And farther south
a tank and a motorized battalion withdrew to the southwest.
In four days, four hundred settlements have been liberated
      (I can hardly contain myself even now as I write this),
and more than thirty thousand enemy officers and soldiers
                      have been killed.
This is the situation on the eleventh of December.

Gabriel Peri,
Moscow has been out of danger for four days now.
Gabriel Peri,
you don't know this,
      and neither does Paris.
Those who swagger down the streets of Paris
           in steel-toed boots,
           clicking their heels,
           have been defeated at the gates of Moscow.

Paris,
city of light, city of revolution,
Paris has been sold out, a POW,
and Gabriel Peri has been jailed.

Gabriel Peri was born in Toulon, France
                (1902):
in the air, the smell of fried fish, pine resin, and jasmine;

in the light, the sane blue of the Mediterranean;
and in the harbor, on the oil-slick sea, the steel
of heavy, ungainly armored ships.

His father was Technical Director of the docks.
His mother wears her hair in a bun
and a silver cross on her breast;
she's devout.

From '14 to '18,
Gabriel Peri grew up fourteen years in four.
And as people killed and were killed,
a fair-haired boy walked the wharfs,
his preteen hand on his beautiful high forehead,
his eyes wide with sad questions,
his amber-black eyes flashing with fury.

In '19 he joined the Socialist Party
and at the end of 1920 helped found
the Communist Party.
He burned all his ships at anchor in gloomy waters,
burned all ships that didn't sail into light,
and conquered the affliction of the self.
And then the life of one man could be read
in the book of a party, a country, and the world.

His laughter soared like white sea birds
over the smoky harbor of his office at *L'Humanité*.
And his head, like a beating heart,
was ready everywhere: Ethiopia, Spain, China.
And he always listened patiently,
with his impeccably tailored suits, pipe, and polka-dot bow tie,
slightly amused and perfectly polite.
And many times he appeared at demonstrations,
bringing people word of happiness
because of and in spite of everything.
And in the Bourbon Palace he defended
France's honor like his sister's.

And one day, defending France's honor

against those forcing the door from outside
and those opening it from inside,
—not in the Bourbon Palace now
but in the streets in the unsurrendered night—
he was sold out and captured.

This is Gabriel Peri's last night.
They've just entered his cell
and stood under the electric light,
flashing their epaulets and short blond hair:
"You'll die," they said.
        "Ask for asylum, and your life will be spared."
They made their point as clear as a drawn blade.
Gabriel Peri listened patiently,
slightly amused and perfectly polite.
"No," he said.

To climb a mountain
and see the blue sea below.
The peace of a death true to the life lived.

He wrote his last letter to his friends and countrymen.
Without a single unnecessary comma,
concise, clear, and direct,
written as ever
with undivided attention.
He signed it
and sealed the envelope.
And he asked himself one last time:
he had no regrets.
If he could do all over again
what began in '02
and would end at dawn
this morning,
the fifteenth of December '41,
he'd start again at the same place,
take the same road,
and, if necessary, end in the same place.
He felt proud and at peace.
He'd entered the fight through his mind and books,

but he'd been as true to it as an honest laborer.

His esteemed friend put it well:
"Communism is the youth of the world,"
and "It awakens singing tomorrows."

The electric light fades,
dawn will soon break.
And facing the firing squad,
he, too, will awaken singing tomorrows.
His is a song of revolution, a rose-scented romance:
"*Adieu,*
et que vive la France!"

They took him out.
Day was breaking.
He leaned back.
Staring down the gun barrels,
he sang the "Marsaillaise."
The French patriot sang the "Marsaillaise."
A volley of gunshots.
And one of the true sons of the Mediterranean fell to his knees:
the Communist sang the "International."
A second volley.
His hands reached out toward the sun,
and Gabriel Peri fell face-down on the earth.

BOOK FIVE

Dawn breaks.
Red hair flares on the pillow.
Halil's wife, Aysha, wakes:
her eyes open big and gold
                in her white face.
The room is ice-cold,
the bed
        warm.
And the woman wants her prisoner husband.

    Across the room, her daughter Leyla in her little bed
    looks like fresh fruit from Iskenderun this winter morning.
    She's curled into a ball,
                her tiny knees touching her chin,
                her hands making fists.

The mother watches her child sleep
and feels her in her womb.

    The windows are bare.
    Aysha gets out of bed
    and puts on the long black sweater
            her husband left behind.
    Fire flares in the brazier.
    Linden tea in the blue enamel teapot.
    Outside, Uskudar wakes up,
            its hazel eyes droopy with sleep,
                its bare white feet in red leather slippers.
    That's how Aysha always pictures
            the neighborhood waking up.

Yesterday some money came from Halil.
Today the letter back to him:
    "My sweet,
    I got the fourteen-and-a-half liras
    with 'I miss you' on the receipt.
                Thank you.

But it pains me to know
you work to support me.
I hate myself for it.

I went into Istanbul yesterday
and heard such strange things on the boat back.
Everyone's smuggling out money:
you wouldn't believe who all
has millions in Swiss and American banks.
They must fear their country:
all they think about is getting out.
Some had their money in Holland,
and it was seized by the Germans,
who later sent it to America
      as a favor to our effendis.
Germany is at war with America,
but they still exchange money.
Money has no country.
Do its owners?
I guess they don't own the money
so much as it owns them.
Then I heard something else
that really upset me:
under the guise of sending it to Switzerland,
      we're shipping wheat to Germany.
Goddamn them
      who feed those cannibals
            our country's wheat!
I don't want to end my letter with a curse.
I'll draw you a picture of my new room . . .

This is our third house you haven't seen.
Here's the chair, the table, the window—
      and here's a pot of winter flowers.
This is the armchair: I'm sitting in it.
This, a little bed: Leyla sleeps in it.
Over here is something like a cupboard
      where I store my coal—when I have any.
This here is both a linen closet and a kitchen.
And here's the bookcase,

             your famous legacy from your grandfather.
Look closely at the wall:
             your picture
                    and mine below it.
My room isn't this big:
either I did the furniture too small,
                    or I drew the room too big.
Anyway, the scale is wrong.
Your wife may make a real home someday,
             a home whose man is no longer in prison,
                    but she'll never make a picture of it . . .

My letter's over, my sweet.
Your daughter's awake and looking at me.
I kiss your hands . . . "

"What's the date today?" thought Aysha.
She remembered: the twelfth month,
             the fifteenth day.
She signed the letter.
And without dating it,
             she sealed the envelope.

The letter reached Halil on the afternoon
of the thirty-first; Beethoven Hasan brought it to his room.
Halil was depressed:
that morning, a peasant prisoner had hanged himself
                    in the third-ward bathroom.
He was in for not paying his road tax,
so he didn't receive any rations.
It was his third time in for road taxes.
The warden announced the death:
they untied the sash and took down the body.
Halil remembered him—
a short, quiet man.
"This time around, no one came to visit him," they said.
"We asked him many times to eat with us, but he wouldn't.
He didn't even open his mouth to ask anyone for a smoke.
The poor man died of hunger."
"Not from hunger," said Modern Yusuf.

"You don't know—
he was a proud man,
he died of grief . . . "

Halil was depressed
until he saw Aysha's handwriting.
Beethoven Hasan watched him, amused,
then asked:
"It's from your wife, isn't it?"
"Yes. How'd you know?"
"Well, I think you read it through twice."
"Not twice, three times."
For some reason, Beethoven Hasan was embarrassed by this answer
                              and changed the subject:
"Well, tonight is New Year's Eve.
What should we do?"
"Hasan, I told the warden
—he'll be playing cards anyway—
we'd get together in my room.
You can sing your symphony 'The Unvanquished'
        and I'll read Jelal's 'Epic of the Independence War.'
Painter Ali can draw our caricatures,
Modern Yusuf and Ihsan Bey can try to tick off Grocer Sefer,
Omer from Aydin can do a Zeybek dance
                and Captain Ilyas a Caucasian . . . "
Beethoven Hasan smiled slyly:
"I smuggled in a liter of raki;
                    can we drink that, too?"
"Why not? We'll drink it.
But where'd you get that kind of dough?"
I didn't buy it.
You know the guard from Izmir,
the tobacco worker?
He brought it.
He said we could all drink it.
We hid the bottle in Yusuf's shop.
Ali knows about it, too.
But don't let Grocer Sefer hear—
            he spies for management."
Beethoven Hasan left.
Halil felt strangely excited

410

and—he didn't know why—a little guilty:
he would drink raki in prison for the first time in his life.
He took off his glasses and wiped them clean,
and read Aysha's letter once more.
It wasn't enough.
He took out her old letters.
They were all undated.
He had numbered them—
Aysha's letters over the last eight months.
He lined them up on the table
        like cards in a game of solitaire.
He read them in order.
It was a journey toward Aysha, into the past.

1.

I'm writing you this letter sick in bed.
If you were here, what good care you'd take of me!
Leyla just turned six.
She's small for her age,
and I make her nap during the day.
I just woke her:
her cheeks are rosy,
        and her hazel eyes look almost grown-up.
(Have you noticed
        how our eyes never change?
Our childhood, good or bad, lives on in them,
        and not just as a memory.)
"I'm writing Daddy," I told her.
She said, "Daddy?"
                and yawned.
She has a hard time waking up.
Everybody says hello,
        Leyla and I kiss your hands.

2.

I'm feeling better.
It's lovely here:
spring.
Fruit trees are the most beautiful things on earth.

Do you have any at the prison?
Are yours there blooming like ours here,
        making your world more beautiful?
Leyla and I talk about you all the time.
She keeps asking: "When will Daddy get the letter?
We'll go to sleep tonight, then he'll get it, won't he?" she says.
We made a cheese pita
        and ate it out in the garden—
                we thought of you.
Our father, we miss you.

They just told me a host of bad things Leyla's done.
I'm stopping this letter to give her a good spanking.

Leyla came in.
I scolded her,
and she started crying.
I couldn't spank her.
I made her sit under the big plane tree.
And she has a scratchy sweater,
                which she hates—
                I made her wear it.
She's going to sit there with her tiny nose, all alone
                                till dark.
By now you must be full of pity.
But what can I do?
        She has to grow up right.
The whole thing gave me a headache.
"Best not to have kids"—
I can't bring myself to say that.
For all their trouble, I still love children.
If I had a dozen, I'd be the happiest woman on earth.
Just think:
what one lacked, another would have;
separately flawed,
        the twelve together would make one perfect person—
                                and me their mother.

I counted:
today it's exactly

                     three years since you went in,
and I've been in my brother's house two years.
"Days pass slow in prison,
          but years go fast," you used to say.
It's the same for us who have people in prison:
          the days go slow,
                     the years fast.
My husband, our father,
we kiss your hands.

3.

What a mess—
camouflaging is all the rage,
everyone's masking their windows.
And I sit reading fairy tales,
not to Leyla but to myself.
Beautiful tales that begin, "Once upon a time . . . ,"
and end,
          "Three apples fell from the sky: one for you, one for me,
          and one for the reader."
Better days, better days—
may anyone who says they won't come choke on his words!

Yesterday
we sat in my sister-in-law's room
when someone burst in, shouting:
"Jemilé Hanum's house—her house is on fire!"
We ran outside.
It was really Shahin Pasha's house burning.
The roof had just caught fire,
          and flames were leaping out when we got there.
The fire truck was late.
They didn't have a hose.
By the time they got everything ready, the house had burned down.
Three firemen fell from the balcony:
one is hurt seriously, two have minor injuries.
It all happened before my eyes.
I was overcome with shock and helplessness.
I didn't really know who lived there:

we never met,
      but I'd known the house for twenty years.
It's as if I've lost an old friend.
I can still see the flames.
And imagine: today it's not a friend, a house, or a city that's burning
                                  but the whole world.
This crisscrossed round thing of ours
                  is burning up, turning in the dark
            (that's how they picture this business,
              and it's always before my eyes).
I heard the news last night:
"The disaster of war is at our door,
we're ringed by fire on four sides"—
                  or some such words.
I can't get them out of my mind.
Fire is so real to me now
that if I steal a look at the night through the window,
I think I'll see the trees ringing the garden all in flames.

4.

My love,
I can't tell you what strange days these are.
I get up very early.
Picking up my room,
    cooking,
        sewing, and so on—and the day is over.
I don't go anywhere.
I sit home, all nerves.
My nerves are bad these days.
And it's not just me
      but everyone.
They look like rabbits—crouched low,
           ears erect,
              listening for something,
and ready to take off down the hill
if anyone says "boo."

My sweet,
I believe in you so much

I want to be like you.
We lived together just five years, really—
                    the rest you spent in prisons.
I'm not complaining:
our life was still beautiful that way, too.
Wherever you are,
                    near or far,
I get addicted to you.
You're the soul of addiction
            (what an odd expression:
            it wears my grandfather's fez on its head
            and a grizzled fringe of beard on its chin,
                            but it's all mine).
As you can see, you "spirit of my flesh"
                            (is that said?
                            Yet that's what I feel),
        I can't present my case in a letter.
I'm full of things to tell you.
To put aside pen and paper,
to be face to face
            and talk with you,
to hear my voice
            next to yours . . .

I kiss your eyes—
no, your hands.
I don't remember saying "I kiss your hands" in my last letter.
Check and tell me.
It takes my breath away:
            how could I forget?

5.

I'm tangled up in so much nonsense.
I've vowed to get through it.
I played the lottery again:
                    nothing.
But I'm stubborn, I won't give up, and you wait,
                            I'll hit fifty thousand yet.
Our neighbor Jemilé Hanum comes over every day,

but just to see me
and maybe my mother.

She stays an hour and leaves.
You don't know her,
but she likes you,
and you would like her, too.
She's quite a lady.
Her beautiful hazel eyes are always made up,
and her tiny mouth is always painted,
yet she's pushing sixty.
She has low blood pressure and a bad heart.
All she does, all she thinks about, is painting.
She's painted since she was a girl.
When her husband died ten years ago,
she sold her jewels and went to Rome at fifty.
It's a good thing she didn't sell her house,
or the poor woman would have starved to death when she returned.
Now she makes ends meet by renting out the first floor.
Her house is another world:
tassels, fringes, knickknacks,
and mountains of paintings everywhere—
oil and pastel nudes,
women one lovelier than the next.
Then she's done some male heads—
all princes out of storybooks.
And what soft, sweet colors:
wine-sediment, dried-rose, baby's-mouth,
all kinds of pinks and off-whites,
lemon-mold-blue, glass-green, emerald,
and deep purple.
Morning to night
she's all wrapped up in painting.
Glasses on her nose
(she only wears them when she paints:
she hates anything that reminds her of her age,
and takes offense at the slightest hint she's old,
and sulks at you for days),
what was I saying,
glasses on her nose,

brushes between her teeth
> (little red-stemmed five-kurush glue brushes,
> because the others cost too much.
> She even makes her own canvas:
>> white lead primer on cambric),

what was I saying,
brushes between her teeth,
her painted eyes squinting,
she wouldn't notice if the world ended
> once she's caught up in the colors.
In fact, she didn't see Shahin Pasha's house burning.
The next day she told me:
"Too bad I missed it, but I was lost in my painting.
> I just saw where the fire was:
> it looks ugly.
Yet flames are beautiful—
> nuances of orange, wine, and crimson
>> and even something of autumn leaves."
That's Jemilé Hanum for you!
P.S. Jemilé Hanum's cat
killed our chicken.
Leyla drew a picture of it
> and insists
>> I put it in the envelope.
Maybe, thank God—
> maybe, what a pity—
> our daughter is growing up.
I kiss your hands.

6.

Leyla is sleeping.
She's much better these days.
But yesterday she climbed up on a chair
> with a stick in her mouth and fell.
The stick went into the roof of her mouth.
We got it out okay,
but at night in bed she cried to herself.
She's very scared of death,
always asking: "Will I die?"

Why does this kid have such a fear of dying?
And tell me:
           how come we don't all go crazy
                      knowing we will die?
Or do people think *they* won't die?
My uncle says
           that's what everyone in the trenches thought—
                                    is it true?
Or do we get used to dying
           the way we do to aging?
I think the reason is this:
although it's short for each of us,
life is stronger than death.

Everyone is abandoning the city,
except those of us who plan to stick it out.

Some news for you:
Jemilé Hanum went into Istanbul yesterday,
I don't know where, to buy some genuine English white lead
because she makes her own white paint, crushing the lead
                                    in walnut oil.
"I got on the boat," she said,
                "and went out on deck.
Sky-blue and gold everywhere,
with a little silver and ash mixed in.
The shadows the palest violet,
the light like filtered honey...
Two young people sit across from me,
a gentleman and a lady.
The lady is plain ugly,
           the gentleman downright beautiful.
What color, what skin, what hair!
He isn't human—he's a pastel.
And he's wearing a light-chestnut overcoat:
the material must be part silk,
           it has such folds
                I can't get enough of them!
I controlled myself, I gritted my teeth,
                then finally I couldn't resist:

I put on my glasses,
first some sidelong glances,
          then a few more, a little more courage,
and then I just gave myself to the gentleman's colors.
I'm lost in a pale green
                    on his shaved cheek
when suddenly all hell breaks loose.
The ugly lady foams at the mouth and almost attacks me.
What she isn't saying!
The gentleman is her fiancé, I'm crazy,
                    she's calling the police.
'You shameless horny old bag!' she says.
The people around us laugh.
The gentleman doesn't open his mouth, he just sits there coyly.
He's a man, no? He's pleased.
Thank goodness it wasn't long
          before the boat pulled up at the Bridge and we got off.
What do you think of that?
The woman was jealous of me."

So that's what happened to Jemilé Hanum.
I noticed
today her eyeliner was heavier,
and when she said, "The woman was jealous of me,"
                    she was happy.

Halil,
how you'd have laughed
at this story last year
or even five days ago.
But now you don't feel like laughing at anything,
and neither do I.
Sometimes it feels like a crime to laugh.
Today is June 27, 1941.

7.

I'm not happy here.
I'm sorry I closed up my house.
But what could I have done?

My brother,
        as you know, is always the same;
my sister-in-law
        is as she's always been—
                lazy, depressed, bored,
                        arrogant, and sometimes awfully aggressive.
She gets up at eleven
        and drags her bloodless, blond beauty around the house
                                like a ghost.
Now I see it's my brother's fault.
She needed a different kind of husband—
                        a calm, strong, gutsy man.
Not my poor short brother with his plump womanly hands,
belly-dancing when he's happy,
        fighting her tooth and nail when he's mad.
Then there's the question of love . . .
Does my brother love my sister-in-law?
                    He does.
It's sad,
but his love
is even heartfelt, like a child's.
But what matters most to him is comfort.
And it's a strange comfort at that:
it doesn't mean a clean house,
                good food,
                      the light of love, or anything.
The house is filthy, everything everywhere;
            we'd all drown in the mess
                if I didn't pick up a bit.
As for love,
        you know.
But I now see
comfort for him
        means things don't change.
But he's gutless.
And the same in business:
all he knows are small-time deals,
he's scared to take on something big.
But he doesn't fear the law or losing money
                    (that never occurs to him);

change frightens him.
And then . . .
Oh, sweet,
am I bitching about my own brother?
But I love him, despite his faults,
and would defend him if anyone, even you,
                              said such things . . .

But anyway
I'm not happy here . . .

My husband,
to cut my ties to the world
        and go live on a mountaintop—
                              can't do it, right?
                              I'd get tired of it.

All I think about is when you'll get out.
Get out,
and I'll gladly die in a week.

This letter got left here
                        and waited two days.
You see the state I'm in—
nervous exhaustion.
Lots of medicines,
        bad-smelling things
I have to take.
And will—if you get out.

This time we've learned how much we mean to each other.
I don't think we'll ever fight again,
                        or will we?

I need you so badly.
It would do me
        so much good if you got out now.

Another letter from you just arrived:
I sat and read it and had a good cry.
I cry these days.

For years I'd learned to suffer without crying.
Now I'm crying again—
I wonder why?
When she saw me, Leyla cried, too.
Mother and daughter see eye to eye:
                    we cry together.

8.

I know where you got the fifteen liras:
          you want to send me your coat money.
Get it made right away.
I don't need money.
I do sewing and stuff.
Some people in Ankara ordered embroidered curtains and bedspreads.
Jemilé Hanum and I work together:
I embroider,
and she draws big roses, violets, or chrysanthemums on them.
We make between forty and fifty a month,
split fifty-fifty.
I've even saved a little.
I'd be almost rich if we didn't have payments hanging.
But enough of that . . .
They say Hitler will beat them all in six weeks.
Fat chance.
The bigger they are, etc.
Can hope be defeated?
They should ask the wives and mothers of prisoners:
it may stagger and slip, but it can't be defeated.
Now take me, a prisoner's wife:
I may suffer terribly, and even weaken
—these days especially, I'm going from bad to worse,
                                        and fast—
but I'll never be beaten.
And then think of humanity
                    and *its* hope . . .

9.

You wrote me lots of things
                    to find out and tell you.
I'm not doing any of them.
I don't want to learn anything new.
You find out,
          and don't tell me.
These days I have to live on hope,
                              not news.

I don't want to do anything.
I'm anxious,
          tense.
I'm waiting for something,
          and I don't know what.
I feel as if
any time now
      the door will fly open
          and this thing will appear out of nowhere.
Or if I get up,
          stand on tiptoe,
                    and part the curtains
(although my window's on the second floor),
                    I'll see its hands on the glass
                              (if it has hands).
Or I don't know it yet
      but I'm about to take a trip—
                they'll call me somewhere.
A book lies on the table.
Maybe it's under that
(it could fit under a book):
who could have put it there?
If I lift the book and look,
      the problem will vanish.
But I don't pick it up,
because my mind stops my hand
or else I want to draw my torture out.

That's how it is, my sweet.

I'm always saying "That's how it is."
Strange, isn't it?

I kiss your hands.

10.

For two days
I've sat on the grass in the yard and read.
I don't have the strength to lift a finger.
Jemilé Hanum's tenant's child plays the violin.
My first year here he'd just started—
                    do, re, mi, fa, sol—
                            and now Tchaikovsky.
So he's done something in all these years.
And what have I done?
My years flow by empty, like a sea without fish.
What do I live for?
Mother's chrysanthemums in the garden bloom all colors.
To watch chrysanthemums,
        to read a novel in Omer Riza's translation,
            to listen to the neighbor's violin—
                        is that enough to live for?

11.

My husband,
to stretch out on my back
        and stare at the ceiling,
to mute sounds and erase colors
        as much as I can—
that's what I need.
Somewhere peaceful, a white room,
a small bed—
no, a big bed, with me in it—
and you sitting there silently watching over me.
And lots of other things like that,
                all having to do with rest.

Rain or no rain,

for three days I've been looking for Kazim from Kartal:
                                        he's left.
I couldn't send you any salted mackerel:
                              they're out.
I can't sell your suit here:
everybody's selling something,
and the rich aren't buying "somethings"
                              but apartment buildings.

12.

Ah my sweet, ah my sweet,
Jemilé Hanum died.
I was with her when she
                    just went.
It never occurred to me she'd die.
She stopped, like a car stops,
                        and that was it.
They're left on the walls—the wines, the sky-blues, the golds.
It's funny:
I never got the expression "breathe your last."
Now I know what it means.
To leave everything
and suddenly go nowhere, to nothing, never to come back . . .
This death woke me up.
The lawyer sent hot sausage and pastrami,
                    I'm sending you some:
                                eat them in good health.

13.

I've moved into a room in my uncle's house.
I'm thirty-five—
                surprised?
I age a year every five years.
You'll see,
I'll have a new life in my new room.
I'll arrange the furniture now.
And there's so much of it!
How did it ever fit into one room,

how will it now?

I read morning to night.
I'm hooked on books:
they're wise
              and foolish,
grown-up
        and childish.
Books make the longest, most beautiful journeys,
but fruitless,
              but without you . . .

14.

It's half-past twelve.
My uncle turned on the radio
        to listen to England.
Rostov has been liberated.

Do you remember
when Leyla had diphtheria at seven months?
We caught it late.
"We'll have to operate right now," the doctor said.
My girl lying there open-mouthed like a fish without water,
loud rasping in her tiny throat,
no movement in her arms,
        just her plump little legs twitching—
you remember now?
Can you see the doctor's instruments?
That shiny thing was a lancet, wasn't it?
And so much gauze and cotton!
Why did you make me leave?
How did I ever agree to it, how?
I waited outside the door,
        biting my nails
                (which I never do).
Suddenly you opened the door
        with tears in your eyes.
The doctor touched me on the shoulder:
"Sister," he said, "it's over."

And it wasn't until the sixth night
        (Leyla was in deep sleep,
                breathing like a small world)
when the doctor—quite happy and a little proud—
        looked me in the eye
and said, "Well, sister, we saved your daughter,"
that I felt overjoyed
                and then, suddenly, strangely sad.
Of course,
just think,
a part of me, something most mine,
was saved without my slightest help.
My child
        was born again without me,
                outside of me.

What do you say?
Why do I
        remember this now?

15.

I want to hear your footsteps inside my house.
I want you to knock on my door
        and me to open it with my own hands.
But take off your shoes in the hall if they're muddy—
        your slippers will be there for you.

I want to cook for you with my own hands
                and set our table myself.
Except
we'll do the dishes together as before.

I want to read the same books as you
(I know you'll still explain what I might miss).
I want to wash your clothes with my own hands
                and mend the tears in them.
And I want to dust your desk myself
(I won't disturb its mess).
But this time

you won't leave your pipe burning on the cushion
                or drop your ashes on the floor.

I want to work by your side
and fight by your side
(not for economic freedom
        or liberation from the slavery of housework and so on
                but to stay right under your nose).

And finally,
my most sacred right:
I want to sleep with you on the same pillow
        and have your kids,
                two more at least...

Halil folded Aysha's letters and put them away.
He lay back on the bed:
four stone walls,
bare iron bars at the window,
cold concrete.
Years
of concrete, iron, stone.
Now the longing for soft cloth,
        a warm wood-paneled room,
and even a lace pillow.
Halil retreated behind his glasses.
Outside in the night, snow fell on the city,
                        hard and steady.

II

On this day in the spring of '42
        they've come down from the foothills
        and sit gazing at the Mediterranean.
The city of X stands on the bluff behind them.
Sun-glare off the water lights up their faces.

Ali Kiraz dangles his legs from the quay,

his big fists resting on his knees.
His eyes glint in his round face like two black bugs.
Ali Kiraz has a good voice:
he reads ghazals
          and the latest news aloud,
adjusting his voice like a gramophone.
Ali Kiraz is brave:
he beat up his guardsman corporal over a woman
and did six months in prison,
where he learned to grow his jetblack hair long
                    and slick it straight back.

Ali Kiraz is talking, his white teeth gleaming,
his voice at once mocking
                and proud:
"When I was an MP in Chanakkalé,
                there was this captain.
I delivered some grapes to his house,
                    to his wife
                        at home.
I handed her the basket.
She went inside and started chomping on the stems
like she'd never seen food before.
I watched her through the keyhole.
Then she brought out a plate of grapes.
'Have some,' she said.
So I started to eat.
Then she asked me:
'How do they eat grapes where you come from?'
I said:
'The way you ate them in there.'
'You pig,' she said, 'you pervert! How did you see me eat the grapes?'
'I peeked through the keyhole,' I said.
She laughed.
You see, she was trying to act refined.
I was only a peasant boy,
and she wanted to make fun of me,
          as if I didn't know how to eat grapes . . . "

Ali Kiraz fell silent.
A weary smile played on his broad, apple-cheeked face.

He picked up a stone and threw it into the sea.
And he said,
      sucking on each word
          like a piece of candy:
"Beautiful woman.
Medium height,
blue-gray eyes,
ivory skin.
And she was foxy:
she had forty devils in her,
and not a one knew what the others were up to.
The captain almost walked in on us once.
Hasibé Hanum hid me in the water jug.
It was a Chanakkalé jug—just huge.
So I got to perform my ablutions, but I nearly drowned."

Ali Kiraz tossed another stone into the sea
and murmured with the sadness of things past:
"Beautiful woman.
Really something else."
"To hell with women—
when you catch one alone, nail her..."
This was Ahmet speaking.
Ali Kiraz objected:
"How can you say that?
Even your better dogs won't bark at a woman—
      just because she's a woman."
Ahmet didn't answer.
He lay back,
      resting on his elbows,
hands behind his neck, head raised like a curbstone.
His patched striped shirt unbuttoned,
his heart seemed to beat
      right under his skin, not under his ribs.

Four years ago Ahmet had abducted Hatijé from a hayfield:
he couldn't afford a wedding.
Hatijé's father was the village carpenter.
Lawsuit, court trial.
In court the girl said she'd consented
and went to live with Ahmet.

That made five heads under one roof.
And before long
        the pots and pans, the ox and the land
                were split in two.
When the property split in two,
            so did the people.
Ahmet, his mother, and Hatijé lived in one half of the house,
and Ahmet's older brother, Osman, and his wife in the other.
Wife beat wife,
the husbands the wives,
and the mother cried day and night.
The ox took sick from grief.
And if the carpenter hadn't helped out,
        Hatijé would have starved to death.
When the time came for her to give birth,
she couldn't.
"It's because they beat my daughter," said the carpenter.
A delegation from the village went to Hatijé's bedside:
the young bride writhed in pain,
all the time swearing she wasn't beaten.
She gave birth that night,
but the child was stillborn.
The carpenter wouldn't let the matter rest.
The blond-bearded carpenter wanted his daughter back.
"My Hatijé," he said, "come home with me.
I'll marry you to somebody with money.
Don't stay here—they're too poor.
A poor man's wife is never happy."
Hatijé went running back to her father's house.
And Ahmet sulked and took off for the city.
Now he worked in Koyunzadé's rice paddies,
and yesterday he'd received the final divorce papers.
Ahmet hadn't cursed women out of anger at Hatijé
but because he was mad at himself for acting like an ass.
Instead of sulking and taking off for the city,
he should have grabbed his runaway wife and dragged her back by
    her hair
or he could now go kill the carpenter.

One-Arm Ismail squatted on Ahmet's right.
A big, brawny man about forty-five,

he'd fixed his hazel eyes on the anchored boats
                    rocking on the green water.
One-Arm Ismail answered Ali Kiraz:
"Those women dogs won't bark at
                    are city women,
                              captains' wives—
not ours.
Our women,
peasants' wives, are donkeys."

One-Arm Ismail's knitted eyebrows were dark and bristly,
and above his thick-lipped red mouth
        his mustache gleamed like polished ebony,
                without a single white hair.

During the Great War, Ismail had been packed off to the army,
        even though he was just sixteen.
He acted brave out of spite.
He got sent to Yozgat as a guardsman.
And when the Armenians were massacred,
        he got up to his neck in blood.
He deserted and became a bandit.
After the war
        he returned to his village with a belt-load
of silver coins, earrings, bracelets.
And his left arm gone at the elbow.
The Liberation Army wouldn't have him.
He married.
He'd been married three days
                when he brought home oranges from the city.
He lined them up on the shelf like gold ingots.
When he got back from the coffeehouse that night,
                he noticed one was missing.
He asked his wife: "Who ate the orange?"
The woman: "I did."
"So you ate my orange," One-Arm Ismail said,
        and beat her till her face swelled up like a drum.
And the woman's life was hell from that night on.
Eminé was a blue-eyed, buxom woman.
The blue of her eyes faded like washed-out denim,

432

and her body shriveled to a dry shell.

One-Arm Ismail looked the same, everywhere and always.
He went around with a dark, long face
        you could hardly bear to look at.
He cared for only two things in the world:
        gambling and his ten-year-old daughter.
When he went into the sheepfold, even the sheep wept.
He hung goats from trees by their legs for whipping
        when they wouldn't stand still for milking.
Summers he worked his son
                and kicked him out of the house come winter.
Ismail's son, Omer, was a mild-mannered, serious youth.
But now and then he thought,
"If anyone but my mother had begotten me by that man,
        I'd have brained her with a rock long ago."
Omer could forgive his mother this lone
                but dreadful crime
because he loved the old woman like his life.
Last winter One-Arm Ismail kicked out the old woman, too.
She took her quilt
and went to her uncle's.
"Go get your mother's quilt," Ismail told Omer.
"Beat her if you have to,
but get it back."
Omer wouldn't go,
and One-Arm beat him unconscious.
He woke in a pool of blood and made up his mind to kill his father.
"I'll shoot him in his sleep,"
he told his mother.
His mother cried:
"Your father has nine lives—
he'll kill us both before you can kill him.
An Armenian priest cursed him to live a thousand years.
Give it up, son.
He's my curse I have to live with.
Go to the city, earn your keep,
        and save your own sweet self."
So Omer left for the city.
When summer came, One-Arm Ismail went looking for his son.

He wanted him back;
it was a busy time in the village.
He found him that morning in the rice mill.
He lied:
"Omer," he said,
"your mother's sick.
She lies in bed
and asks for you.
Come, Omer, let's go home.
Take your time—finish up here first.
I'll wait for you at the Cretan coffeehouse by the sea,
                    not inside but right close by.
Ask the agha for your pay.
Did you make good money?
You can buy some cotton cloth and stuff for your sister.
And I could stand a new shirt, too.
Your mother said, 'I want to see my son.'
But take your time—finish up here first.
I'll wait for you by the sea till dark."

And he waited.

The wrestler Kadri, sitting on Ali Kiraz's left, asked:
"That German plane crashed out near you—that true, Kiraz?"
"It didn't crash—it landed."
"Did it run out of kerosene?"
"Planes don't burn kerosene, wrestler; they use gasoline."
And Ali Kiraz thought:
"'When a horse is slow, it moves like an ox;
                    when men are slow, they're jocks.'"
And he continued, with a knowing air of mystery:
"They were coming back from bombing the English
when they had engine trouble
—you know, with the propellers.
But it was night,
and they thought this was Rhodes,
so they landed.
They just missed the thicket at the lower end of Hasan's field.
In the morning the pilot found an empty matchbox
—you know, the captain of the airplane.

434

The box had a star and crescent.
'Oh, no,' they said, 'we've landed in Turkey!'
We heard about it and all went out there, the mayor and everybody.
We saw them destroying their code boxes
and called the township.
Just then, one of the Germans . . . "

No one listened to Ali Kiraz but the wrestler Kadri.
"How can I get the money from the boy?"
                              One-Arm Ismail wondered.
And Ahmet, still lying on his back, thought of Hatijé's breasts,
which he would never smell or kiss again.
But about fifty meters off, in the Cretan coffeehouse,
              the same plane was discussed.
The customs officer, Kamil Effendi, said:
"Orders came from Ankara
to treat the Germans well
and put them on a train to Ankara.
Orders are orders.
Koyunzadé gave a banquet for them at the club:
the governor, the regiment commander,
                              the police chief were all there.
Orders came from Ankara:
'Treat them well.'
Orders are orders."

Kamil Effendi came from Prishtina.
He'd served as a guardsman and sergeant in Yugoslavia.
He had an incredibly long thin neck,
              especially from the back.
His voice boomed like a trumpet.
And he was hard of hearing,
       so his mouth always hung open.

The Cretan owner of the coffeehouse
                    put a Greek record on the gramophone.
The trill of mandolins shivering with pleasure filled the room.
Ramiz, the new waiter
from Istanbul,
stood stroking his neat sandy mustache.

Then he grabbed the towel draped over his left shoulder:
"*Elado vre,* my black-eyed beauty," he said, *"elado vre, Eleni.*
The islands, Arnavutkoy, Samatya—
ah, Istanbul!
Que quieres, buenos?
Its water, air, fish, strawberries.
Its Turks, Armenians, and Greeks,
                    plus Jews.
I can almost taste it. *Ahparin girlas?"*

A voice behind him
asked with envious contempt:
"If Istanbul is so great, why'd you leave?"

Ramiz spun around as if knifed in the back.
His drawn, wheaten face flushed scarlet.
He dug his chin into his chest
and was about to rip into the guy
when the shoes on his sockless feet caught his eye:
they were in tatters,
only the pointed toes intact,
and under the frayed cuffs of his baggy pants
        they looked like two fish out of water.
Ramiz swallowed the curse on the tip of his tongue
                    and grinned:
"Istanbul is great," he said, "but I had no choice.
Cruel Fate stuffed my bells with straw.
Blind Fate
        —*katalavis?*—
gives sweet melons to some, bitter to others.
[And fixing his yellow cat-eyes on the ceiling now,
                    he went on,
                        rolling his r's.]
Hunger hit Istanbul hard this winter—
and when I say 'Istanbul,'
            I mean the real Istanbul.
And what a winter!
Freezing winds,
knee-deep snow.
And no coal.

They finally let us have five kilos a month
                                  and one bar of soap.
I lived in Beshiktash with my brother.
He had a wife and kid.
He was a quilt-maker.
With the winter so hard
and bread rationed
and no work,
he told his wife he couldn't support her.
Folks were down to eating barley.
A neighbor, Murtaza Effendi,
his son Memet (a scale inspector for the city),
and his mother
—they all starved to death within eight days
at 21 Hill Street, Beshiktash.
Not that neighbors didn't help one another,
but if they helped today, they'd go hungry tomorrow.
So my brother took off.
We sent the kid to relatives in Tuzla.
The wife ended up a streetwalker in Beyoghlu.
I stopped by my aunt's in Ferikoy.
Same thing there, hunger and so on—
                        nobody home.
Everyone out hunting for bread and coal.
I sold my coat at the flea market
and went to Osmanbey.
The non-Muslims
        from Kurtulush and Galatasaray
            had looted the Osmanbey bakery.
Mounted police had cordoned off the street.
A man wearing glasses
came out of the bakery
with bread,
and they grabbed it from him the minute he stepped out.
I heard there was a place in Kasimpasha selling roast chickpeas.
I went.
More crowded than the bakery.
I kicked my way through.
Laid down the dough
and bought four hundred grams of chickpeas.

Kids chased after me.
I went up to Kojamustafapasha.
Ihsan Hanum had four kids.
May all four rest in peace.
We got help to bury them.
And at Modern Cemetery,
          what did I see,
                    what did my eyes see?
The dead lying in the snow,
some wrapped in white shrouds,
                         others stark-naked.
I went to visit a Christian friend in Kurtulush.
His wife and two daughters were home.
No bread, no coal.
They all started bawling when they saw me.
I gave them two-fifty from the coat money
and left.
Three times I counted the money in my pocket:
                    ten liras and twenty-one kurush.
I made up my mind:
'In Istanbul I'll die of hunger or the cold,'
I said to myself, 'I'm getting out of here.'
And I migrated south, like a swallow."

Ramiz had stopped talking at some point in his story
—he had no idea where—
and had told the rest to himself in one breath.
The mandolins still played on the gramophone,
and a Greek girl lisped a song.

The guardsman Master Sergeant Aziz called to Ramiz:
"Turn off that noise, Ramiz.
I don't get that stuff.
If you have an Arabic record, put it on.
For me, Arabic is it.
No language on earth is as eloquent.
Twelve years I've been with the government,
                    and I haven't gotten there yet:
Aleppo, Baghdad, Egypt.
Especially holy Mecca.

When you spin the globe,
all places are about equal.
I spent a lot of time with the four A's in my youth.
My father was a hodja, turban and all—
God rest his soul.
It's knitted into my bones and marrow,
                 it's built its nest in me—Arabic, Arabic,
                                  Arabic, Arabic.
Use your ounce of brains,
Ramiz, and put on an Arabic record . . . "

Ramiz changed the record
and stepped outside.
He sighed deeply
and raised his eyes:
the sea,
bay,
and harbor.
Out beyond the anchored barges, fishing boats, and motorboats,
a sudden wind came up and blew in low,
                 the water shivering and spangling
                                  between the rocking hulls.
Two people in a dinghy pulled away
from Dursun's motorboat,
one rowing and one standing in the stern.
They headed for the public olive groves
at the foot of Pomegranate Mountain
                 on the left strand of the bay.
On the right, the point ended in jagged, red rocks.
Straight across stood the ruined breakwater
        built by the Romans or maybe even the Phoenicians.
Kids swim out there
        to steal gulls' eggs.
Beyond the breakwater lay open sea
                        as dark blue
as it was deep.
It spread out, dense and thick,
until glistening white rows tracked the dark blue
        as if ships sailing out had left their trails.
And then way out at the horizon

the sea surface shimmered under the sun,
   flat as if it had just been planed.
Out there the sea wasn't soft and slippery
   but strong and sure, like a stretch of sheet metal.

Ramiz sat on the doorstep,
feeling all alone
   and unhappy.
Suddenly
he saw two tiny
  black hulls
round the rocky red point.
Their sails were down,
and oars flailed at the water.
Ramiz yelled into the coffeehouse:
"Two more launches are coming from the islands!"
The men bolted out of the coffeehouse.

The launches carried about a hundred people, fifty or so each:
men, women, and children,
even babies in swaddling clothes.

The peasants on the quay also spotted the boats.
Ali Kiraz (who'd performed his ablutions
   in the Chanakkalé jug) said:
"They're Greeks from the islands, escaping the Germans."
The wrestler Kadri asked: "Why?"
Ali Kiraz glared at the wrestler:
"Why?
Because they got tired of eating baklava, that's why!"
Ahmet (the ex-son-in-law
   of the blond-bearded carpenter) stood up.
He stretched and yawned:
"I'd sure like to escape somewhere."
One-Arm Ismail (who waited for his son Omer)
      looked at the launches
and mumbled under his breath
  (either to himself or someone else):
"Now these heathens would have money
  and watches with silver fobs and stuff,

and the wives all wear gold crosses on their necks."
Then he licked his ebony mustache
                with his thick red tongue.

The quay was crowded.
The hamals at the warehouses put down their sacks of wheat
                and stood gazing at the sea,
taking this chance to rest.
The crew loading rice and olives on the big motorboat
                                stopped work.
The smell of the Adana frycook Haji Sami's grilling meatballs
and the hum of bees buzzing over the tall fruit baskets filled the air...
The launches passed the ruined breakwater
                and dropped anchor in the harbor.
The customs patrol boat left
with the lieutenant governor,
        the chief of police,
                and the Guard commander.

The people on the launches
        hailed them, all talking and crying at once,
        waving their hands and arms
        as if trying to grab hold, clutch, embrace . . .

Some knew Turkish;
the lieutenant governor was Cretan anyway
                and spoke the best of Greek.

The men needed shaves.
The women didn't notice they were half-naked.
        Their eyes were all on fire,
                their faces all pale and translucent as parchment.
Hunger, fear, exhaustion, and hope
                made them all look alike, like twins . . .

On the quay, the wrestler Kadri asked Ali Kiraz:
"What happens to them now?"
"They'll be turned away—
        that's what happened last time."
"When they get back,

won't the Germans butcher them for escaping?"
"They will."
"That's terrible . . .
I'll bet the poor guys are starving, too.
Is it against the law to give them food?"
"No.
Last time we all collected stuff to give them.
See, Ahmet's back with some bread already . . . "
Ahmet
      (the blond-bearded carpenter's ex-son-in-law)
      stood beside them
          with two loaves of bread under his arm
      and yawned away,
        eyes glued to the launches.

The wrestler Kadri asked another question:
"How do we get the stuff to those guys?"
Ali Kiraz had taken a leather billfold out of his pocket
         and counted his money:
         5 liras and 62 kurush.
"Let's go—
      buy whatever you like,
      and don't worry, it'll reach them . . . "

The customs patrol boat returned
with the announcement:
"Citizens are permitted to help out.
The city will also render assistance.
No one will be allowed ashore.
They will depart in three hours at the latest . . . "

The two anchored launches had fallen quiet.
The hamals took up a collection among themselves
         and sent a man into town for provisions.
The waiter Ramiz passed a tray around the coffeehouse
and then, outside, stopped Koyunzadé's accountant by the warehouse
         and, yelling and screaming, squeezed 25 liras out of him.

Loaded with provisions, the boats rowed out
         and pulled alongside the launches.
The launches remained dead silent.

One-Arm Ismail was the only man on the quay who paid no attention.
He thought about Omer, his son:
"If he doesn't come soon, the stores will close,
and there'll be no cloth for the girl or shirt for me.
Then another night here,
and more money for the inn.
Omer has money.
But how to get it out of him . . . "

Omer appeared
with a long face.
When he sulked, he looked just like his father.
He kissed One-Arm Ismail's hand:
"Let's go, Father," he said.
"Let's go, Omer.
But we'll stop in the market first."
"Are you going shopping, Father?"
"I'm not buying anything,
        but you can buy your sister some cloth and me . . . "
Omer cut his father off with sweet vengeance:
"Can't be."
"Why? Didn't the agha pay you?"
"He paid me."
Omer was silent.
One-Arm Ismail glared at his son
and felt the same rage that made him hang goats from trees:
"So why can't you buy your sister some cloth?"
"I got paid, but nothing's left.
        They took up a collection for the refugees
                        from the islands:
                                I gave them the money . . . "
"Who? You gave who the money?
You idiot, they're heathens, not refugees.
Who'd you give the money to? Tell me, you little swine . . .
We'll get it back . . . "
"No way, Father.
The bulgur they bought with the money is already out there."

Omer was half lying:
he had donated only half his money,
and not just out of pity for the refugees

but also to spite his father.

One-Arm Ismail raised his right arm with all his fury:
                    one blow.
                    Omer reeled.
                    Then three quick kicks.
                    And Omer collapsed.

Out on the water, the launches weighed anchor.
Oars flailing, they pulled out of the harbor.
Tears in his eyes, Ramiz watched them grow
smaller and smaller in the evening light
until they were two specks on the open sea . . .

III

Halil had taken up woodworking in prison:
he carved mirrored sewing boxes,
                    thin walnut cigarette cases,
                    salt shakers, coffee and sugar canisters.
He had Pater sell them on visiting days
                    and one of the guards on the town's market days.
He also took some wholesale orders.
It amazed the prisoners
how Halil's hands mastered the craft so fast;
only his eyes balked,
          his vision more blurred each day . . .

Pater walked into the woodworking shop.
His chubby baby-face beamed.
"Papa," he said,
          "you've got visitors, Papa—
                    I showed them to your room."

Halil's visitors were the worker Kerim
                    —the heart of my heart!—who'd just turned fourteen,
and the honeyseller Remzi Effendi.
Kerim sat cross-legged on the bed,

notebook clutched tight under his arm.
The honeyseller Remzi Effendi sat on the chair,
                quiet, his basket at his feet.
His shapely hands rested on his knees,
and his head inclined to the right,
                his hair close-cropped under his cap.
He was of medium height and pudgy.

A Balkan War refugee,
Remzi Effendi
had attended the School for Orphans
and had worked in Sultan Reshat's tile factory.
Now, under a big white umbrella
        in the town market, he sold
        molasses, grape syrup, olive oil, and honey,
and he was the only student in the French class at the Free School.

One day,
with the district attorney's permission,
                Halil had visited the public baths.
On the way back, they passed through the town market,
and Remzi Effendi asked the second guard, who brought up the rear:
"That's Halil Bey, isn't it?
I recognized him right away—
I have photos of him
        cut out of the papers.
Could I visit him?"

The guardsman—a tobacco worker from Izmir
        and a friend of Halil's—
        looked Remzi Effendi up and down:
"Could be," he said, "could be.
You could sell olive oil, molasses, and stuff,
                but here's a better way..."

And Remzi Effendi started visiting Halil.
He gave the warden and head guard good prices
                on honey and molasses
and had no trouble entering the prison on visiting days.
At first Halil feared he was the police.

Then he stopped being suspicious.
From head to toe, Remzi Effendi looked at ease—
more than any undercover agent could ever be.
His head, hands, and little blond mustache were all at ease.
You can tell right away:
      a good man's ease
                 is like the ease of good health.

They had agreed—
Remzi Bey would prepare ten questions for Halil on each visit.
Otherwise, with his angelic blue eyes
             he'd have sat across from Halil
                   silently the whole day,
                   shy and worshipful.

"Remzi Bey, do you have your questions?"
Remzi Effendi readily blushed to his ear lobes:
"Yes, I do.
      I prepared them."
And he took out his little grocer's notebook.
"I've got questions today, too," Kerim said.
"We'll answer your questions, too, Kerim.
But first Remzi Bey's."

Remzi Effendi swallowed hard.

"Why don't you take off your hat, Remzi Bey?"

He removed his cloth cap
and blushed again.
With a happy, childlike curiosity, Halil asked:
"What's in the basket?"
"Some olive oil, grape syrup, and molasses . . . "
"Thanks, Remzi Bey, thanks.
I'll pay you next week—put it on my tab.
We'll clear up my account next week."
Remzi Effendi stammered:
"But these, I wanted to . . . "
"No, no."
Remzi Effendi looked hurt,
then said, very decisively,

with an awful question in his soft voice:
"Do you suspect me?
I mean, do you think I'm a spy or something?"
"Not at all.
It never even crosses my mind now."
"But it did at first?"
Halil smiled:
"Yes,
I was suspicious."
They were quiet.

The worker Kerim, the heart of my heart
                who'd just turned fourteen,
listened wide-eyed
                to the conversation.

Remzi Effendi took an envelope out of his pocket
                        and handed it to Halil:
"You can send this to your prison friends who need it most."
Halil opened the envelope:
        there, crisp as if hot off the press,
                was a shiny fifty...
For some reason, Remzi Effendi explained, without raising his eyes
                (maybe he feared
                Halil wouldn't take the money
                and he'd be humiliated):
"Sales have been good the last two weeks,
        and I wholesaled grape syrup to a merchant.
I mean, this money
                is on top of my profit..."
"Thank you, Remzi Bey.
I'll send it on to my friends tomorrow."
As if he'd just spotted something very beautiful and bright,
Remzi Bey's angelic blue eyes lit up with a happy smile.

Pater appeared with two glasses of tea.
Kerim and Remzi Bey gulped their tea with loud slurps.
"If they just wouldn't slurp so," thought Halil.

The visiting area downstairs filled up,
and the prison hummed louder.

The honeyseller Remzi Effendi opened his notebook
                   and asked his ten questions of the day:

"1. They say Germany started the war—
the Nazis, that is.
Well, if there had been a revolution
and the Communists had come to power
instead of Hitler,
           would Germany still have started a war?
And would that revolution
           have been as bloody as this war?

2. They say Germany started the war.
Well, who got Hitler started?
If the German banks and trusts hadn't felt threatened
and backed their partners in England, France, and America
           in their fight against the Communists,
and if they hadn't all together
           put the Nazis in power,
and if the German middle class hadn't been wiped out by the last war,
and if hordes of vagabonds
ready to be bought with a pair of boots
or a ring of sausage
                   hadn't wandered the streets,
                   wretched, hungry, and hopeless,
and if the Social Democrats hadn't sold out,
           would Hitler be what he is today?

3. For the second time in 25 years there's a world war;
           don't the capitalist regimes have any responsibility here?

4. Roosevelt and Churchill:
     'We fight'
           —they say—
     'not to gain land
           but for people's freedom.'
Well, will the people of Java, Sumatra, India,
           the African colonies, and so on
—I mean, great masses of people,
           more than a billion—
enjoy independence after the war?

Will they be spared becoming markets for the trusts?
Or do only white peoples count as people?

5. Roosevelt and Churchill:
        'We fight for nothing'
                —they say—
                        'but the Four Freedoms.'
Well,
when the war ends,
        won't there be unemployment in, say, America?
Or will they hand the veterans a few dollars
and tell the workers in the war-plants,
                'Take care of yourselves'?

6. Isn't unemployment necessary
        for the capitalist economic system?

7. Social systems have always changed,
                essentially and incidentally, throughout human history
and have given way to new systems.
No one would deny it.
But has this process reached perfection in the capitalist system
                                and come to a dead stop?

8. Those who supported the rise of fascism in Italy and Germany
are now, like teeth-mothers who devour their own children,
                busy bringing them down . . .
Doesn't this contradiction say something?

9. Today there are six major imperialist powers,
six big effendis of capitalism:
America, England, Germany, Japan, France, and Italy.
How many will be left after the war?
What does this process of elimination say?

10. Before the war, why couldn't the capitalist-imperialist world
—chiefly America, England, Germany, Japan, France, and Italy—
join forces against the Soviet socialists?"

The honeyseller Remzi Bey finished reading
                and fell quiet.

He shot Halil a dumb-like-a-fox look.
Halil was a little taken aback.
"Your questions are very different this time, Remzi Bey," he said.
"And many of them answer themselves.
You've clearly thought a lot. And even . . .
                    ["And even had someone else write them for you,"
                                        he almost said
                                        but didn't,
                    for fear Remzi Bey would take offense.]
And even read a lot last week . . . "
"Not just last week—
                    I'm always reading.
I got hold of a few good books,
a couple of them your banned books.
Plus, I've been your student three months.
And I've worked on these questions a long time.
I wanted to surprise you . . . "
Remzi Effendi blushed so deeply and was so at ease and happy
that Halil felt like getting up and kissing him on his button nose.
"Remzi Bey, I won't answer
your questions.
You write your answers
and bring them next week.
Now it's your turn, Kerim.
Did you resolve the fractional problem I gave you?"
"I didn't 'resolve' it; I *solved* it.
And it's not 'fractional problem' but 'fraction.'"
"You're right.
Let's see your notebook."

Kerim had solved the problem correctly,
and Halil gave him a new one.
"Now let's get to my question," Kerim said.
"They say you're paid by the Russians,
                    you're a traitor."
"Who says?"
"The accountant at our factory, Seyfi Bey, says so."
"And what do you think?"
Kerim fired back:
"It's a lie."

The time between Halil's question and Kerim's answer was less than a
    second.
But in that split second
            three memories flashed through Halil's mind:
one recent,
        one farther back,
            the third very old.
The recent one:
Ten days ago he'd mailed his wife, Aysha, some money—
            fifteen liras saved up from woodworking.
The postal clerk asked the guard:
"How come Halil Bey just sends ten or fifteen liras?
Halil Bey," he said, "must be rolling in dough."

The one farther back:
Years ago,
fifty of them were thrown in prison together.
Most were workers and poor tradesmen,
more than half of them bachelors.
Dirt-poor,
they'd sell their tobacco rations to buy tomatoes and onions
                            to eat with their bread.
And sometimes Halil, who couldn't live without tobacco,
            would have to scavenge butts from the ground.
One day, the "agha" of the fifth ward approached them.
"The warden calls you," he said,
        "enemies of your country
and says that Moscow feeds you milk and honey.
But I've been watching:
        nothing ever cooks in your common pot.
And some of you were even wounded
        fighting for our country."
Later, that man quit being a ward "agha"
and transferred to the weaving shop . . .

The third and oldest memory:
Halil had been brought before the commissioner.
The short little man, round and oily like the inside of a hazelnut,
                grinned, baring his pointed teeth:
"In your faith," he said, "women are used in common—

something like the Kizilbash, eh?"
And Halil picked up the inkwell on the desk
            and threw it in the bastard's face . . .

These three memories flashed through his mind like lightning,
his dark bony face flushed slightly,
and he asked Kerim with a sad smile:
"It's a lie, then?"
"Sure, it's a lie—
            I just wanted to ask why
                        they slander you this way."

The honeyseller Remzi Effendi
            —maybe for the first time in his life—
                        said as if accusing a criminal:

"They're scared, Kerim,
they fear the Turkish people.
In the capitalist regime today, the leaders
                        and the bourgeoisie everywhere
                                    fear their own people."
Remzi Effendi used the French terms
            haltingly, as if learning to use new tools,
            but with immense pleasure.
He finished his speech
            by discussing dialectics
                        and class warfare.
"Kerim," Halil said,
"praised be the glory of the Turkish people and humanity
            [He laughed:
            it struck him
            how old-fashioned his terms were,
            compared to Remzi Bey's.
            He repeated:]
praised be the glory of the Turkish people and all people
            and, thanks be, *I'm a Communist*—
            to the core
            and more so every day,
                        each day a little more of a Communist,
                                    a Communist . . .

[As he repeated *Communist*,
                    he felt he could breathe easier.]
Thanks be, I'm a Communist.
That much is true, Kerim.
And like all Communists, I'm a true patriot,
                    with a love for my country more real, more advanced,
                    than any in all history,
                    encompassing a whole era,
                    and all of humanity...
It's the love of those who don't live off others' labor,
                    the love of working people.
It's how you love your country, fourteen-year-old worker Kerim.
I don't consider other peoples
                    better or worse than my people.
I'm no internationalist.
But like all Communists, I call on the proletariat
                    of all nations to unite.
That's true.
Now, Kerim,
        about the Soviet Union:
if I'd been born a hundred or a hundred-and-fifty years ago,
                    I'd have respected and admired the French Revolution.
Who knows, they might have said then
                    I was a tool of the heathen, seditious French.
I didn't live in that era,
                    but I'm still excited to sing the 'Marsaillaise.'
Now go back twenty years:
imagine yourself a child in an African or Asian colony,
I'm sure you'd have loved and admired us Turks
for ripping our independence from the claws of imperialism.
Now take the Soviet Union:
the exploitation of man by man, and nation by nation, is abolished.
I'm certainly going to respect and love
                    those who laid the groundwork of socialism.
We're in the twentieth century, Kerim,
and in our hearts live the 'Marsaillaise'
                    and our national anthem
                        and the 'International.'
As for the lies and slander:
guardsmen, police stations, prisons, and so on aren't enough—

453

in some places, they can't quite resort to such solutions.
The enemy also needs lies:
newspapers, radios, movies, books, and coffeehouses
                              are all mobilized.
Lies are like lice:
they go through seven beds a night,
                          especially those of the poor . . . "

Remzi Effendi blushed and whispered another proverb:
"But the liar's candle . . . "
Kerim, confused by most of what he'd heard,
                          happily finished his sentence:
". . . doesn't last two hours past sunset."
Halil added sadly:
"But sometimes sunset comes a little later."
He laughed:
"Well, a couple minutes . . . "

Downstairs, the bell sounded the end of visiting hours,
and Kerim and Remzi Effendi left.
Halil took the olive oil, grape syrup, and molasses from the basket.
He looked at them, swallowing hard.
He picked up the tin of grape syrup, turned it around and around,
                          and put it down.
Grape syrup was his favorite sweet.
"Aysha loves grape syrup, too;
I should send her this tomorrow as is."
Reaching for the spout of the olive-oil jug,
                  he poured a drop on his finger and tasted it:
"And I'll send Suleyman this,
and Remzi Bey's fifty liras to Fuat.
He's getting out in twenty days—
                  he can use it to go home."
The molasses came in a bottle.
He eyed it darkly:
"So this is left for me,
        and I can't stand the blessed stuff . . . "

IV

Fuat was released on a Thursday,
                              late
                                        at night.
He walked away,
                    swinging his arms and whistling,
        and never looked back at the prison.
Those he left behind
              saw him off through the iron bars
                              with a little longing,
                              a little sadness,
                              and "Have a good trip . . ."
Fuat turned the corner
and came face to face with the city
he'd only seen from a distance for the past year.
Rows of poplars,
                    green fields,
                    pastures,
                    and the white highway leading to the city
                              stretched before him in the evening light.
The young man's heart pounded
                    with an excitement he couldn't contain—
              the desire to catch up with something,
              to give someone good news.
He stopped
and looked around
—right and left, up and down—
as if he were the center
the whole world spread out from.
No worries like "I'll bump into a wall"
                    or "If I swing my arms,
                              my hands will hit the bars."
The world had no lines or corners.
Fuat suddenly felt himself floating in space.
The feeling was so strong
                    it made him dizzy.
He bent down and grabbed a handful of grass.
He jumped a ditch.

Two armed guardsmen walking toward the prison
called out "Good luck!"
Fuat looked after them.
His lips trembled under his fine black mustache:
"Damn it,
             even this much freedom is beautiful.
I should head straight to the baths," he thought,
"and just lie back on the stone . . .
Then get loaded at some nice little neighborhood bar.
Suddenly he wanted a woman again—
dark,
       firm,
              voluptuous,
the creature of all his dreams in prison.
Her face is a blur,
                but not her body.
Yet Fuat could neither hit a bar or get a woman:
                                    he didn't have the money,
                    even counting what Halil had sent him.
So never seeing by day the city
                he'd spent a year in,
Fuat caught a train
early the next morning
                and headed for Istanbul
as scrawny, wasted women cloaked in black
                walked barefoot along the tracks
                            to the tobacco nursery.
On the second day of his freedom
                he forgot all about prison.
But on the fifth day,
                as the train approached Istanbul
and the Yeshilkoy shore appeared in the distance,
Fuat felt dizzy as if hit with coal fumes,
                and sadness overcame him like nausea.
All those left behind in their separate prisons
—especially Halil, Suleyman, and Melahat
and even the friends he had made inside
                            (the murderer Murat,
                            Huseyin the rapist,
                                Mehmet the bandit) —

flashed before his eyes,
now distant,
                    pained-looking ghosts
                    as if they were dead,
now close enough to touch, happy and alive,
now all blending together,
and now one or another
                    standing out
                              clear and distinct.
At that moment
the fitter Fuat wished himself
          back in prison with any of them,
but especially with Halil.
He rubbed his forehead
               to hide his tears.

An hour and a half later
                    he stood on the Bridge,
     at the heart of Istanbul:
he saw the Galata Tower, the Golden Horn, the Suleymaniyé Mosque,
freighters, barges, trolleys;
he looked at the people crossing the Bridge;
and the black jewels of his eyes filled with blue light
                    as he breathed in the city.

A siren screaming out of Karakoy
          shot across the Bridge like a white flame:
                         an ambulance.
The white van with the red crescent
          seemed airborne
                    as it streaked over the water.
The paramedic Hasan Kilich sat next to the driver—
                    eyes shut tight,
                         dark circles under them.

His head was bare:
curly dark-chestnut hair;
pale but handsome shrewd face;
and a dull headache
          from no sleep.
His white shirt was wrinkled and stained.

The smell of burnt gasoline
    and the heat of the engine rising to his knees,
the paramedic Hasan Kilich tried to pull himself together,
    not physically
    but mentally.
Eyes still shut tight,
    he could see the streets they passed through:
doors, windows, store windows, and people
    all running together
and the siren wailing nonstop.
This lasted 15 minutes.
Then the crowd slowly thinned out,
the buildings grew smaller,
the people fewer,
and the siren less loud,
    dying down as the wheels stopped.
The paramedic Hasan Kilich opened his eyes.
They were at the police station,
and the guard outside shouted:
"You can't take the ambulance.
Get the stretchers,
it's not far anyway . . . "
With Hasan Kilich and the guard leading the way
and the orderly and driver following with stretchers,
    they set out on foot.
His torn white shirt flapping, Hasan Kilich walked
    with heavy-lidded eyes,
    aloof yet hurried and officious,
    silent yet self-important.
Not a sound anywhere,
the sky was clear
    warm
    and happy.
The neighborhood houses were wood,
unpainted
    and weathered
    but clean.
A barefoot girl scrubbed some steps.
It felt as if one world ended here
    and another would begin

just around the corner...

Rounding the corner,
they found themselves at the top of a hill:
the street plunged straight down,
                      long and narrow,
and far below at the very bottom,
           as if seen through the end of a lead pipe,
                                    was a patch of sea.

They started down.
A crowd had gathered outside a wood door:
clothes ragged,
          skin pasty,
                    sallow,
most either too young
                or too old to work.
At that hour, everyone else
            —in the same clothes and skin—
                    was at work:
factory workers,
            apprentices, salesclerks,
                       street vendors,
and two young men stationed far away in the army.
The tax collector lived on the first floor
                    of the house on the left, facing the fountain.
The prettiest girl of the street
              was probably working in Beyoghlu again—
           in a theater loge or at Madame Athena's.
And the carter's no-good son
                was off in prison.
The police chief greeted the paramedic.
They entered the house.
It stank.
Six families in five rooms.
Although it was twice as crowded now,
       the stark emptiness of the rotting damp boards remained.
They went into the back room on the second story:
two mattresses on the floor,
          a tablecloth and a forlorn cooking pot in the middle.
Five people lay sprawled on the floor.
The paramedic turned to the police chief.

The chief said:
"They were poisoned.
My investigation shows the guy poisoned himself and the others.
Looks like arsenic.
A family suicide.
What can you do?
The man worked at the tannery
for 110 kurush a day.
But look, the mattresses are fairly new,
        and the pot is worth something, too.
They didn't sell them.
They're all dead, except maybe the girl.
The people came in when they heard her screaming."

The girl was in fact alive:
barely thirteen,
                she was like a withered plum branch.
Hasan Kilich gave her a shot of apomorphine,
put her on a stretcher, and sent her down.
He examined the others one by one:
the man had a long face, bushy black eyebrows,
and an expression as if he'd been suddenly
                        and badly scared.
His wife was about thirty-five.
She had torn her dress in the throes of death;
her breasts hung down like two shriveled hands.
The old woman—the man's mother—was bent double,
                her toothless mouth gaping.
The fourth body was a five-year-old boy,
a rickety bag of bones in blue pants.
The police chief talked constantly,
mostly thinking out loud
and turning over the idea in his mind:
"They still had a lot left to sell—
the mattress, the pot,
the boy's blue pants are brand-new,
and the woman has underwear.
It wasn't time for suicide.
People with a lot less go on living.
Not everyone can beg, but still . . .

The man was beaten down . . .
It was defeat, my man, defeat . . .
But the guy had his pride . . . "

Hasan Kilich headed for the door:
"Let's go, chief."

They left.
Only an old man stayed behind,
one of the tenants in the room across.
Barefoot,
he wore a tattered homespun sash around his waist.
Pus oozed from his left eye.
And his face looked innocent and forlorn, like something abandoned.
He bent over the man with the bushy black eyebrows
and rifled his pockets.
He found the man's bread coupons
and stood up,
        slowly straightening his back.
The door burst open.
It was the neighborhood alderman.
They stared at each other.
The alderman held out his hand,
and the old man turned over the ration coupons.
His hands didn't shake,
but his face looked twice as innocent and forlorn.
The alderman counted the coupons,
tore out five, and put them in the old man's hand:
"That's half," he said, "we'll split them.
Pay attention to their dates:
you can buy from the Laz baker up the hill.
Keep your mouth shut about this.
Don't even tell your daughter-in-law or the kids.
Buy it and eat it yourself."
He was quiet.
He thought a minute
and stuck out his hand again:
it was soft, dark, and hairless,
the skin at the base of his nails glistening as if oiled.
"Or you can sell me yours—

I'll give you 150 kurush.
Or—no, keep them.
Or—
no, you'll botch it.
Here, take this seventy-five
            and give them back.
No—
no, I don't want them.
Put your hand down—I said I don't want them!
And you can keep the seventy-five kurush:
                        I don't want it.
Go on, get out of here . . .
Goddamn
        the both of us!"

The old man left the room.
He stopped in the hallway
and walked back to the half-open door,
his face wearing the same innocent forlorn look.
He peeked in the door
        to see what the alderman was up to inside.

The ambulance took off.
The girl on the stretcher kept vomiting.
The orderly swore to himself
                by force of habit
                        but said nothing.
And next to the driver sat Hasan Kilich, thinking:
"The maitre d' of the Park Hotel must be at the office by now,
                        but he won't leave:
his waiters' vaccination certificates
                have to be stamped.
That's ten liras there.
And Tokatlian's will probably come the day after tomorrow.
That's seven and a half.
I don't know where I'd be if folks weren't so scared of shots.
I've got to stop by the doctor's tonight:
he'll have the quinine ampules filled with distilled water.
Twenty liras in commission there
makes thirty-seven and a half.

I'm loaded this month."

The driver stopped at Jerrah Pasha Hospital.
"No room!" they said.
The ambulance moved on.
The girl vomited in the back,
and Hasan Kilich thought:
"I just hope she doesn't die in the ambulance
                    like the one this morning,
but I've never seen TB this bad.
You either kill yourself,
croak from TB,
or get smart like me."

Hasan Kilich thought himself very sharp.
The ambulance stopped outside Gureba.
"No room!" they said.
The ambulance moved on,
climbing up from Chapa toward Aksaray—
Yusuf Pasha, Murat Pasha,
the street narrow, run-down, and tired.
The grocery store, chickpea shop, and wool fluffer
and the red-ochre kiosk up from the coal place . . .
Hasan Kilich was still thinking:
"The apomorphine will keep the girl vomiting.
Nuri Drug Supply has put some calcium on the black market:
the ampules and labels are European, the contents local.
Now show your stuff, my boy.
The guy is smart, but you're smarter—
                    get in on it."

And Hasan Kilich grinned,
his thick red lips parting
        to bare two rows of glittering white teeth.

GLOSSARY

A short history of Turkey during the period Hikmet's epic chronicles may be helpful in sorting out the events it relates. During World War I, the Ottoman Empire sided with the Central Powers. Although their army, under the leadership of men like Mustafa Kemal, won all its major battles, the Ottomans lost the war along with their allies. After the war, the Montreux Pact of October 30, 1918, dismantled the Empire and divided Turkey among England, France, Italy, and Greece. The English concentrated on the area around Istanbul, the French moved into southeastern Anatolia, the Italians were handed the coastal regions in the south and southwest, and the Greeks occupied Izmir in the west. While the Ottoman military was disarmed and the central government in Istanbul had given up any ideas of armed resistance, local guerrilla groups formed throughout Anatolia to regain Turkish lands. The people took up their own defense, and the Liberation Army evolved from these groups.

To organize a national resistance, keep alive the idea of an independent Turkey, and coordinate the various local forces required central control and a strong leader, and Mustafa Kemal emerged as that leader with the requisite power, knowledge, battlefield experience, and faith. Foreseeing the implications of the Montreux Pact, he left Istanbul for Anatolia in 1919 and set out to organize an army for a war of independence. The strengthening of the Anatolian forces, together with the success of guerrilla warfare against the French and the Greeks, scared the Allies and led the English to officially occupy Istanbul in 1920, dissolve Parliament, and exile the supporters of a Turkish independence war. Mustafa Kemal announced that the closing of Parliament in Istanbul marked the end of seven hundred years of Ottoman rule, and he opened the Turkish National Assembly on April 23, 1920, in Ankara, a small town on the steppe that would become the Turkish capital. The Sultan proclaimed Mustafa Kemal a traitor, and the Caliph, declaring the Independence movement to be anti-Islam, issued a *fatwa* for his death. Airplanes dropped fliers announcing the *fatwa* all across Turkey at the same time the National Assembly was convening, and the *fatwa* caused many guerrilla gangs to switch sides and oppose the nationalists.

The Independence War was fought on many fronts. Major battles on the western front include the First Inonu Battle, the Second Inonu Battle, and the decisive Sakarya Battle, which lasted twenty-two days and ended with the Greeks' retreat. The French withdrew from southeastern Turkey following this victory. All forces then concentrated on the western front. The Great Offensive began on August 26, 1922. The Greek army was decisively defeated, and Turkish troops entered Izmir on September 9, driving the stragglers into the sea. Nine days later, all occupying foreign troops had been driven out of Anatolia. The Lausanne Treaty of July 1923 made the Turkish victory official, and the borders of modern Turkey were drawn.

Following Independence, Mustafa Kemal became the first president of the new republic and carried out major reforms designed to make Turkey a nation on the Western model. State and religion were separated; religious schools were closed, and a secular educational system was established; language reforms purged Turkish of Arabic and Persian influences; women were granted equal rights, and the Islamic practice of multiple wives was outlawed; and last names, Western dress, and the Roman alphabet and calendar were adopted. Although Lenin made overtures of friendship to Mustafa Kemal, he outlawed the Turkish Communist Party, a ban in effect to this day.

During World War II, Turkey managed to remain neutral. That was not an easy feat, since both sides coveted the Straits. The country was nevertheless mobilized during the war and, with bread rationing and shortages of fuel and medicine, still experienced the economic and moral trials of war.

Abdul Hamid II (1842-1918): made Sultan in 1876, he closed Parliament in 1878 and ruled as an absolute despot until he was deposed in 1909.

Agriculture Office: established in 1938 to protect farmers and consumers alike, this bureau is part of the Commerce Department and sets the prices of grain and other farm products.

Akif: Mehmet Akif Ersoy (1873-1936): author of the Turkish National Anthem.

Ataturk, Mustafa Kemal (1881-1938): Turkish general and founder and first president (1923-38) of the Turkish Republic.

Balkan War: in 1912 and 1913, the peoples of Bulgaria, Greece, Macedonia, Serbia, Montenegro, and Albania successfully fought the Ottoman Empire for their independence.

Book of Ahmet: title of four books recounting Mohammed's life, one dating from the fourteenth century, two from the fifteenth, and the fourth from the eighteenth.

Constitution: in 1908, Sultan Abdul Hamid II reinstated the 1876 Constitution, and general elections were subsequently held to convene Parliament, which became known as the "Second Constitution."

Delibash, Mehmet: guerrilla leader who switched from the nationalist side to the religious faction, gathered deserters around him, and battled the Liberation Army near Konya in 1920 before he was killed in 1921.

Enver Pasha (1881-1938): Turkish general and statesman.

Ethem the Circassian: guerrilla gang leader who first worked with the nationalists but then, impressed with his power, established his own army, which the Liberation Army defeated in 1921.

Fikret, Tevfik (1867-1915): Turkish poet known for his social criticism.

Gokalp, Ziya (1876-1924): Turkish sociologist and man of letters.

Hashim, Ahmet (1883-1933): Turkish formalist poet.

Inonu, Ismet (1884-1973): Turkish general and second president (1938-50) of Turkey.

Kemal, Ali (1867-1922): Turkish journalist lynched during the War of Independence.

Kemal, Namik (1840-1888): Turkish poet imprisoned and exiled for his liberal views.

Koroghlu: warrior hero of popular Turkish folk epic by the same name.

Lame Osman (1883-1923): head of Ataturk's security forces, who had an anti-Ataturk Representative from Trabzon killed and was killed in retaliation.

La Pasionaria, Dolores Ibarruri (b. 1895): Marxist Spanish orator and writer, in exile from 1939 to 1977.

March 31st Affair: in 1909, certain reforms during the Second Constitution disturbed reactionary and fundamentalist factions who, encouraged by Sultan Abdul Hamid and the English, incited the people and part of the army to revolt; the Movement Army was called in to put down the uprising.

Nasreddin Hodja (1208-1284): legendary Anatolian humorist now part of Turkish folklore.

Night of Revelation: night the Koran was revealed.

Peri, Gabriel (1902-1941): French Communist journalist and politician executed by the Nazis for his activities in the Resistance.

Rebiulahir: fourth month of the Arabic calendar.

Sultan Reshat (1844-1918): succeeded Sultan Abdul Hamid in 1909.

Suphi, Mustafa (1883-1921): Turkish journalist who founded the Turkish Communist Party in Baku in 1920 and was subsequently assassinated.

Tahir and Zuhré: the Romeo and Juliet of Turkish folklore.

Talat Pasha (1874-1921): Turkish general and statesman opposed to Abdul Hamid's regime.

Tanya: code name of Zoe Kosmodemianskaya (1923-1941), celebrated Russian partisan executed by the Nazis.

Venizelos, Eleutherios (1864-1936): Greek statesman who fought in the Balkan War and in Turkey in 1918.

Vrangel (1878-1928): White Russian general who, along with General Denikin (1872-1947) and Admiral Kolchak (1874-1920), fought the Bolsheviks.

466